I DRAW FASHION

SHOPPING TIME

100+ PROFESSIONAL FIGURE TEMPLATES
FOR FASHION DESIGNERS

VOLUME 14

© 2019 I DRAW FASHION

CONTENTS

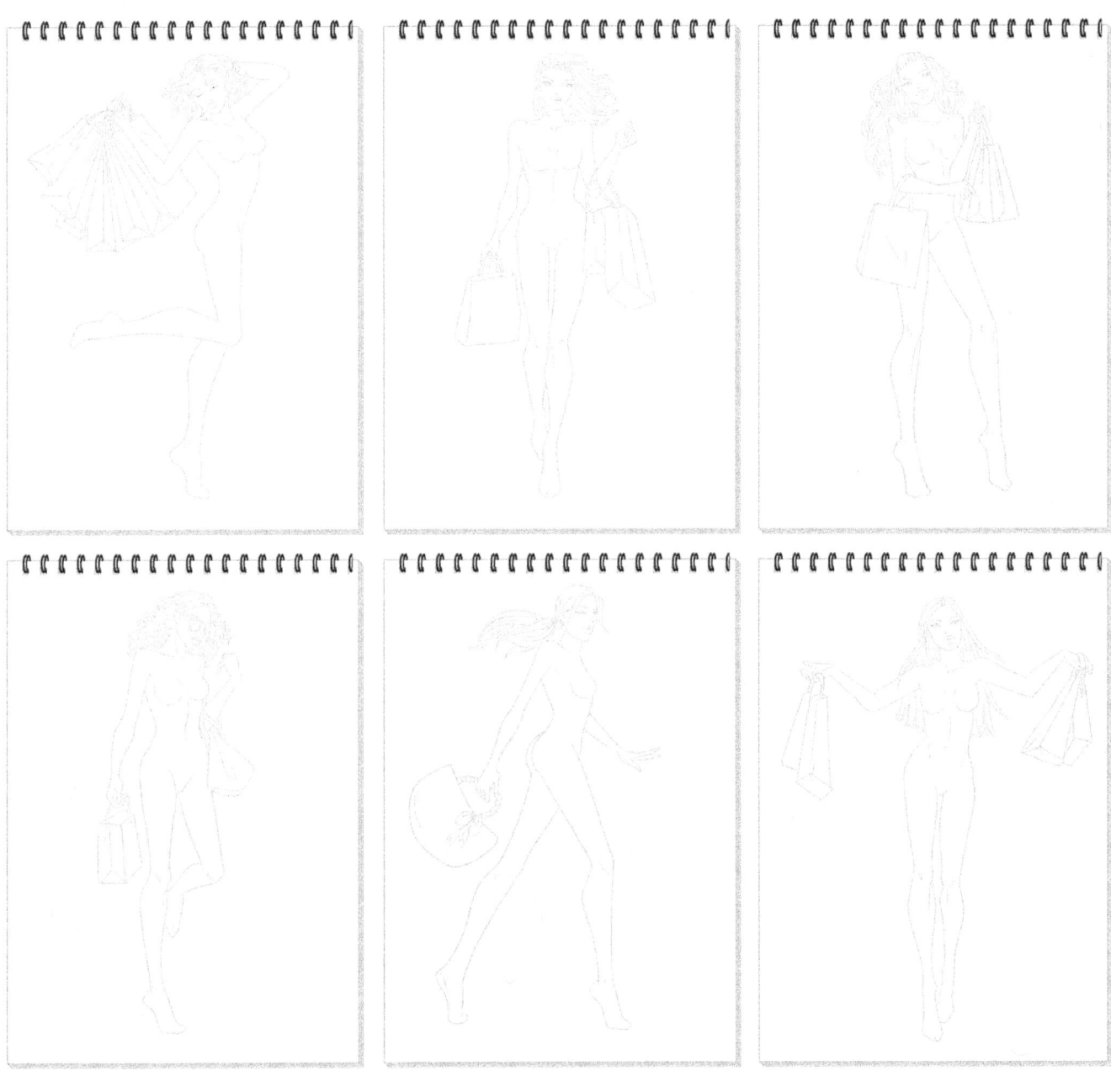

FULL DETAIL FIGURE TEMPLATES

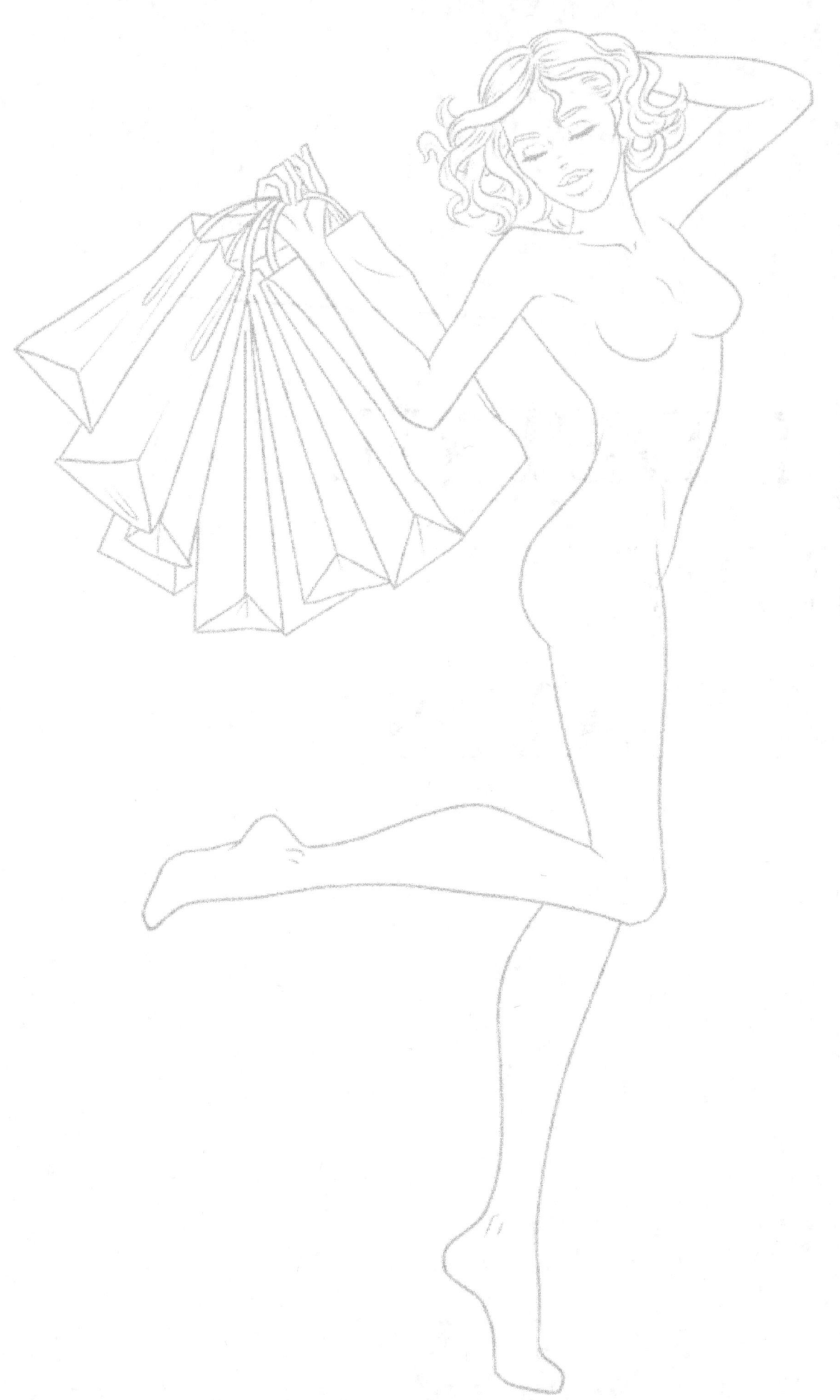

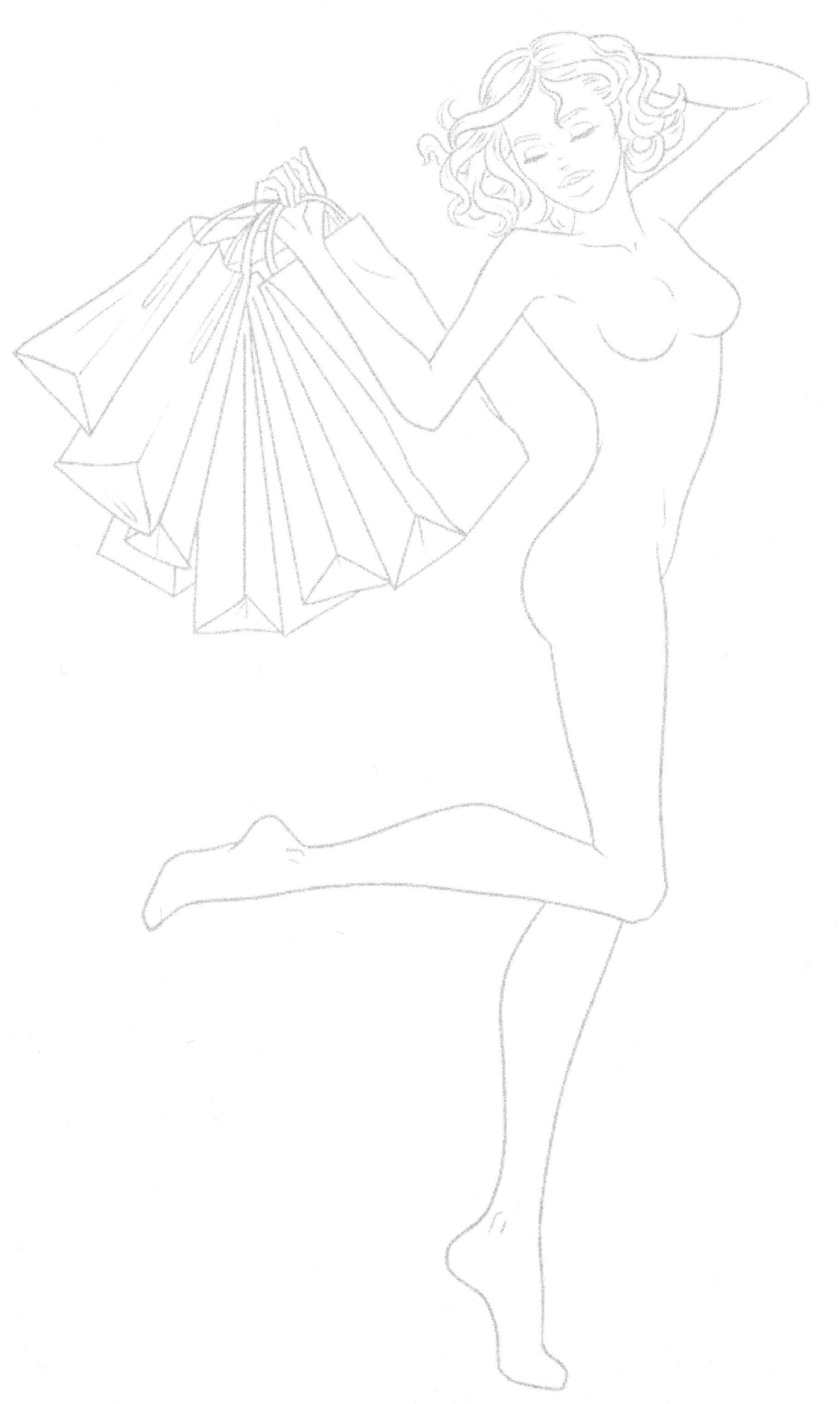

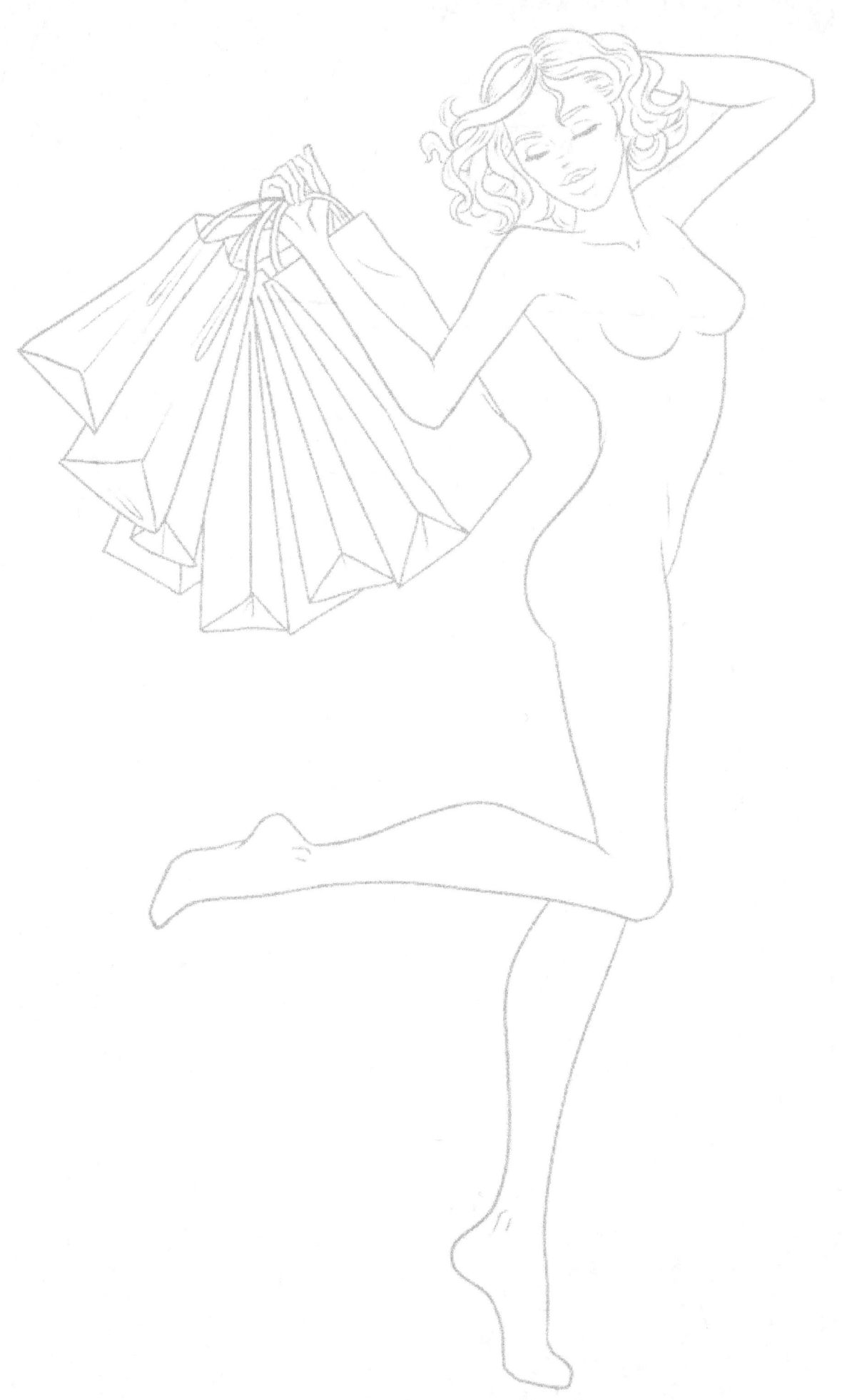

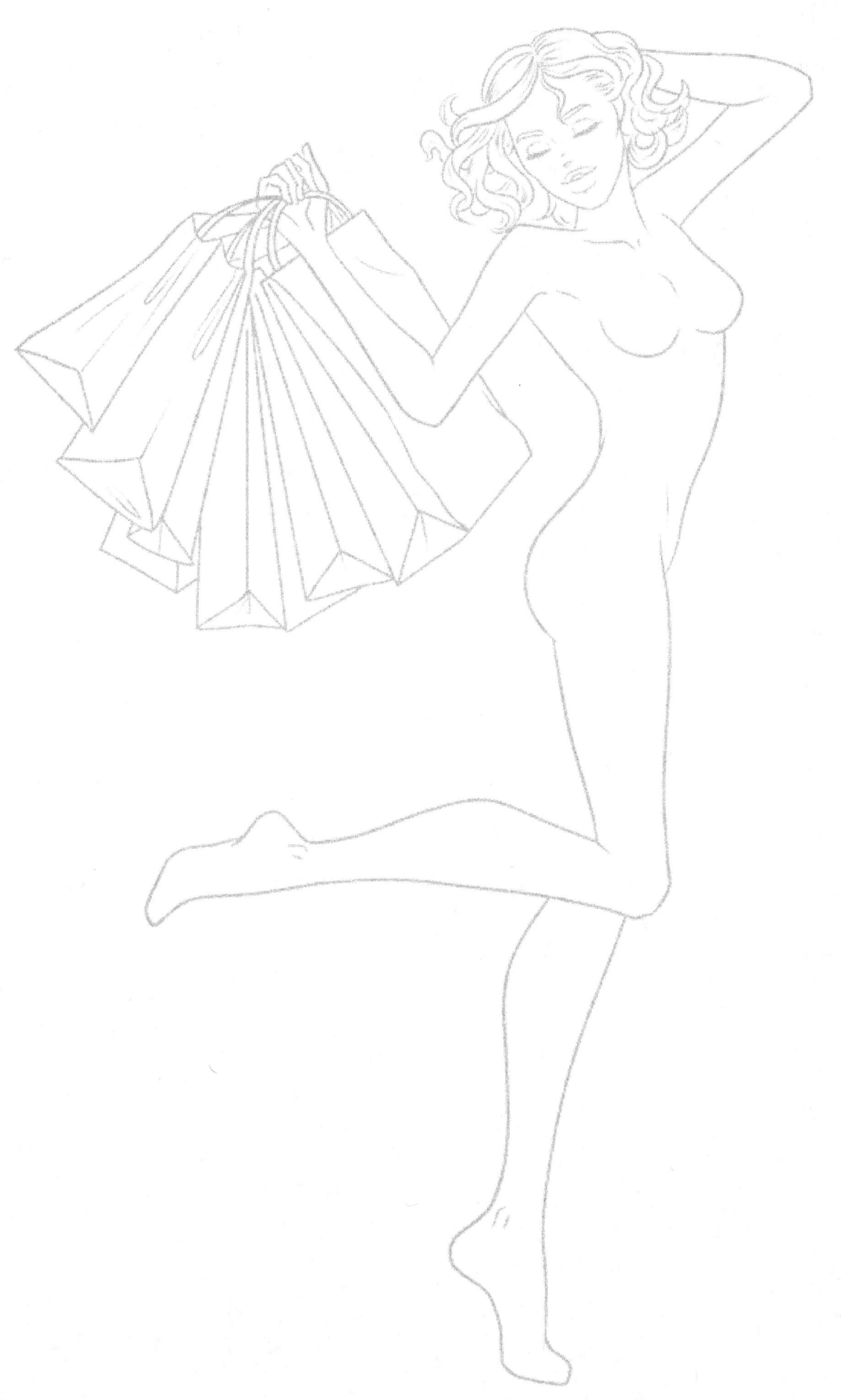

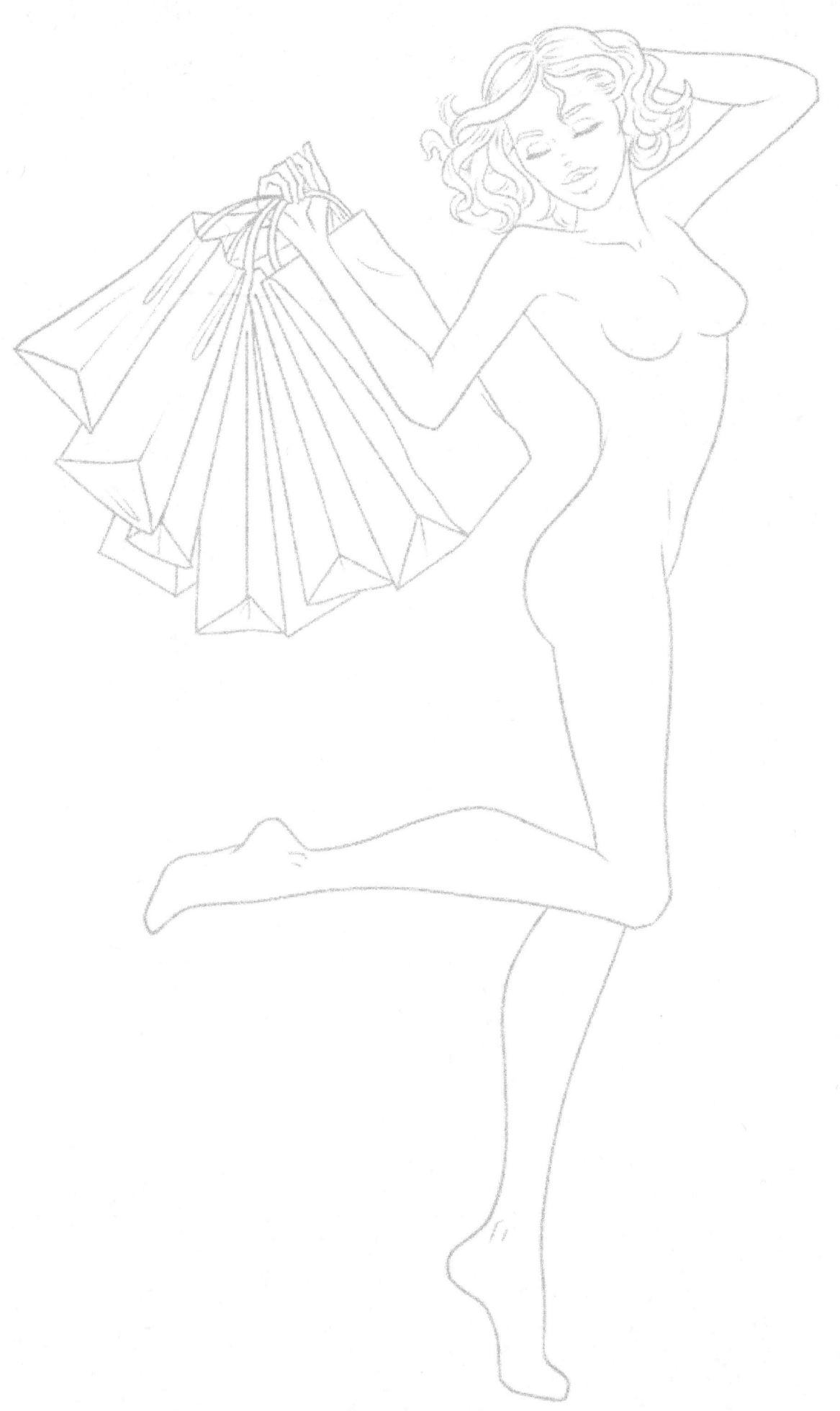

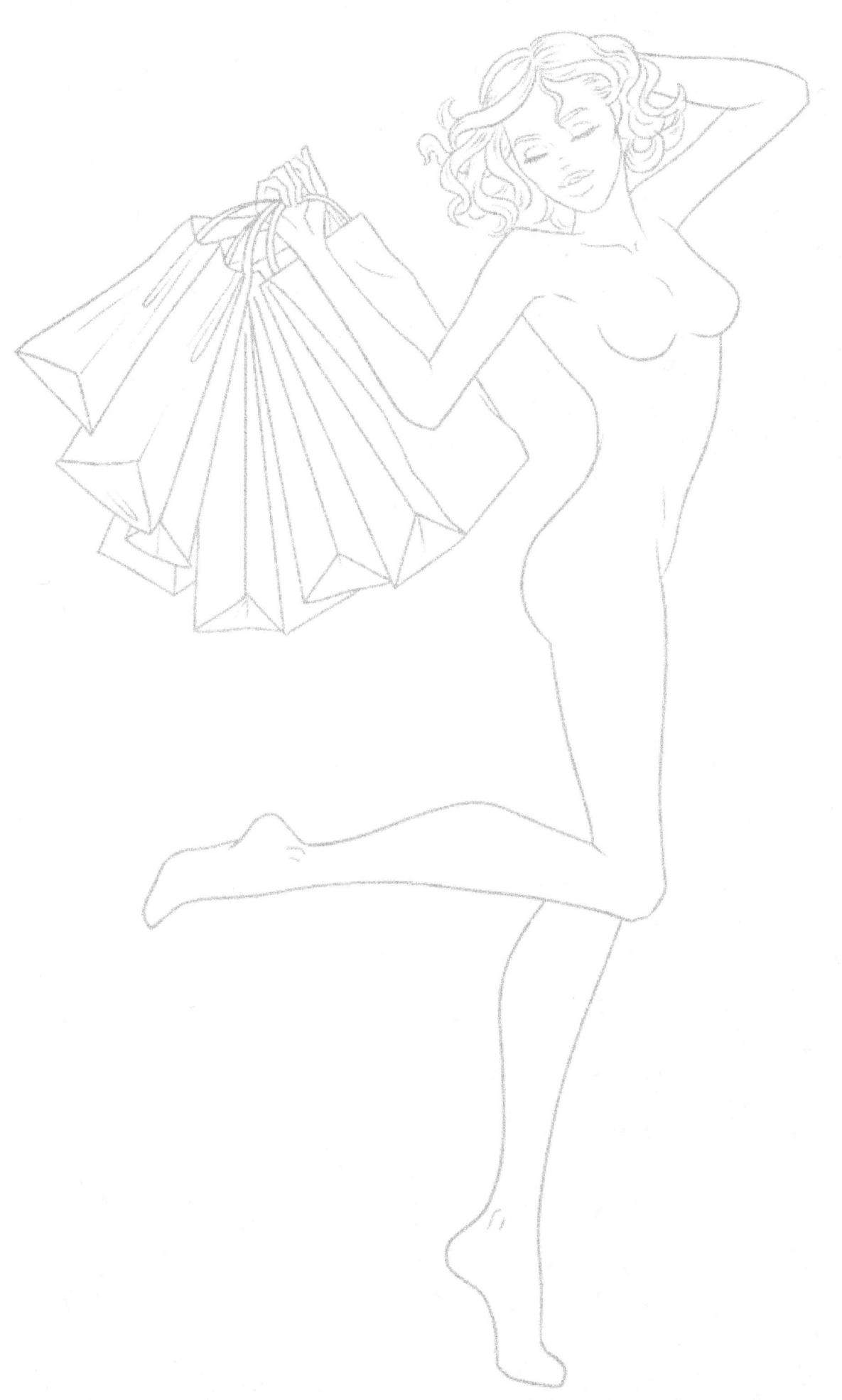

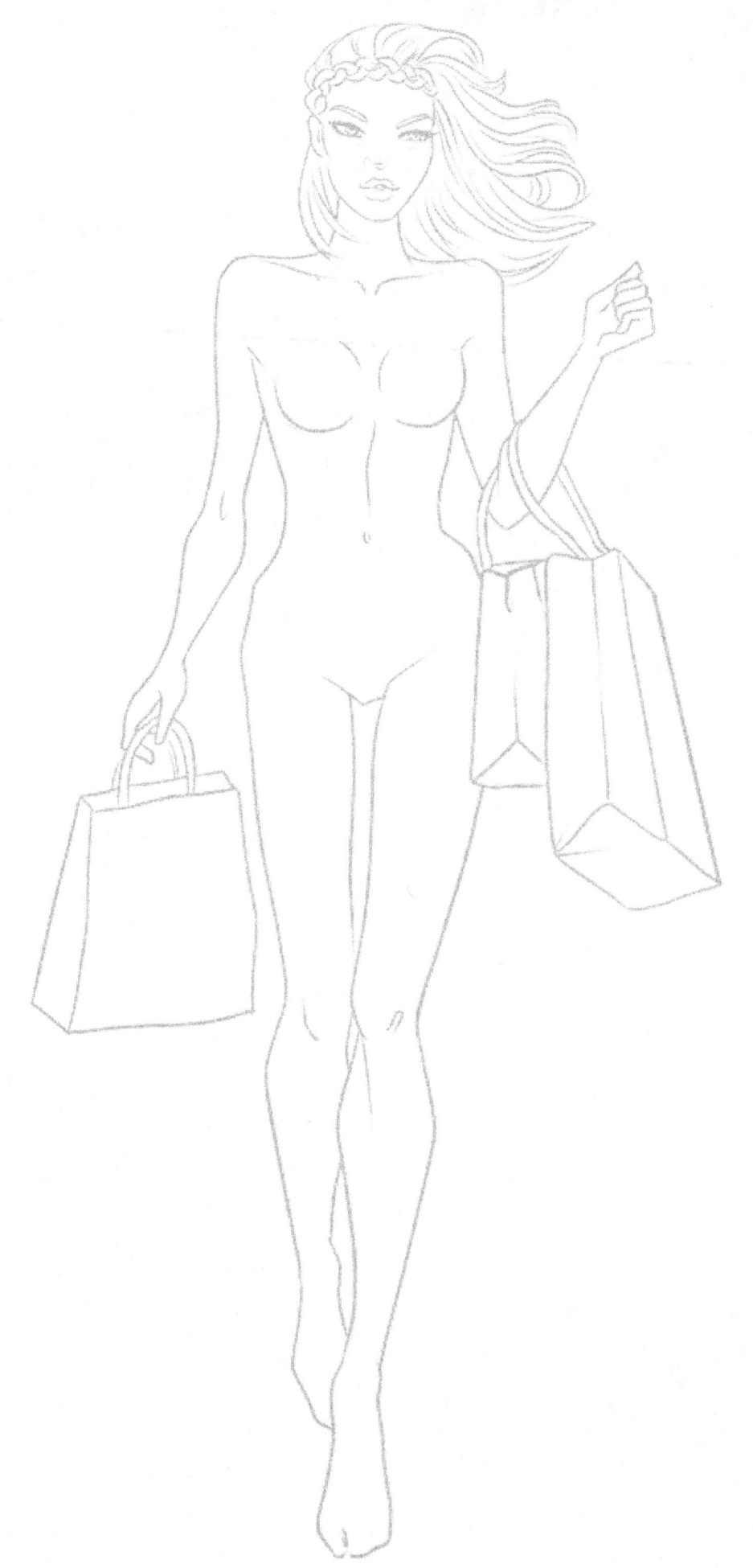

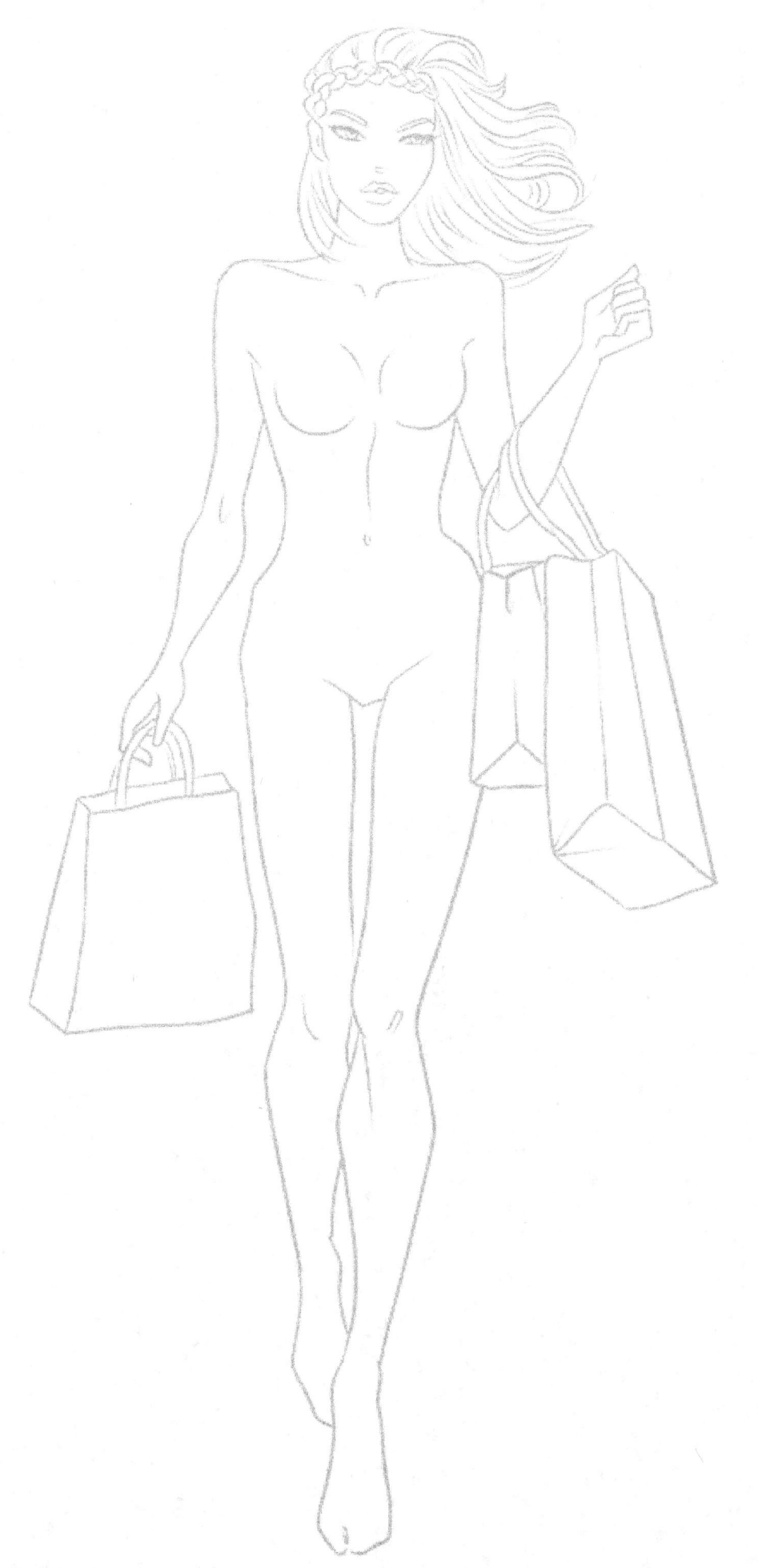

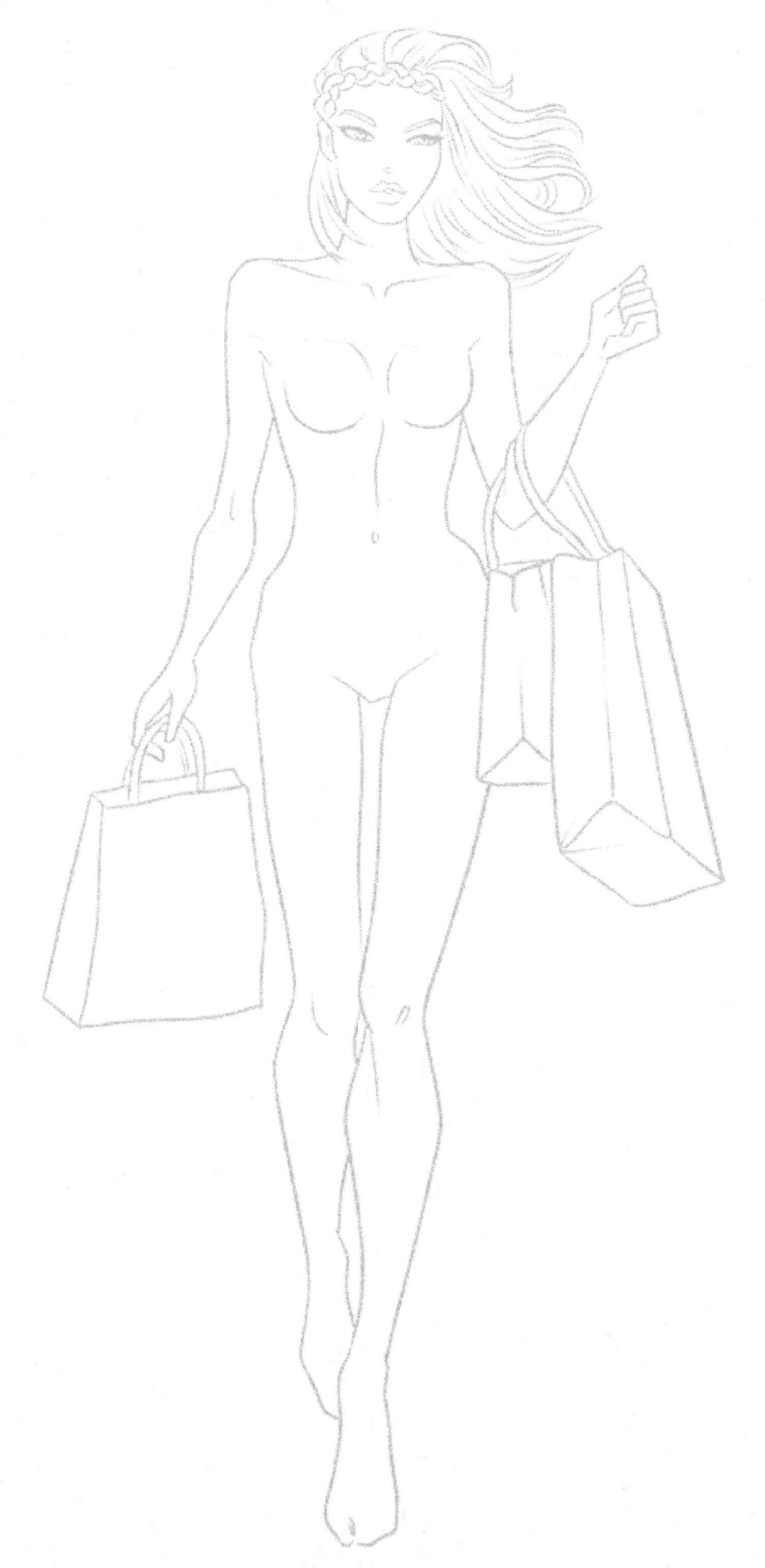

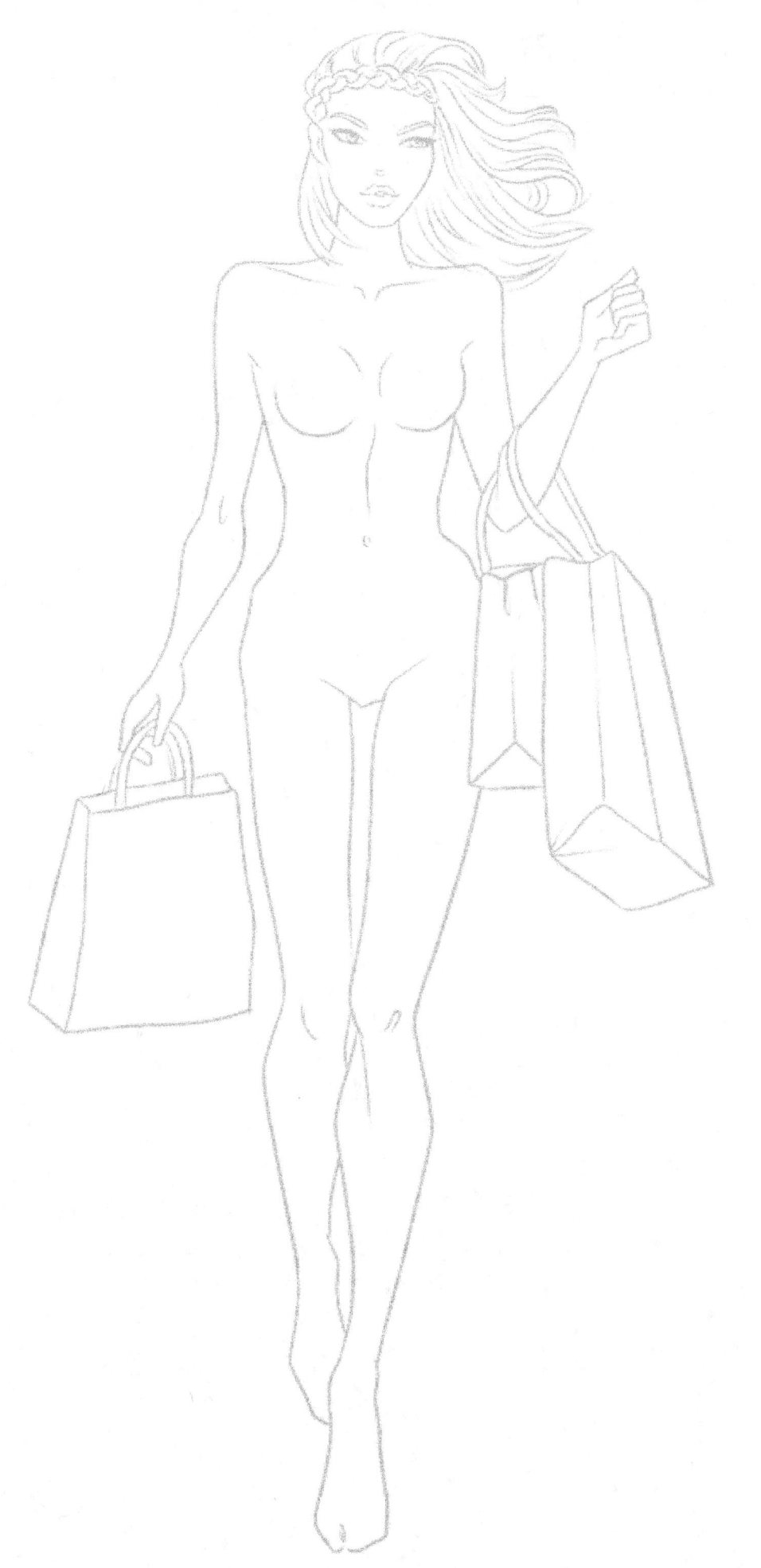

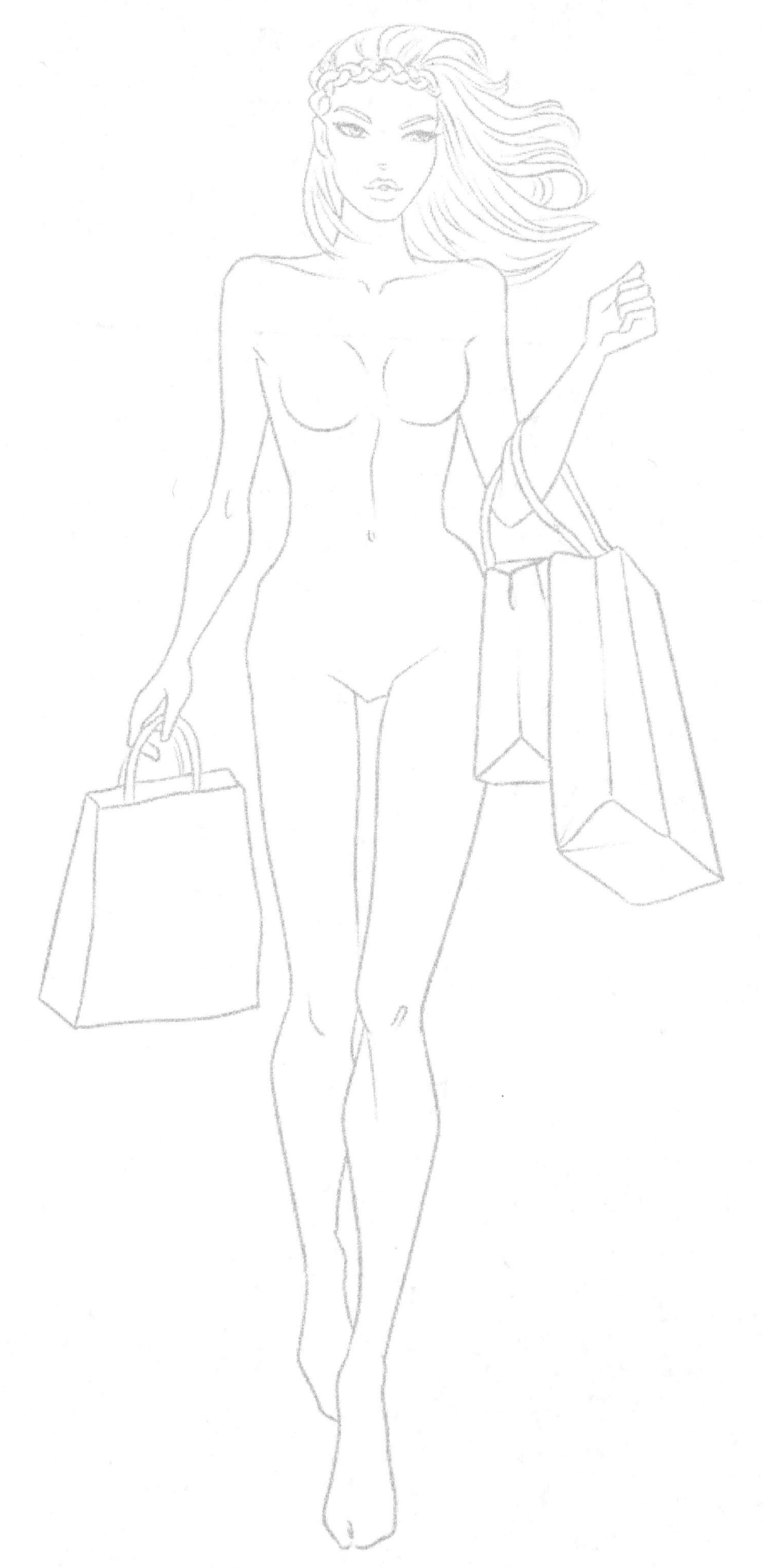

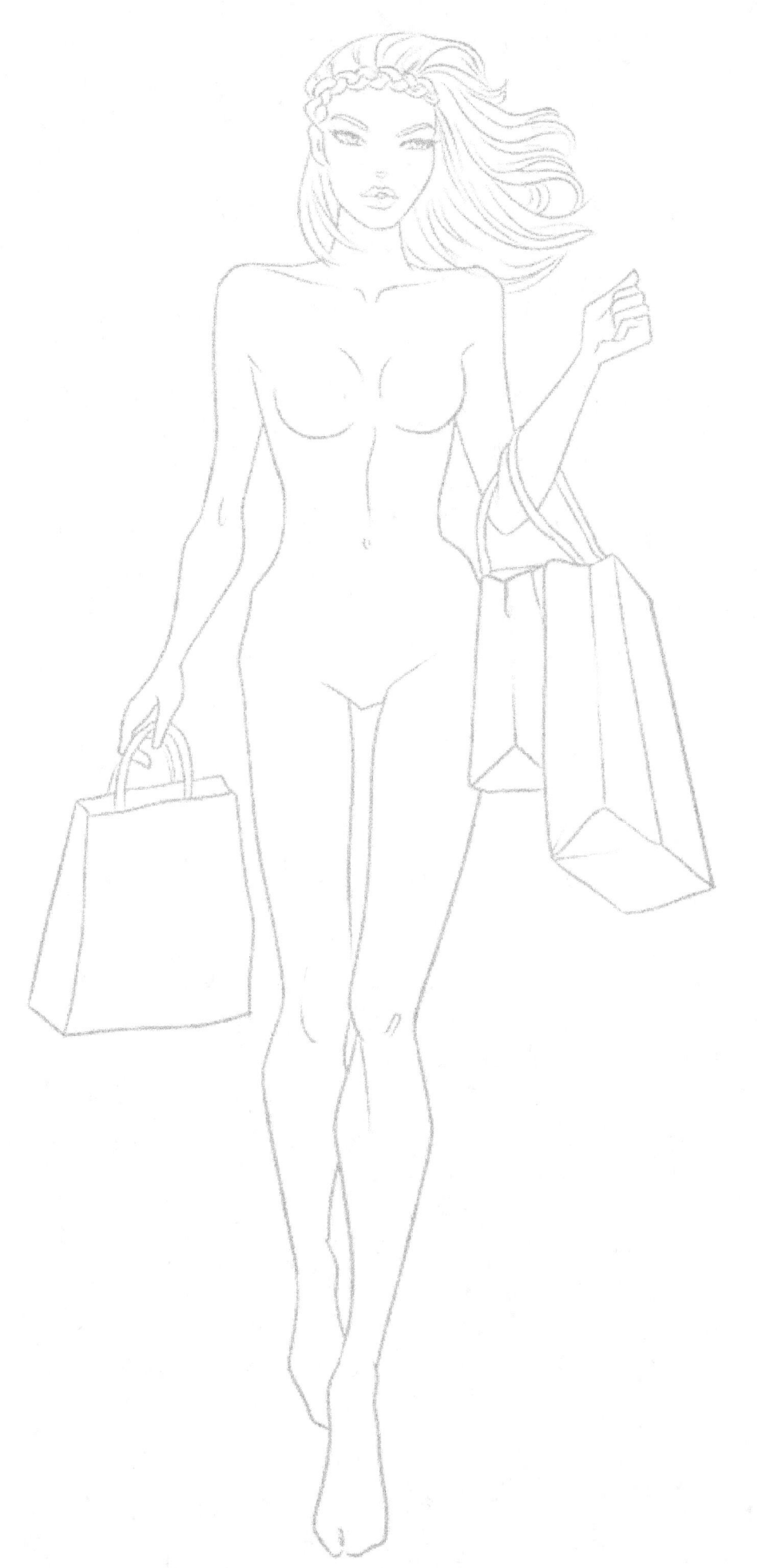

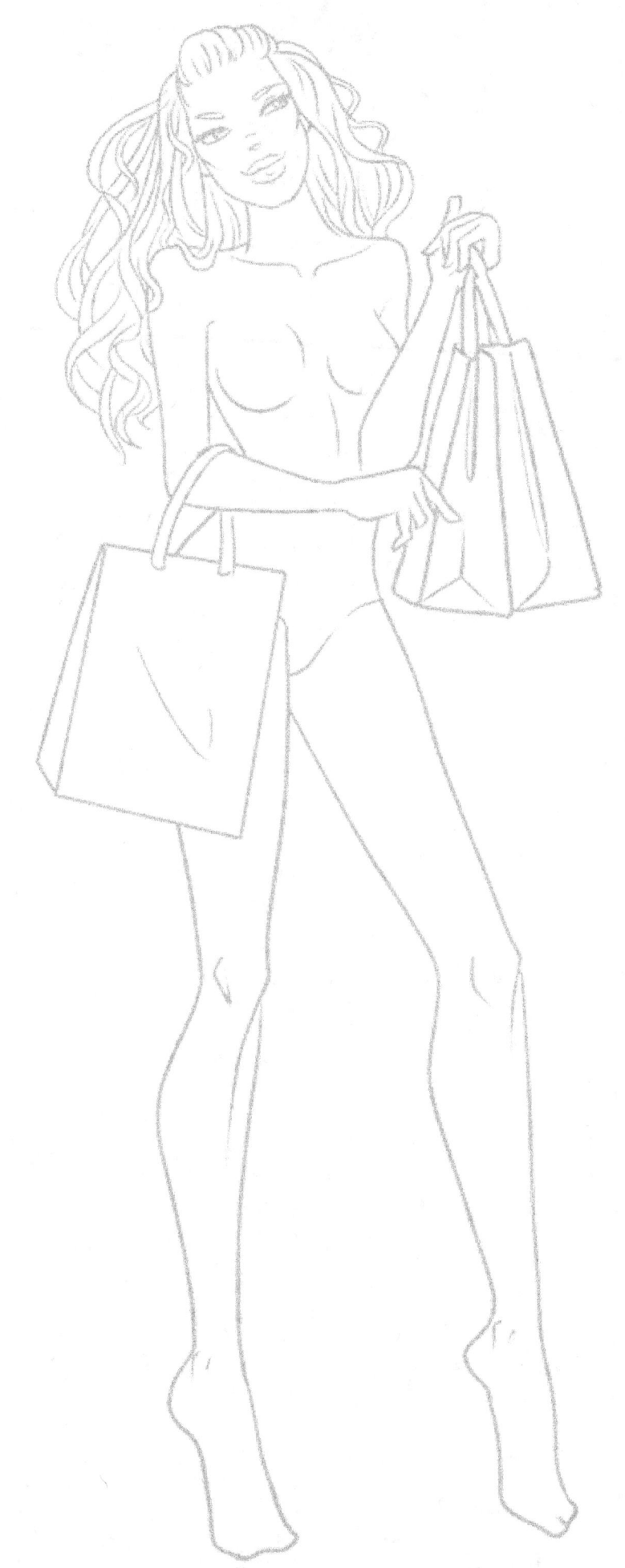

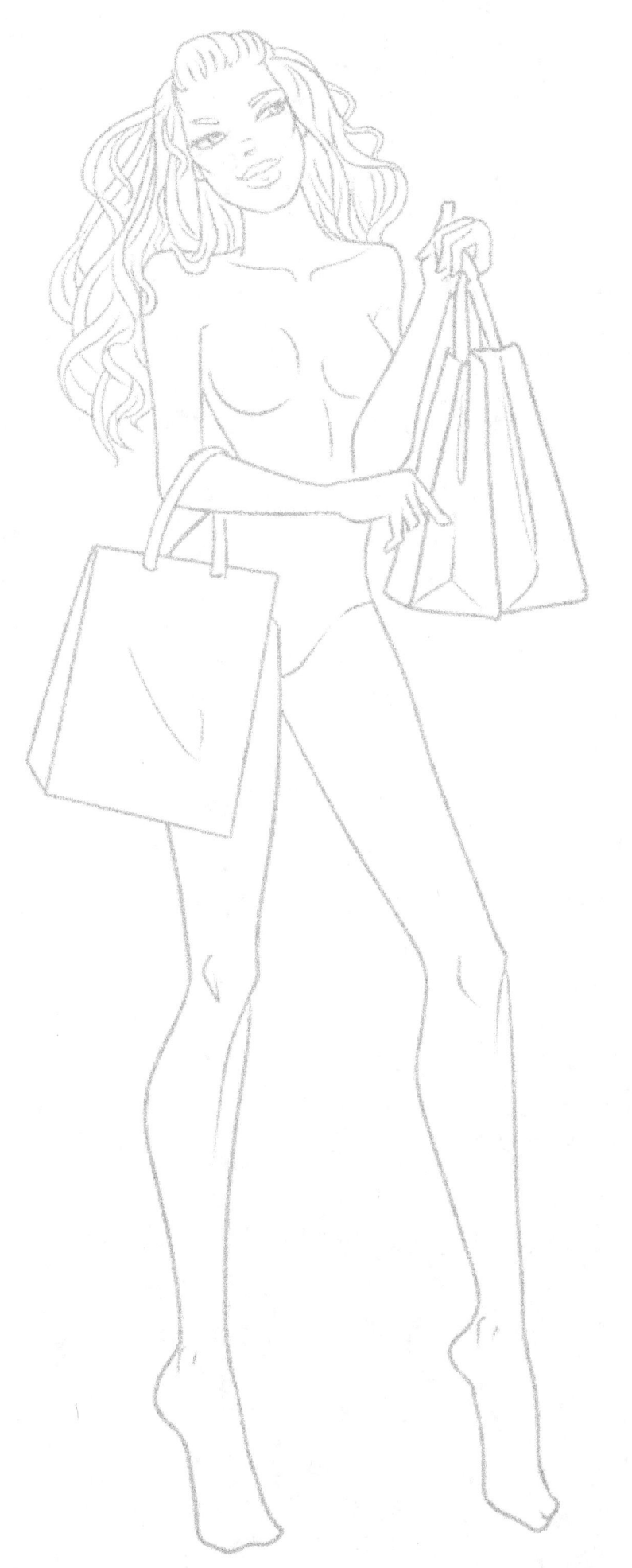

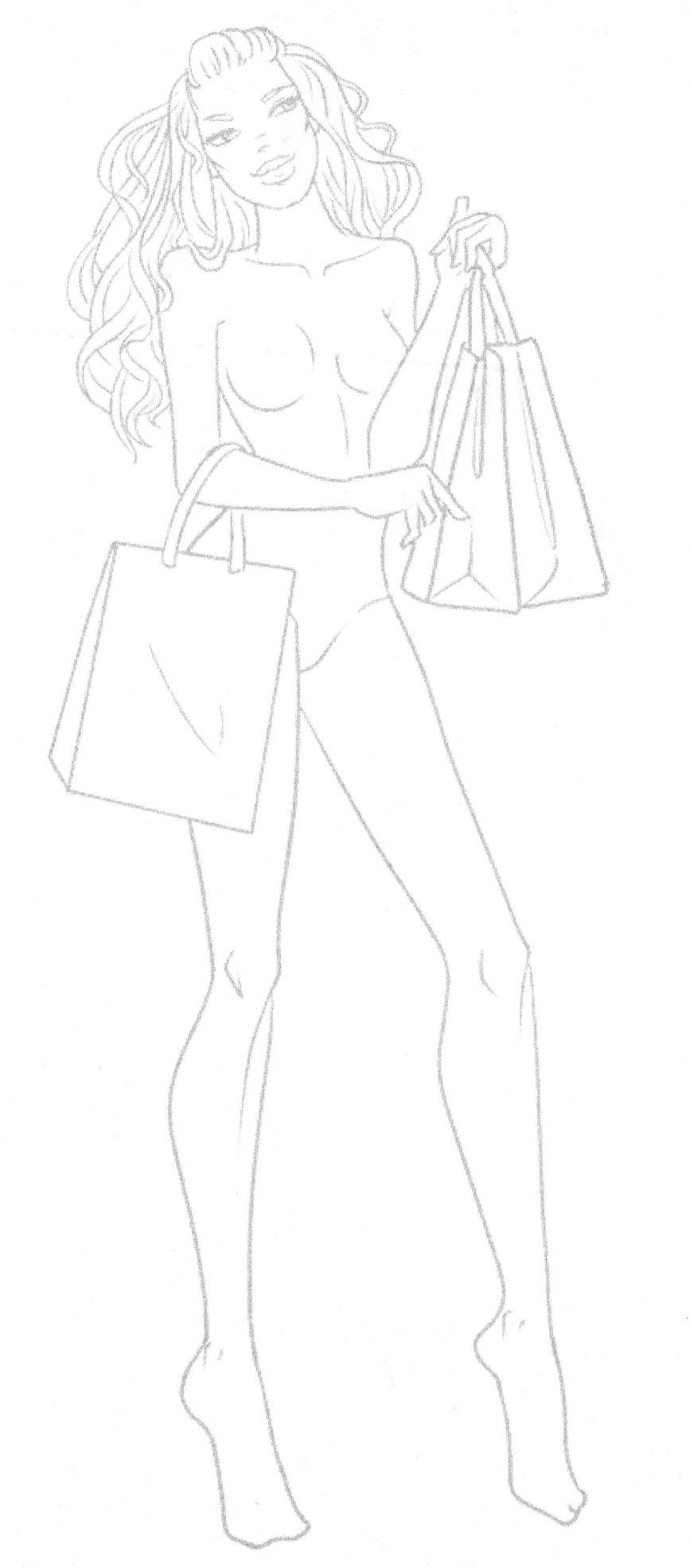

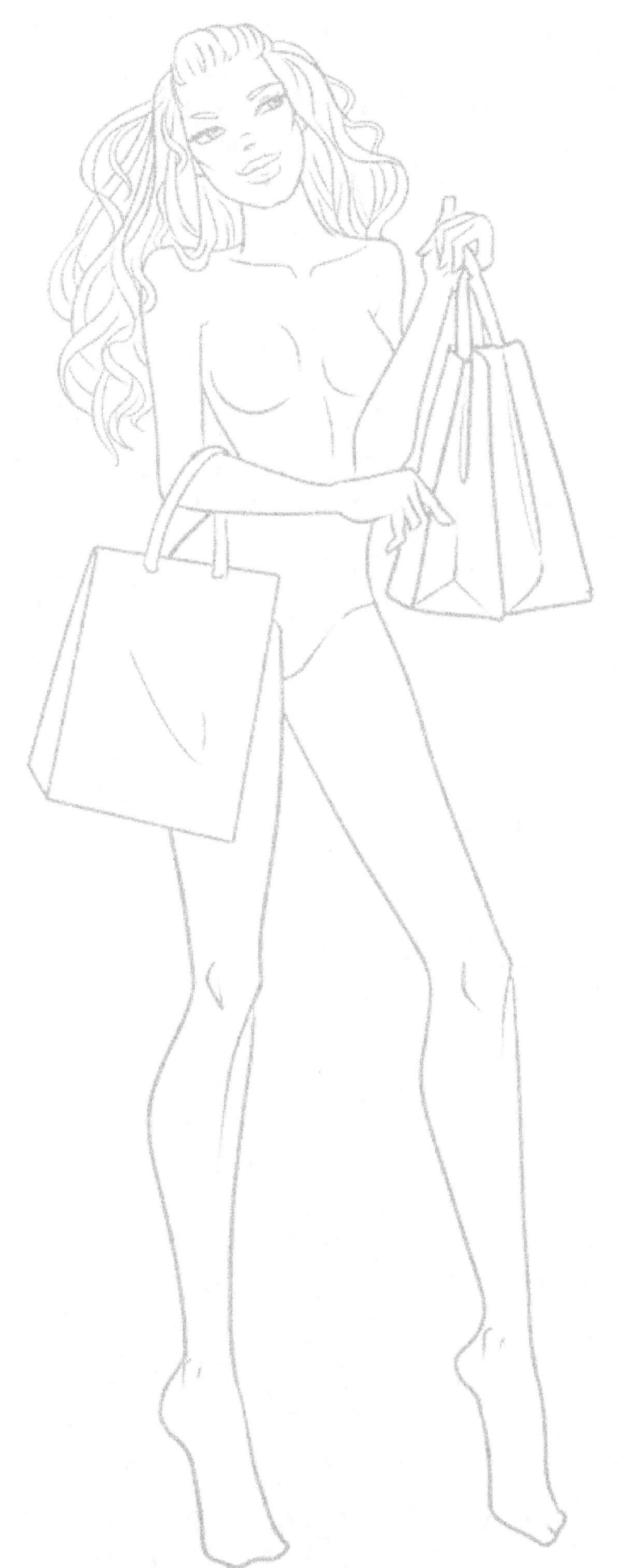

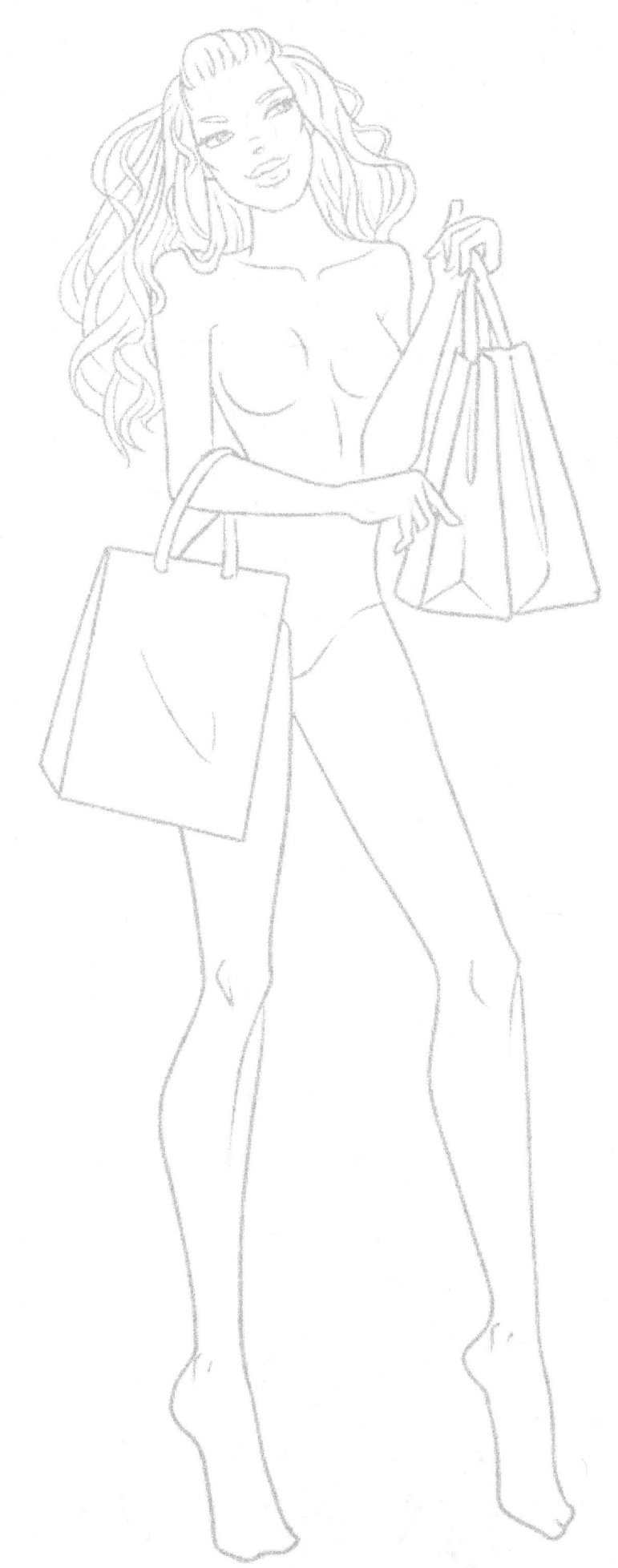

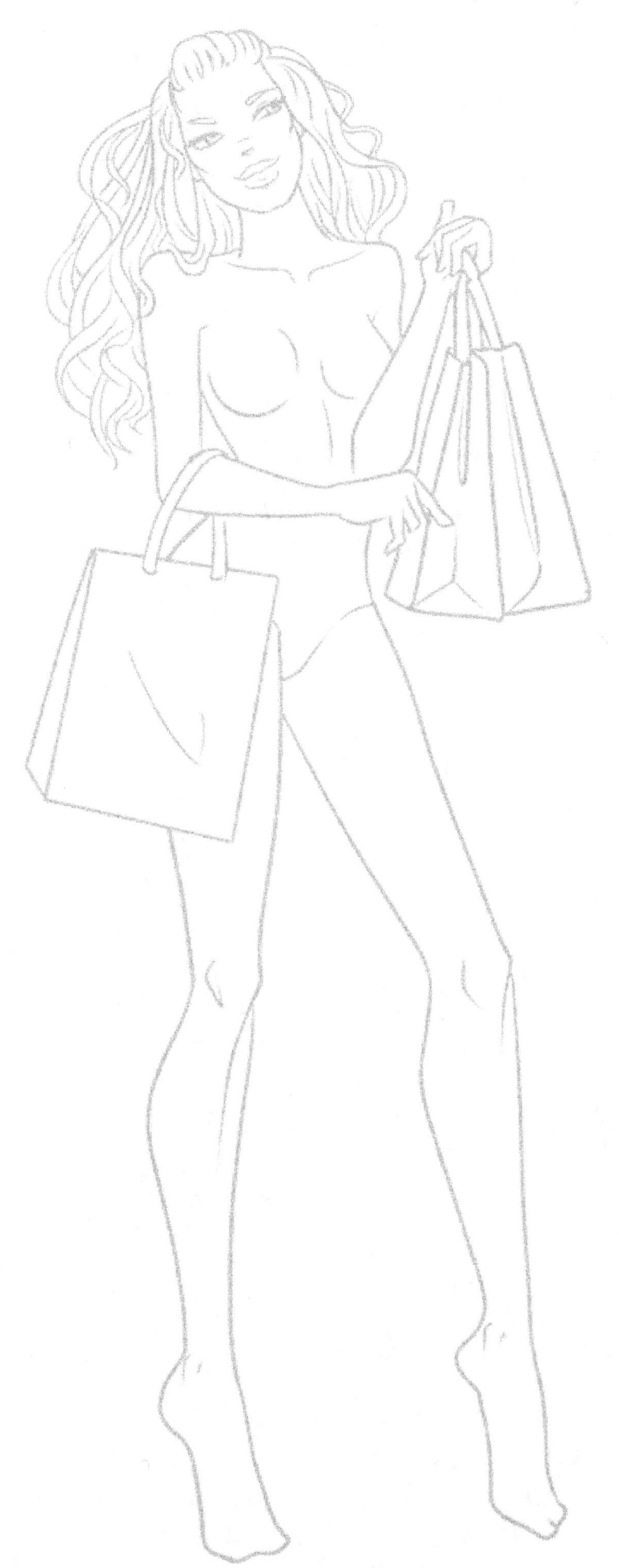

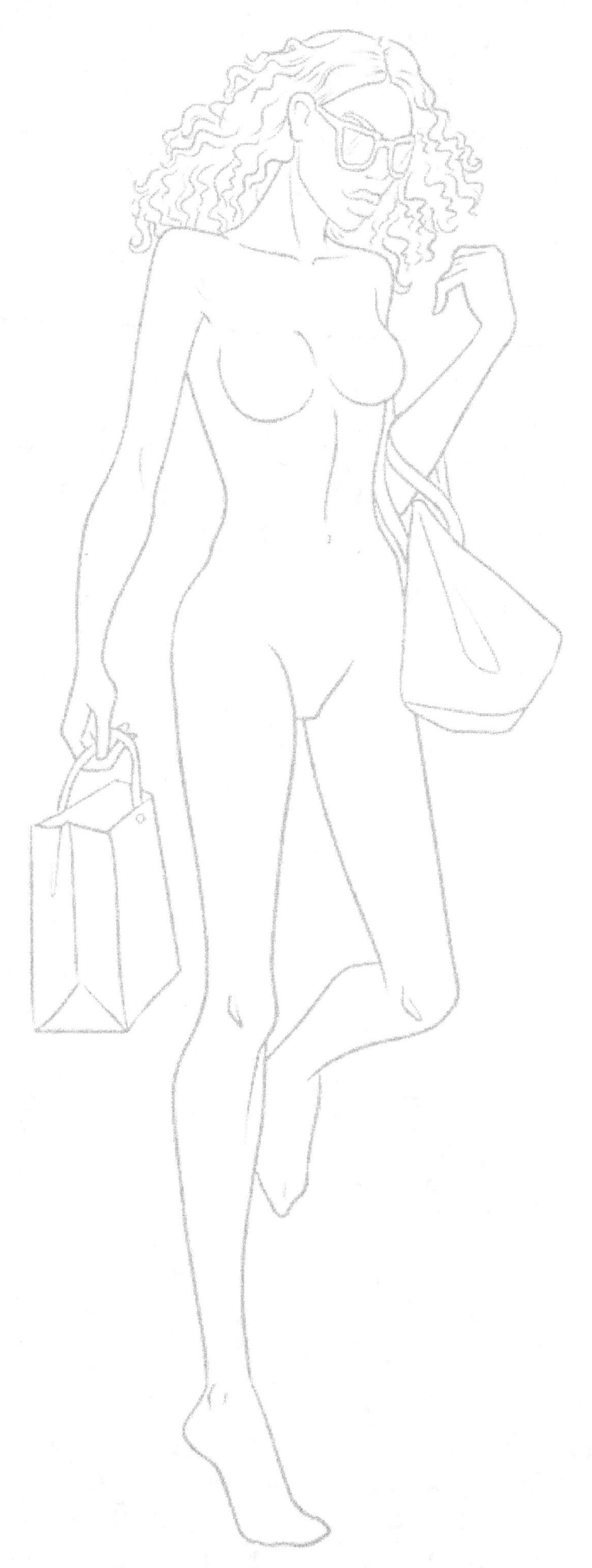

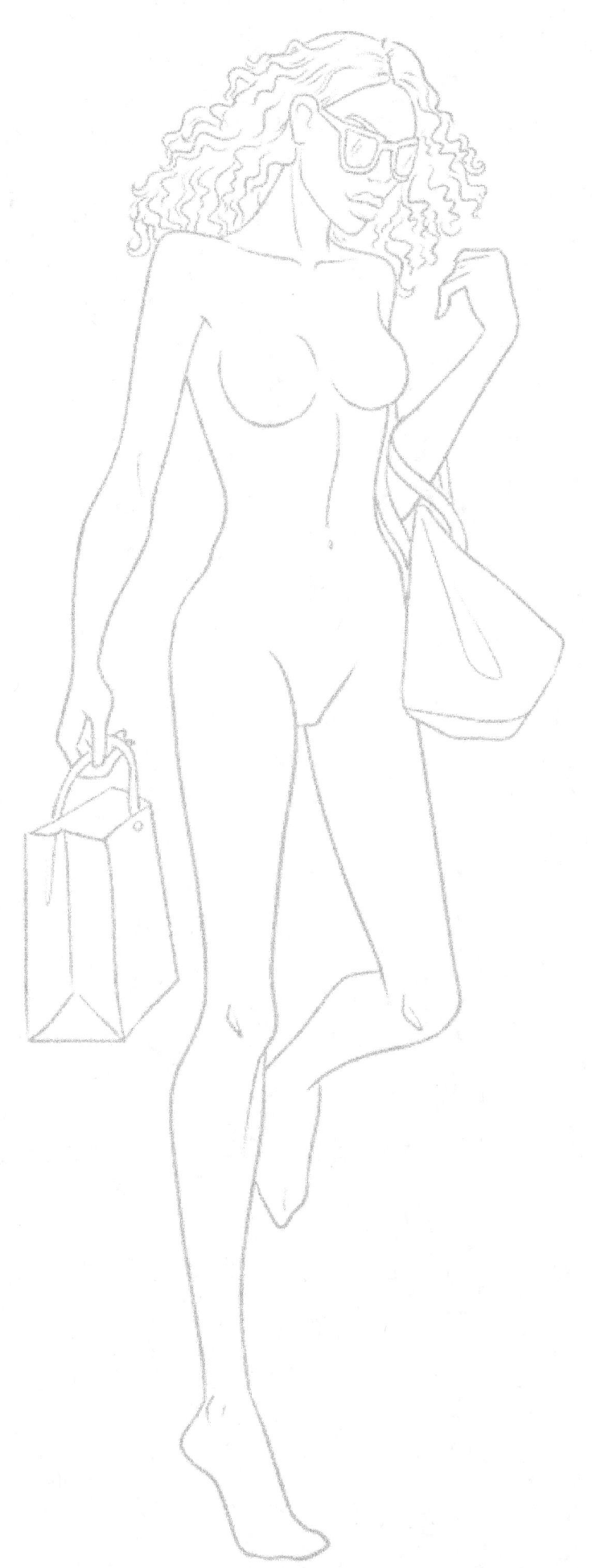

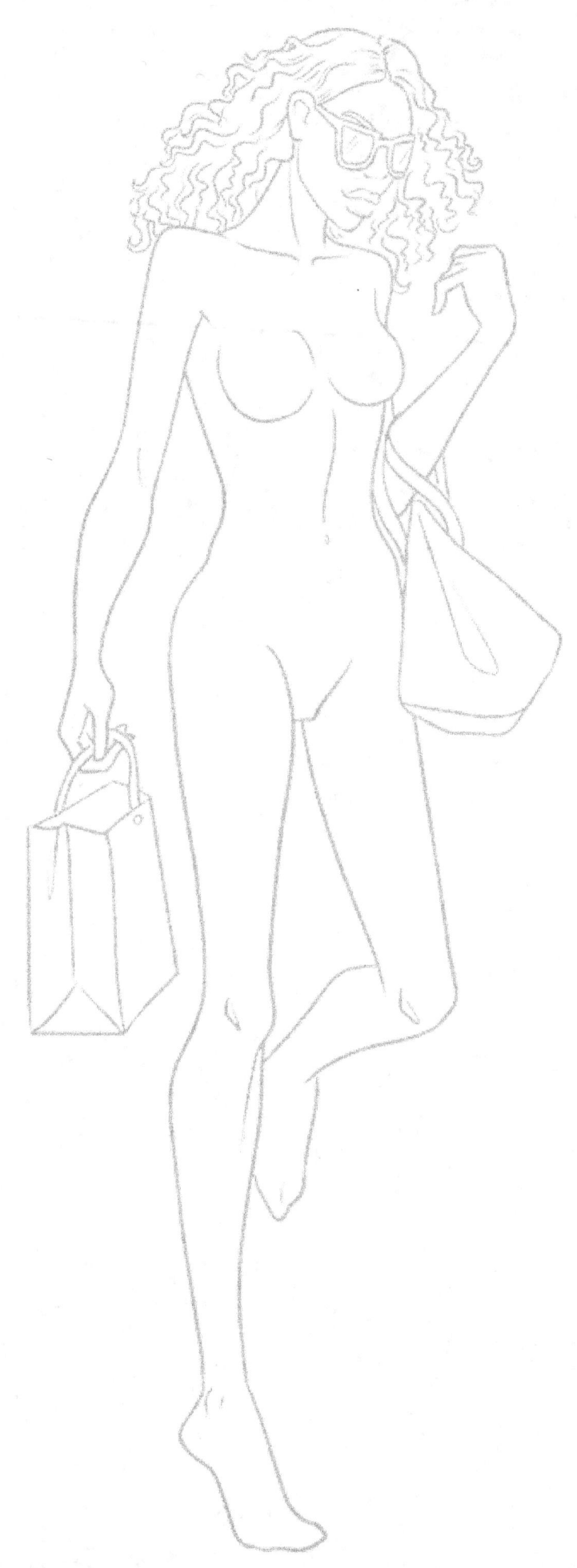

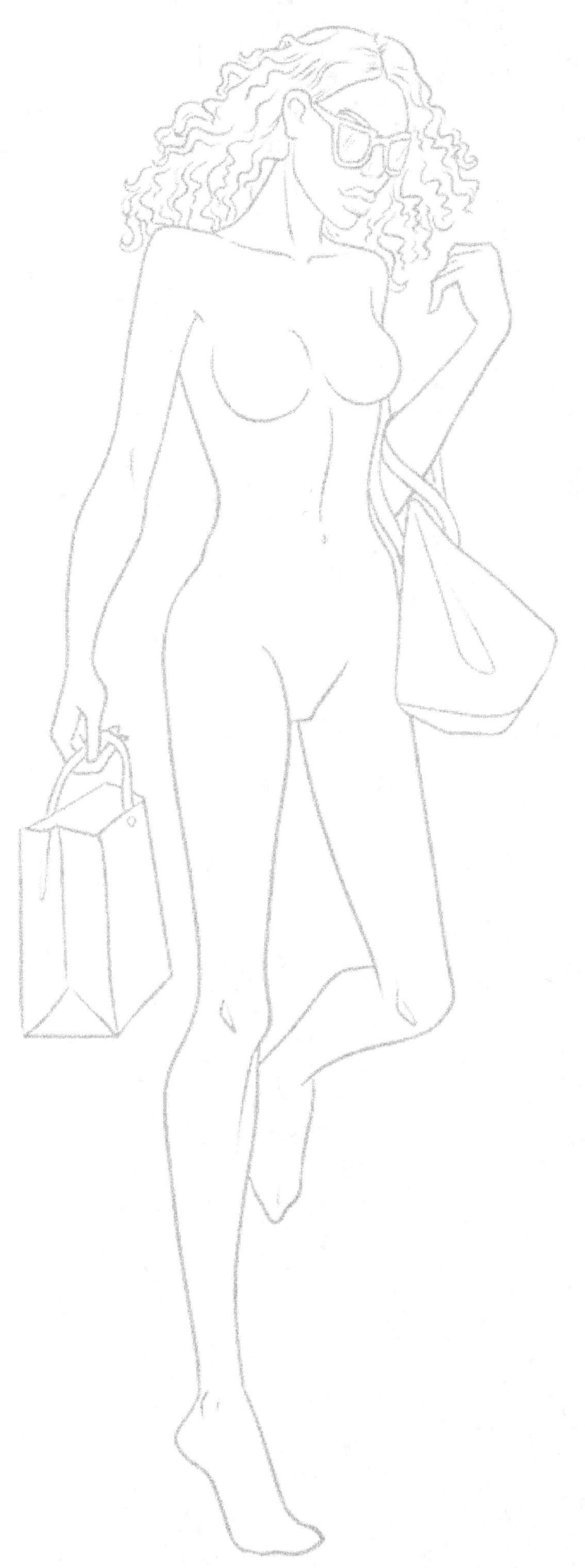

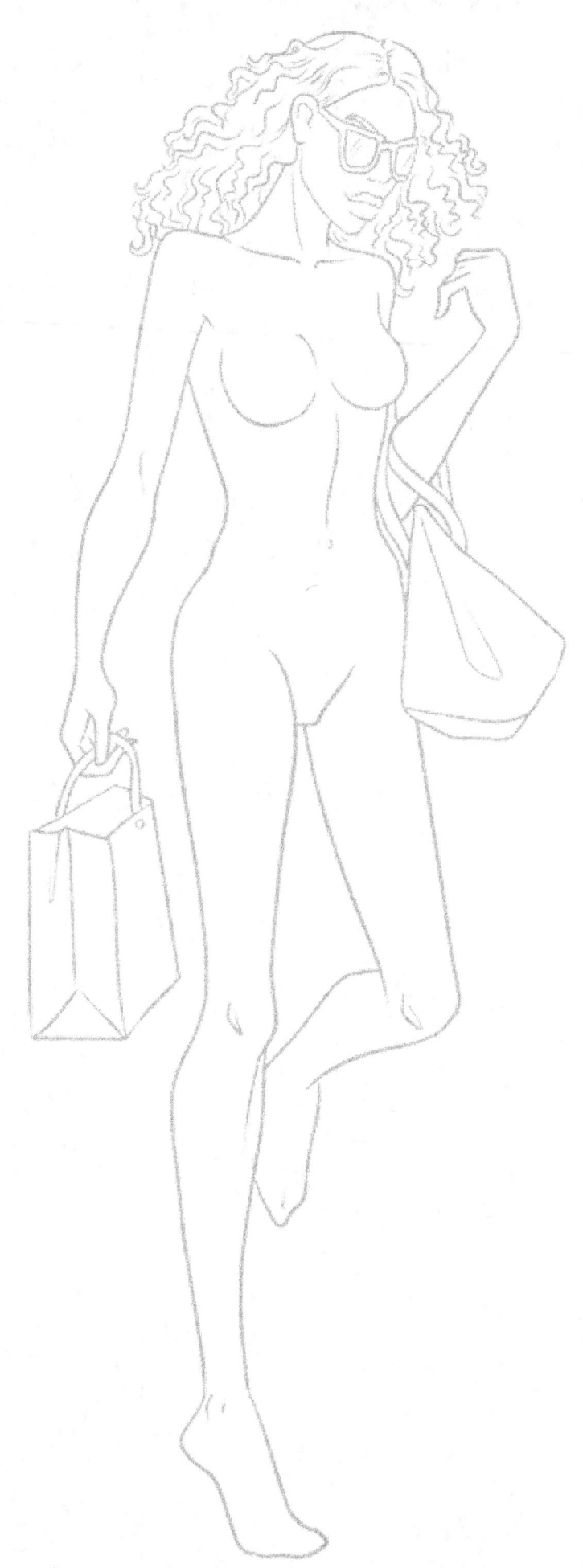

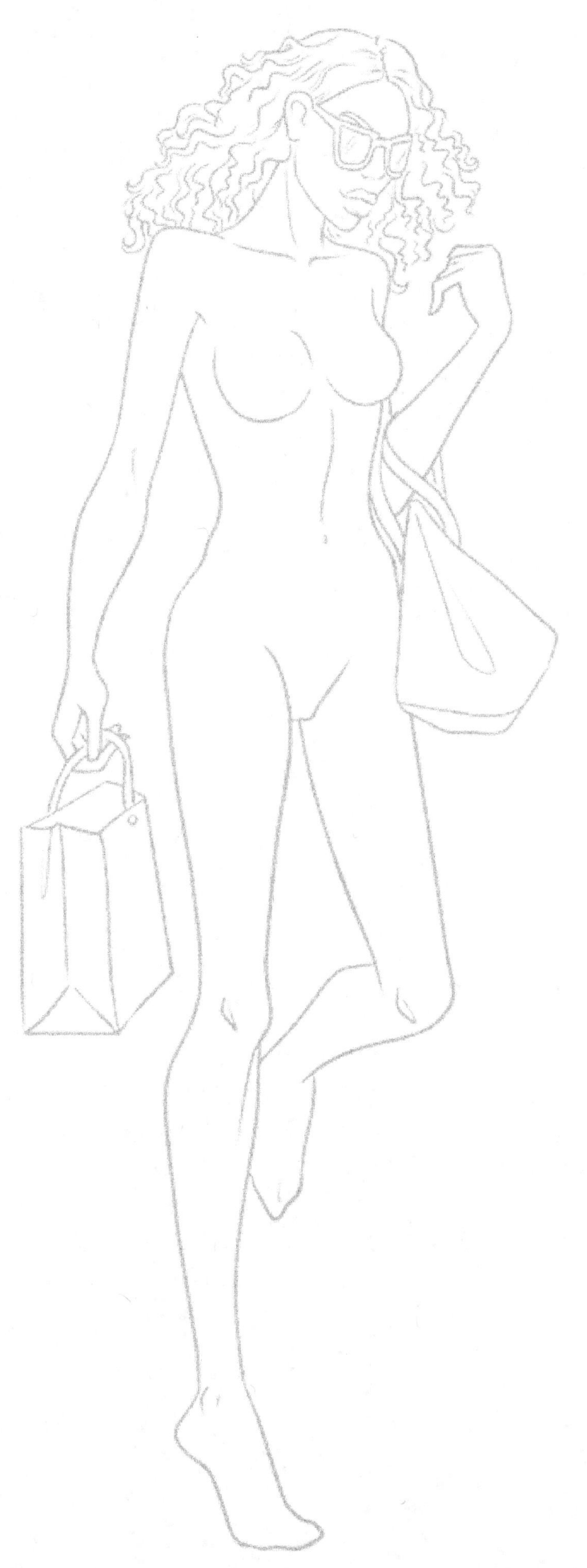

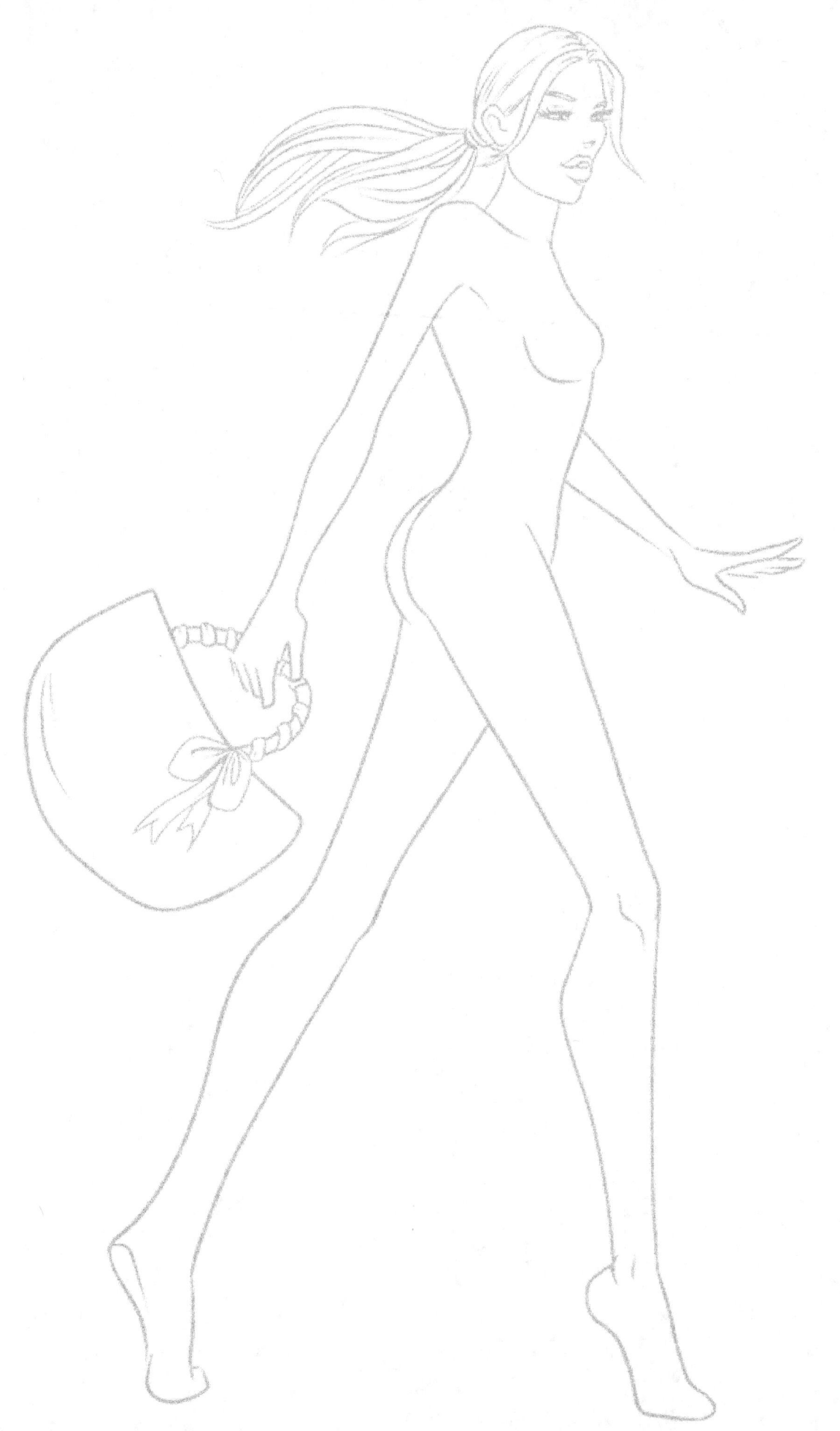

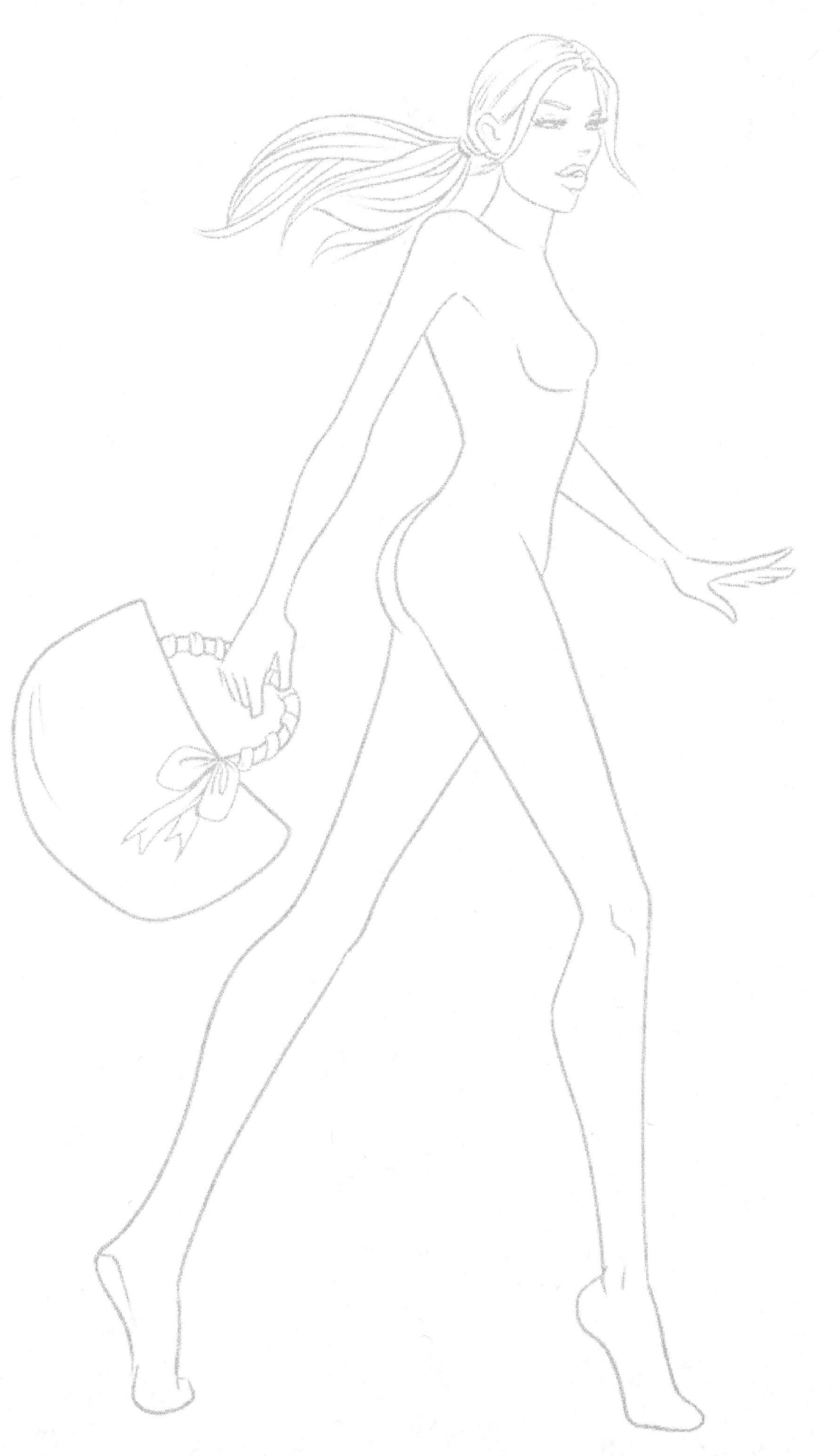

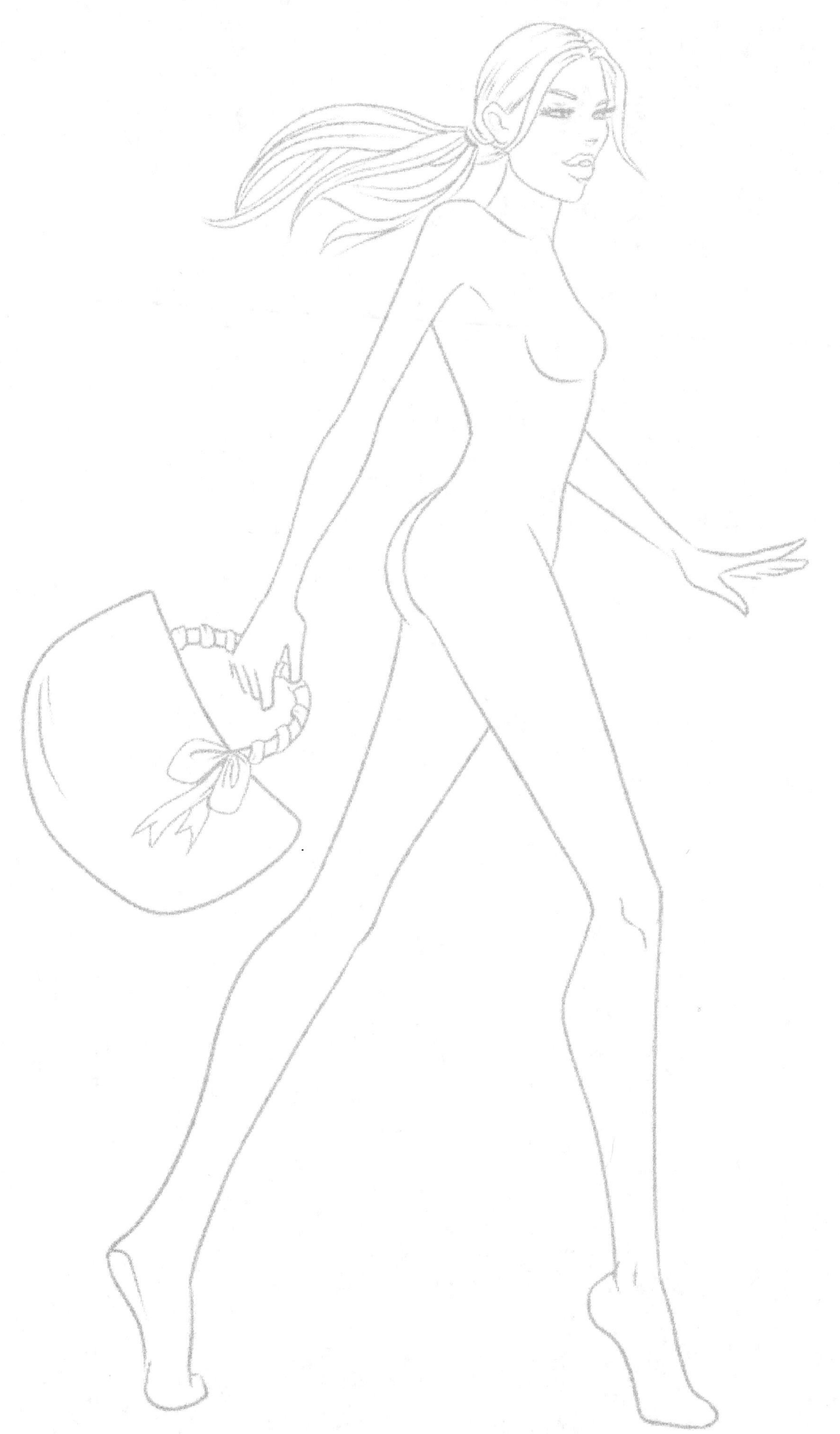

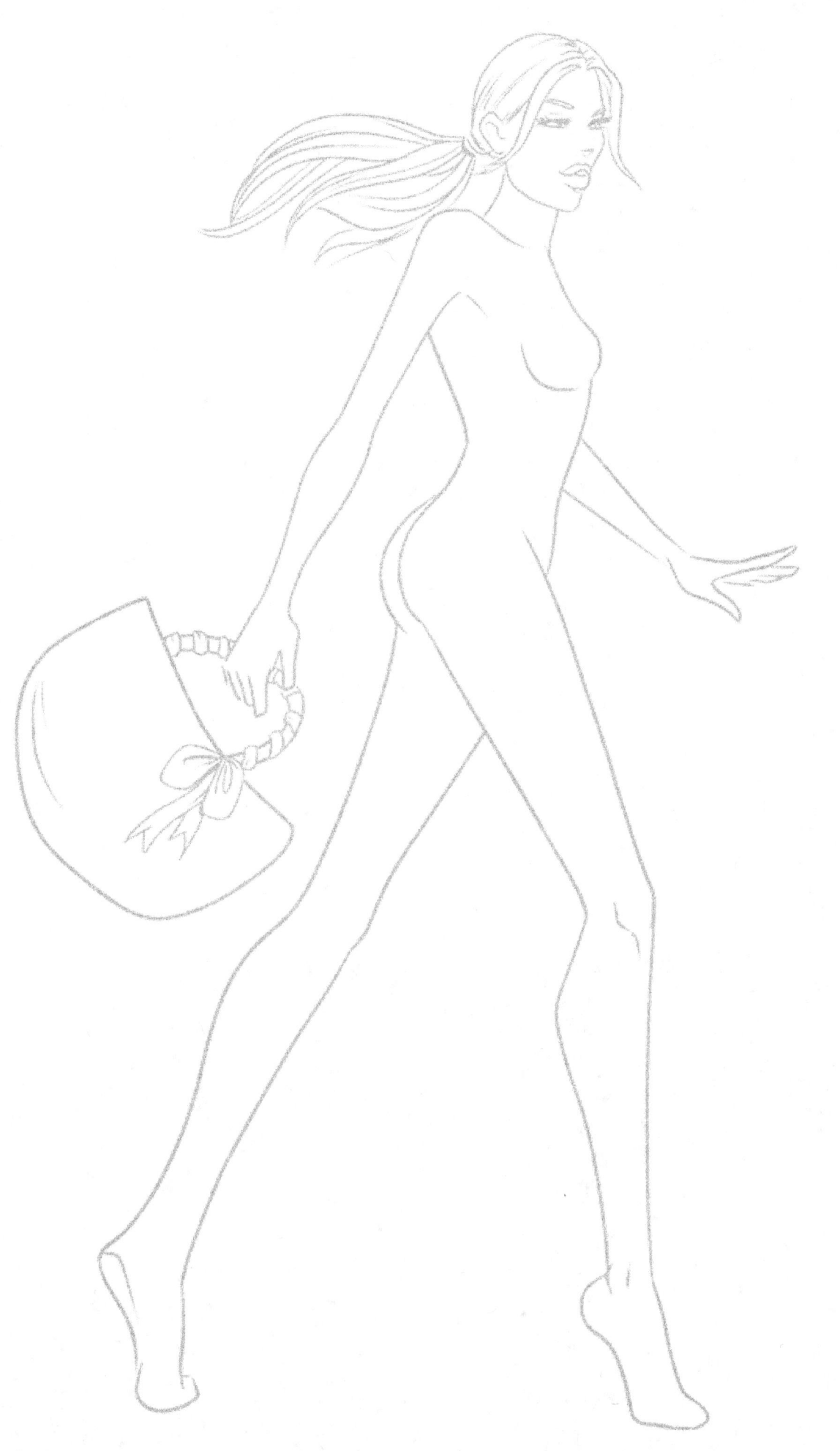

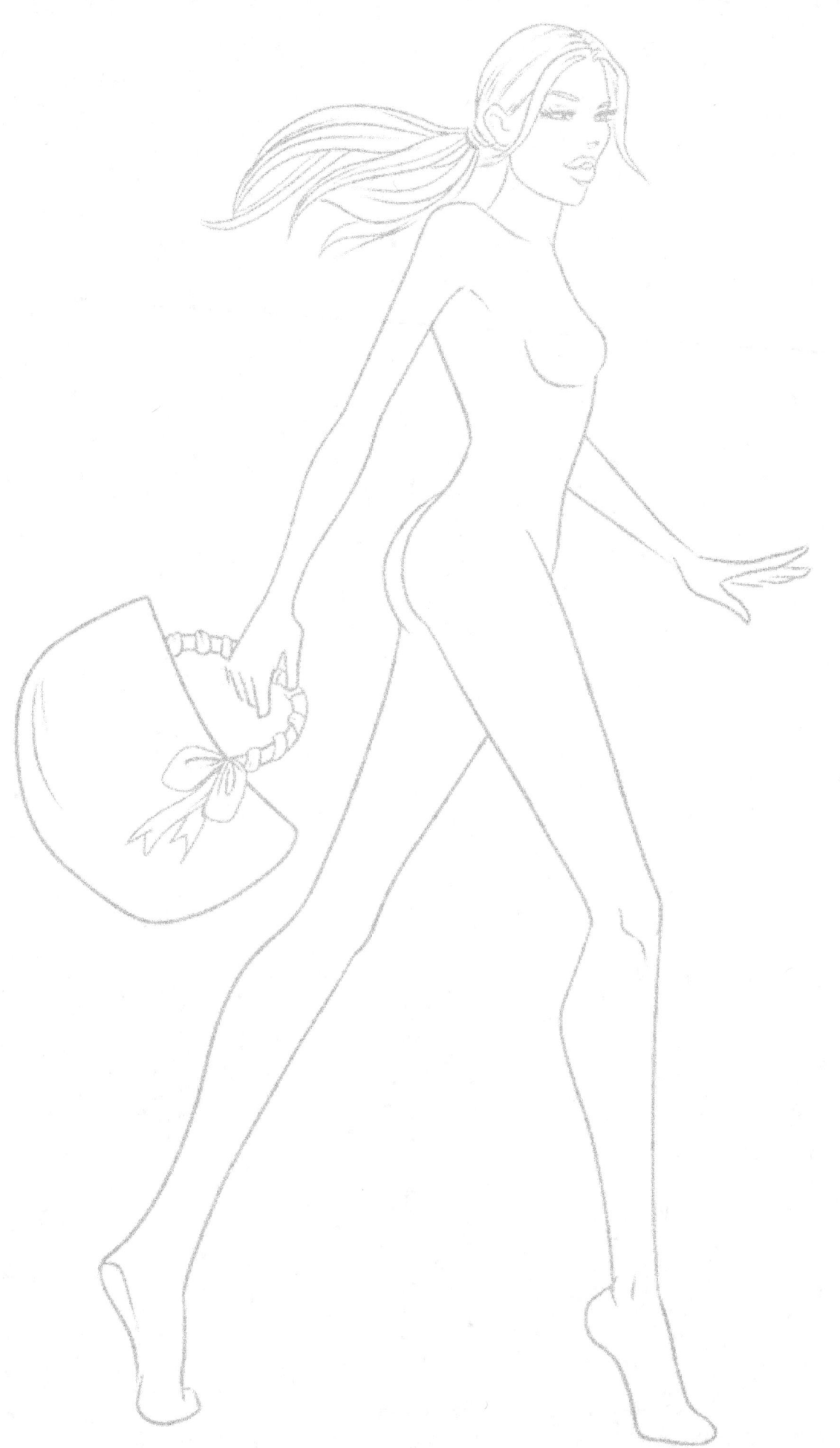

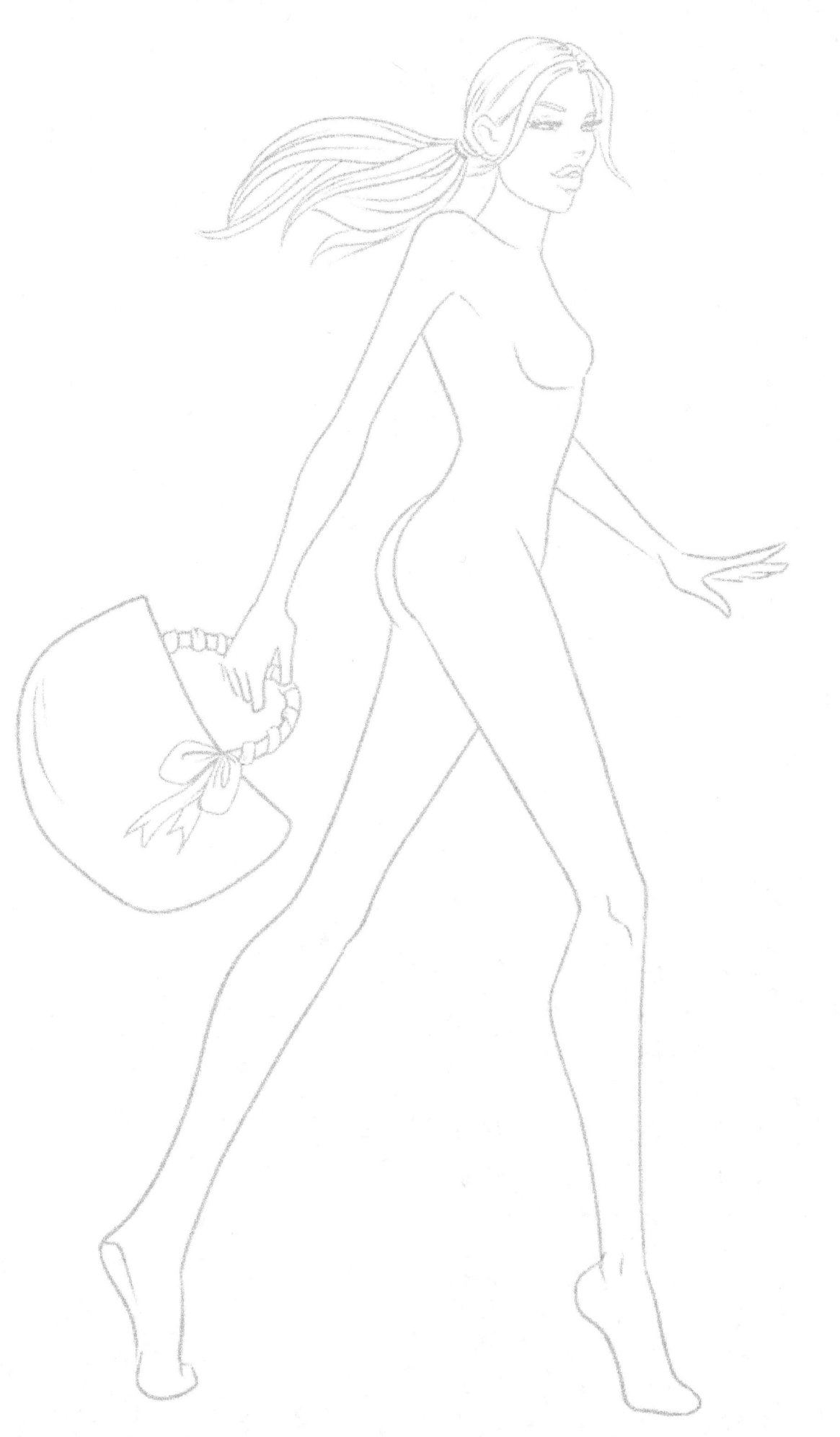

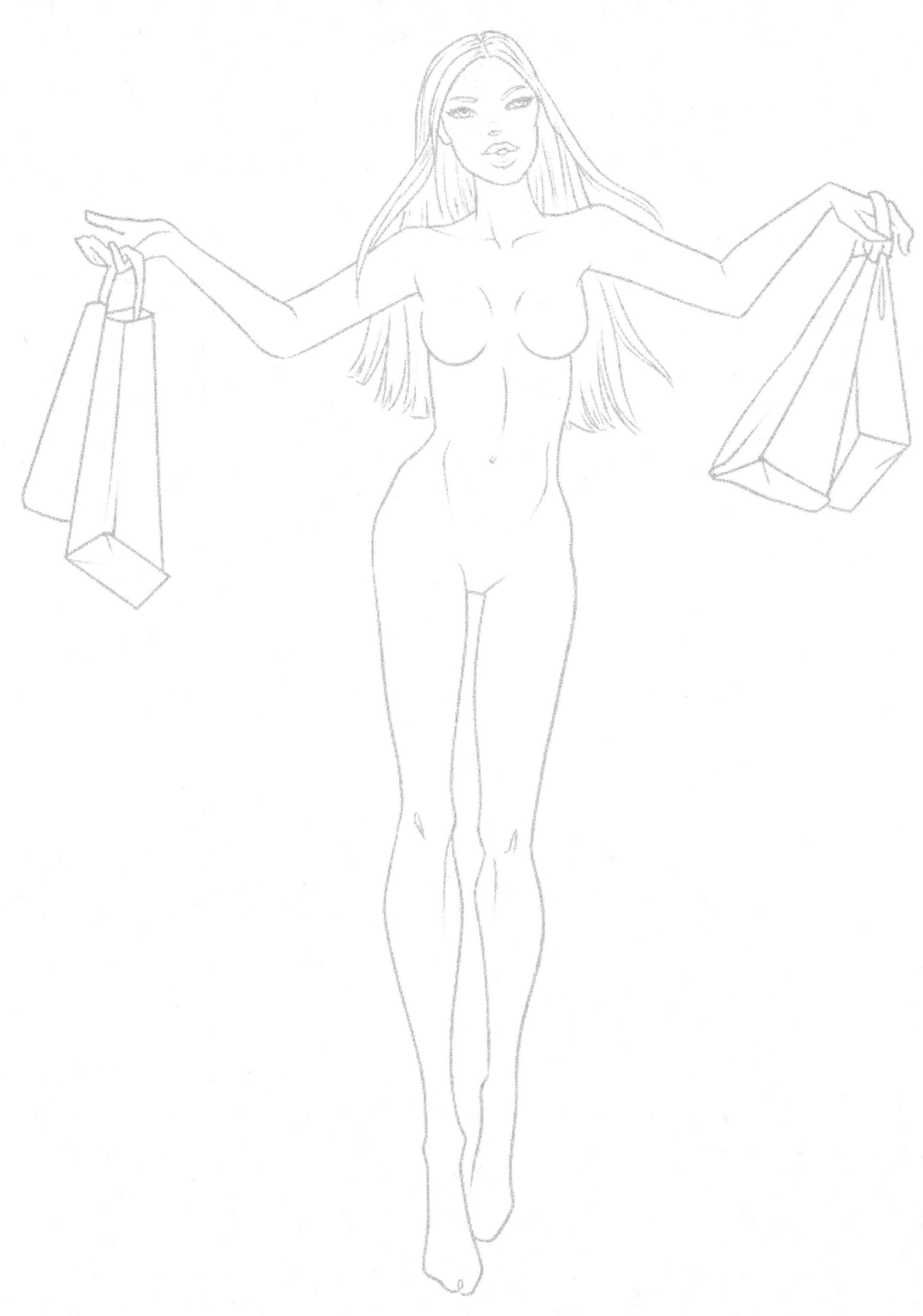

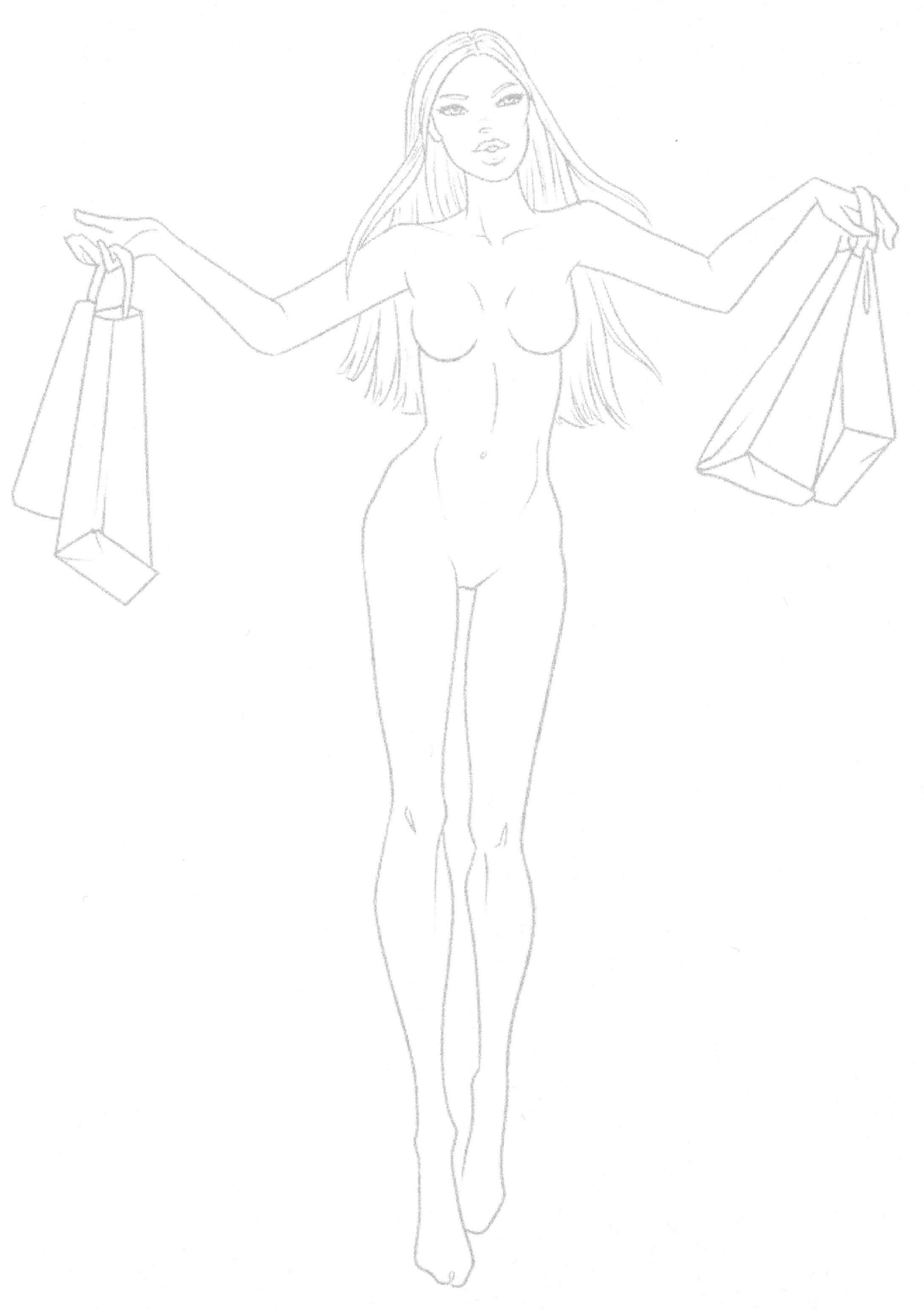

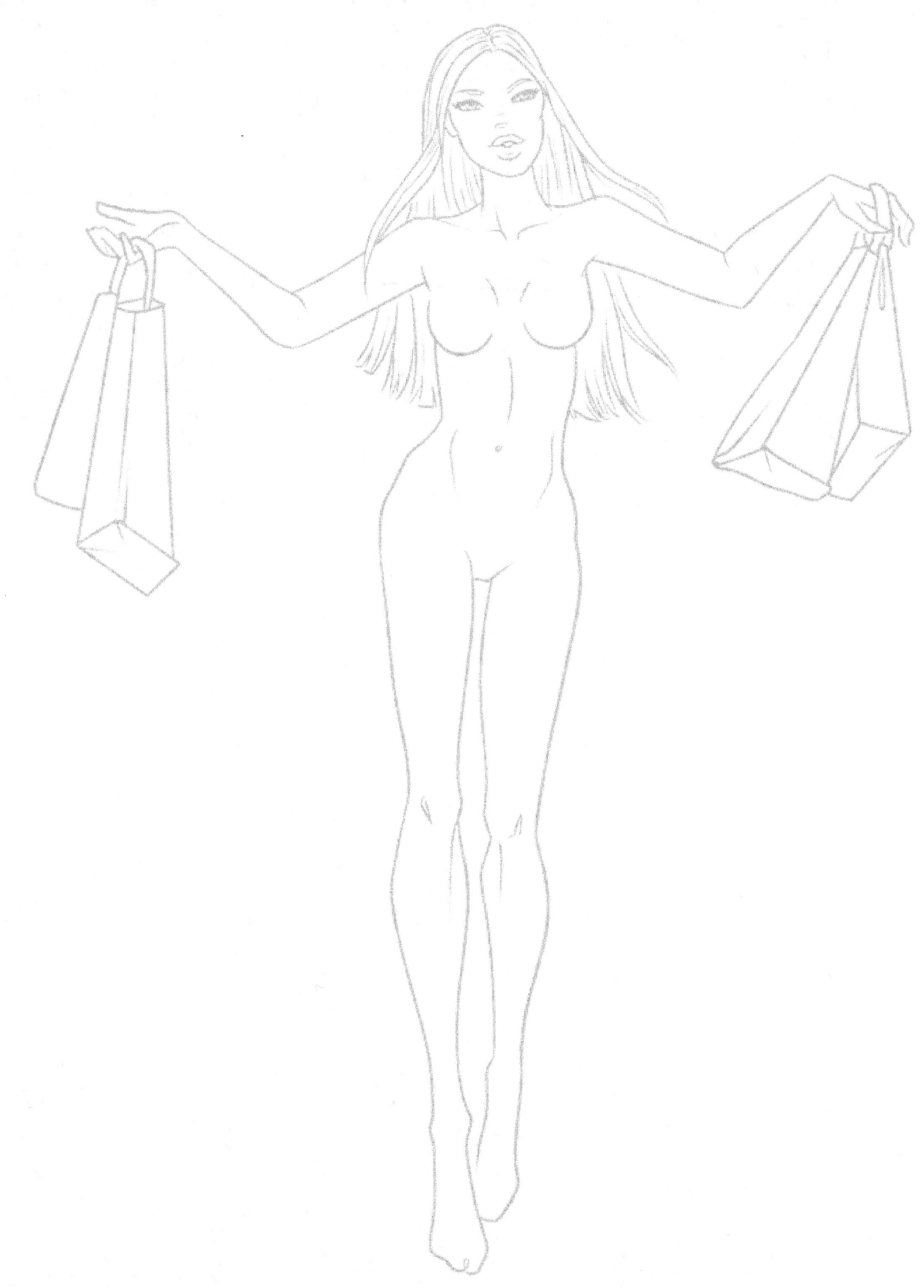

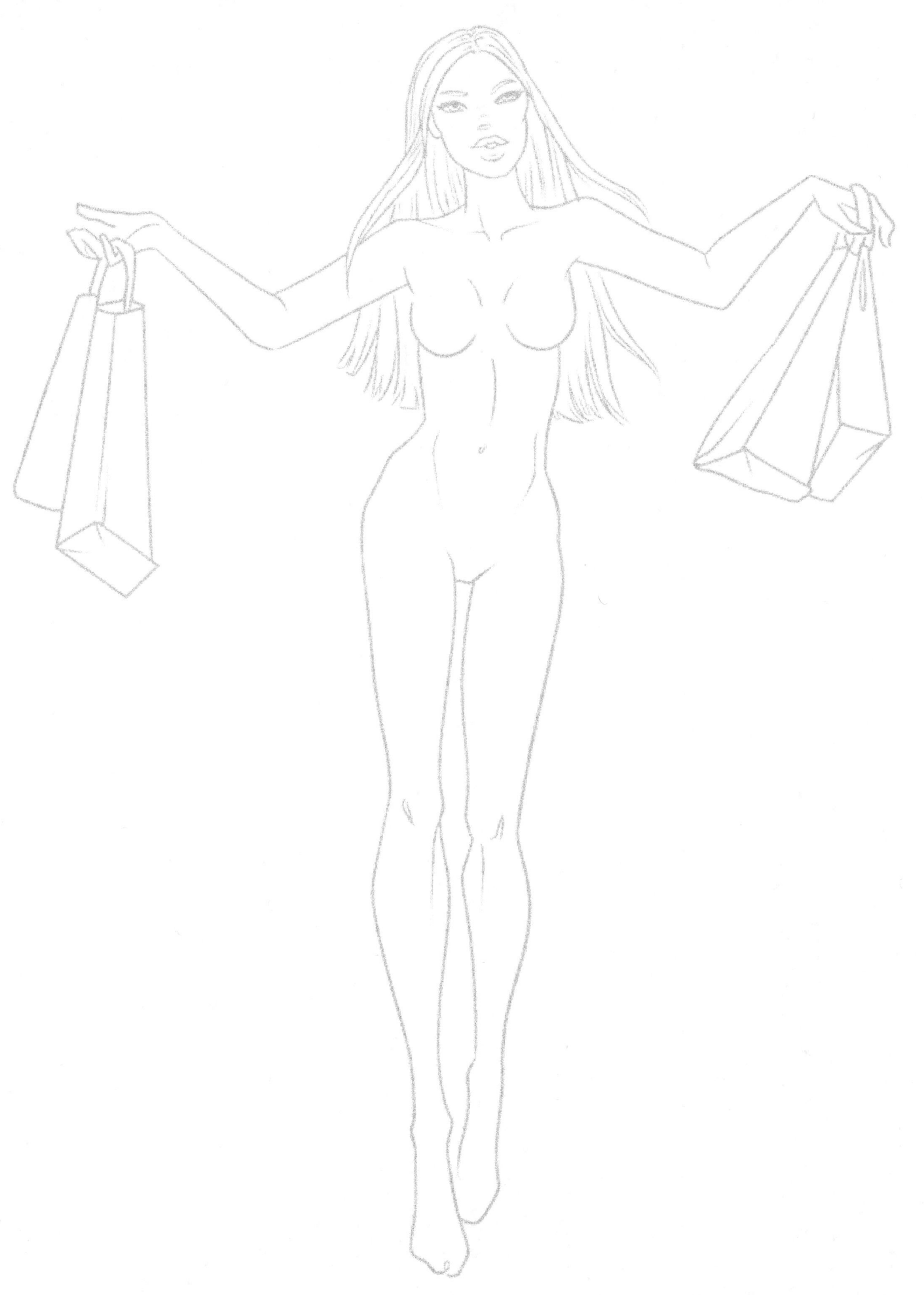

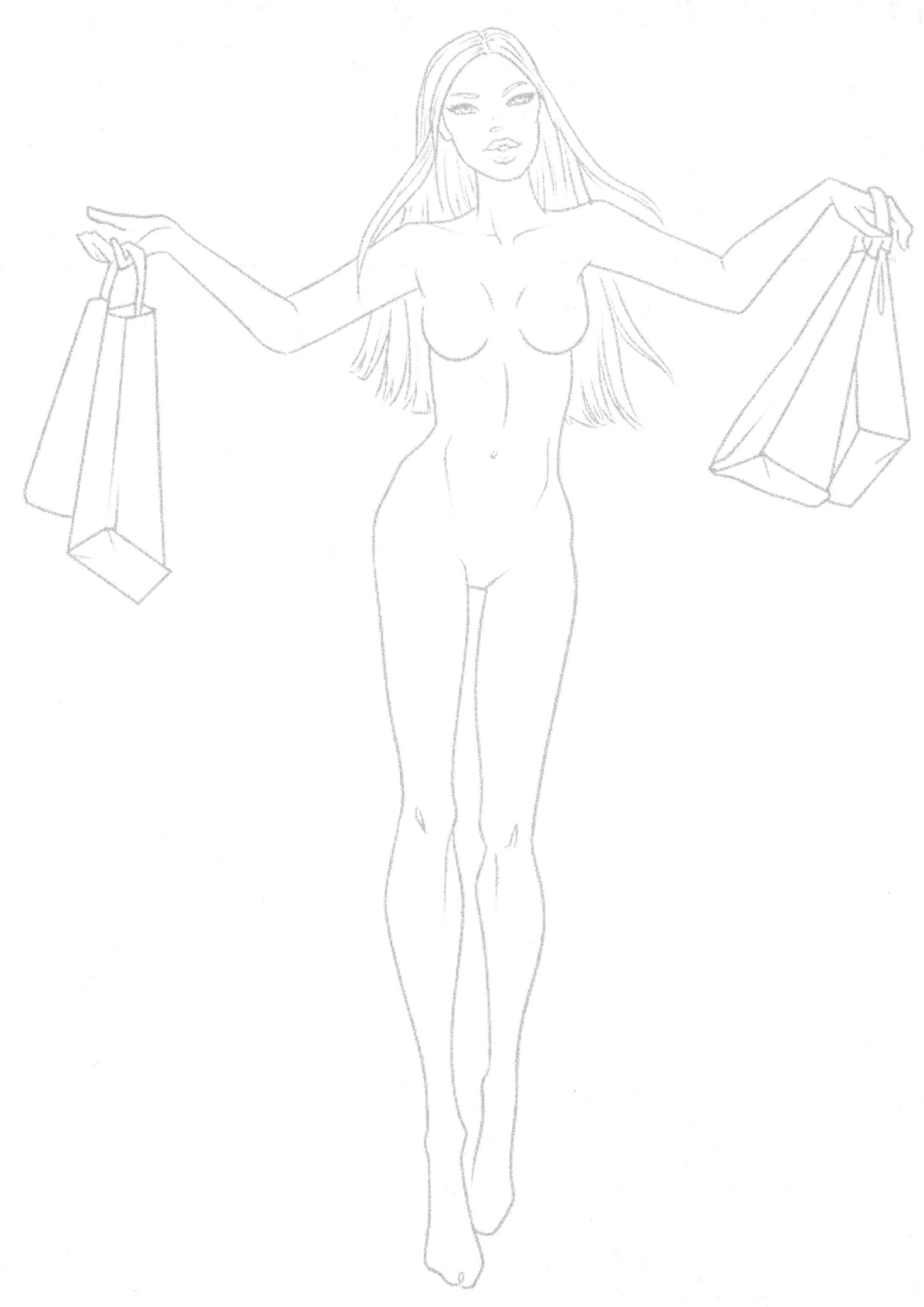

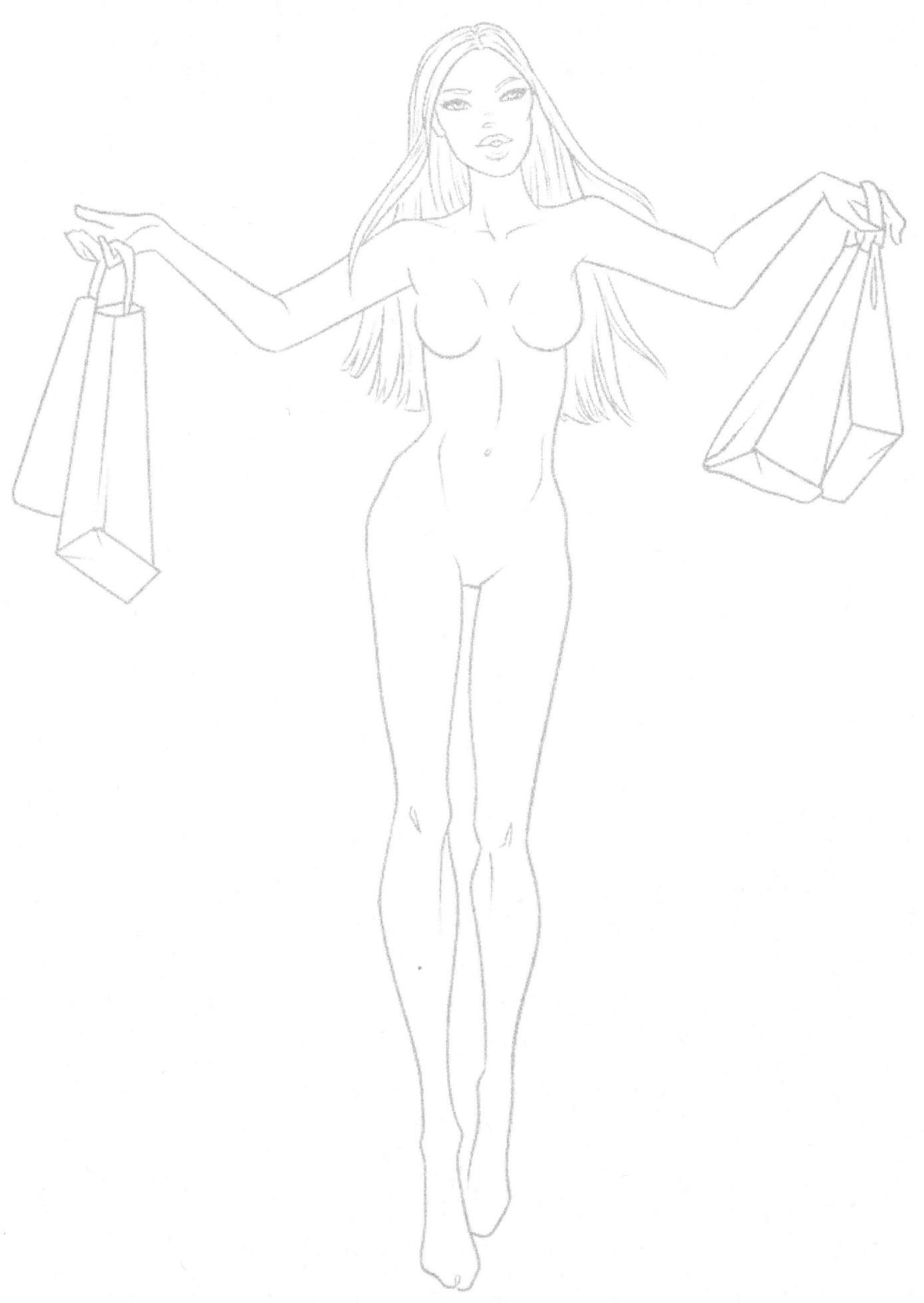

JUST OUTLINES FIGURE TEMPLATES

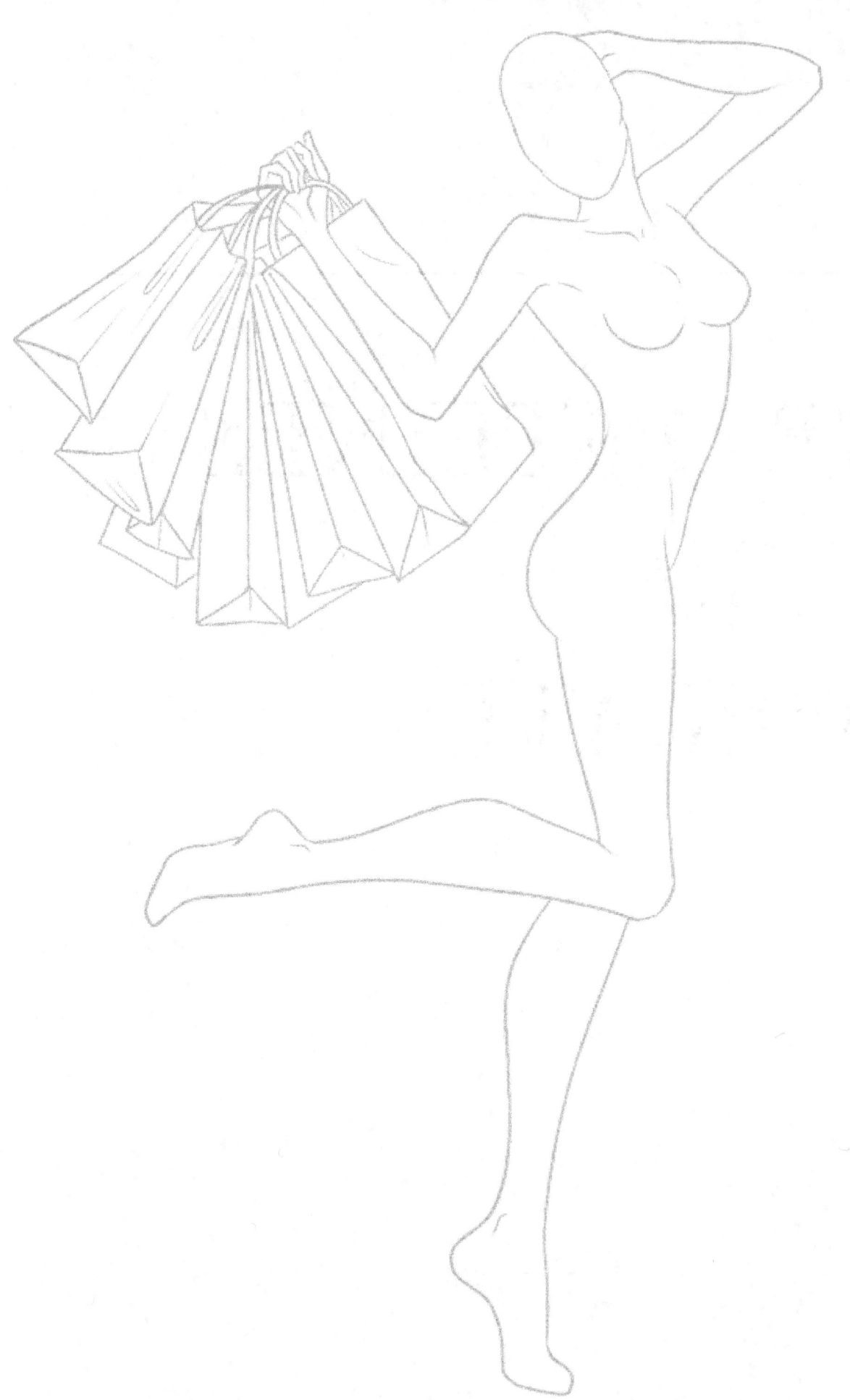

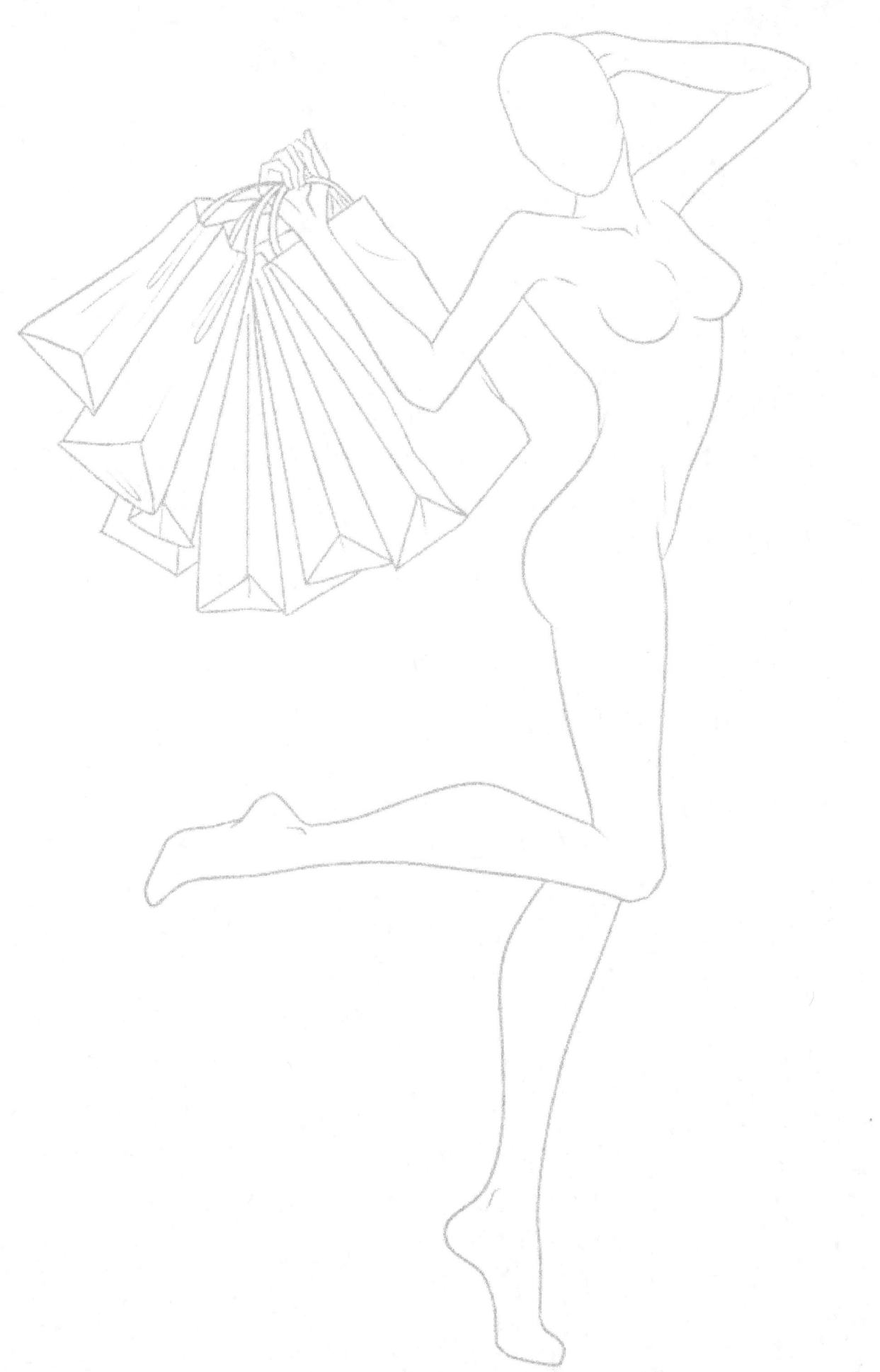

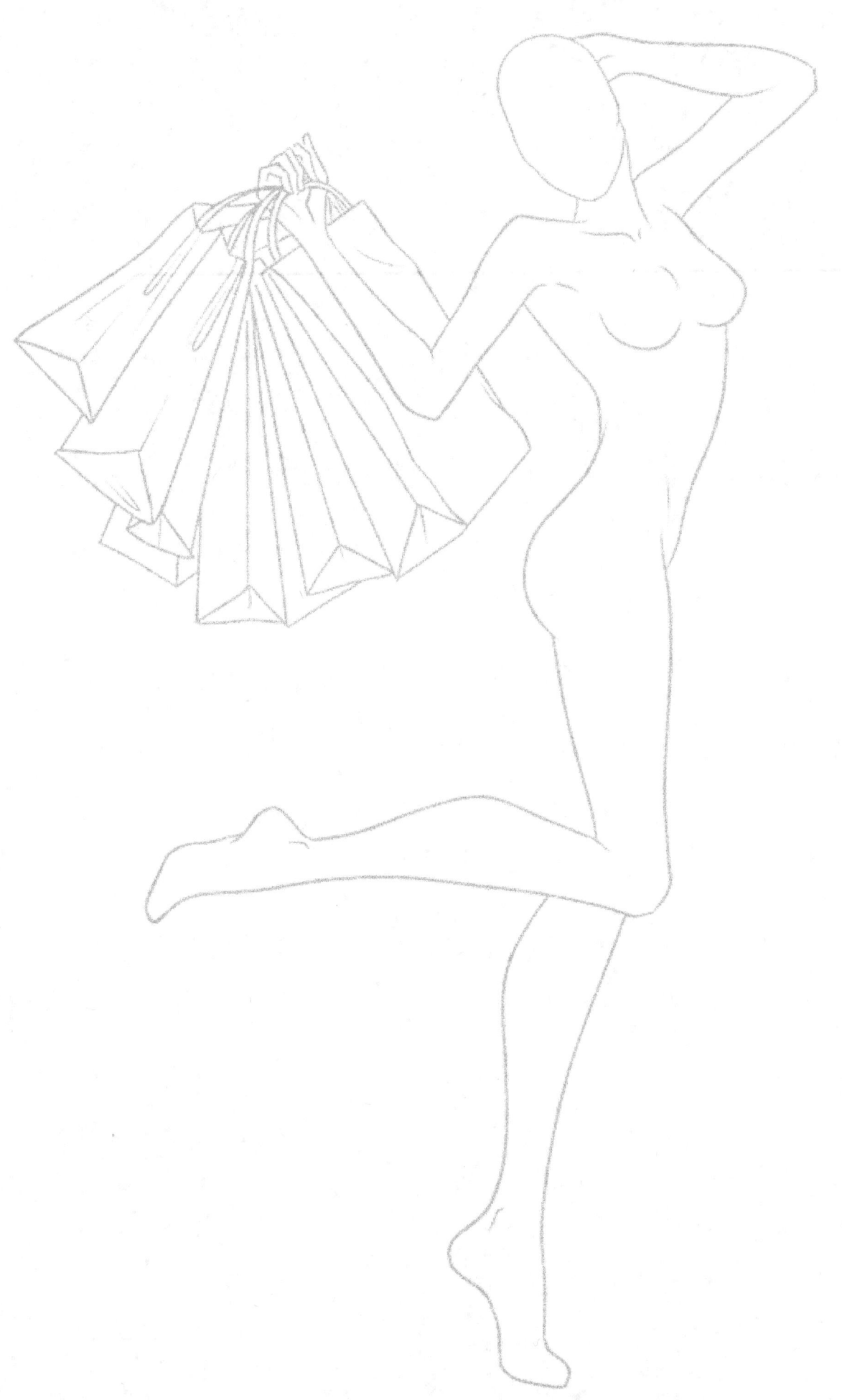

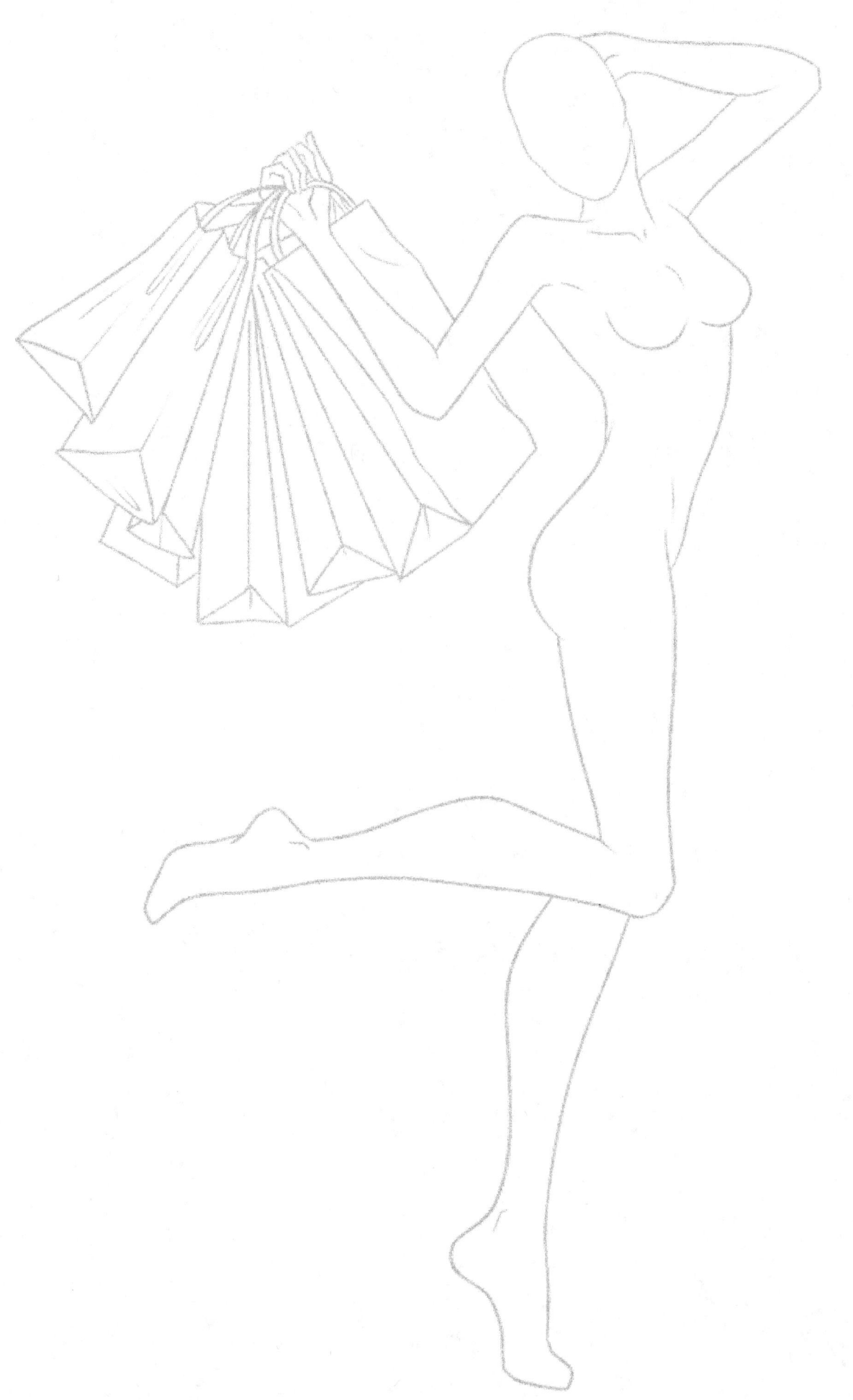

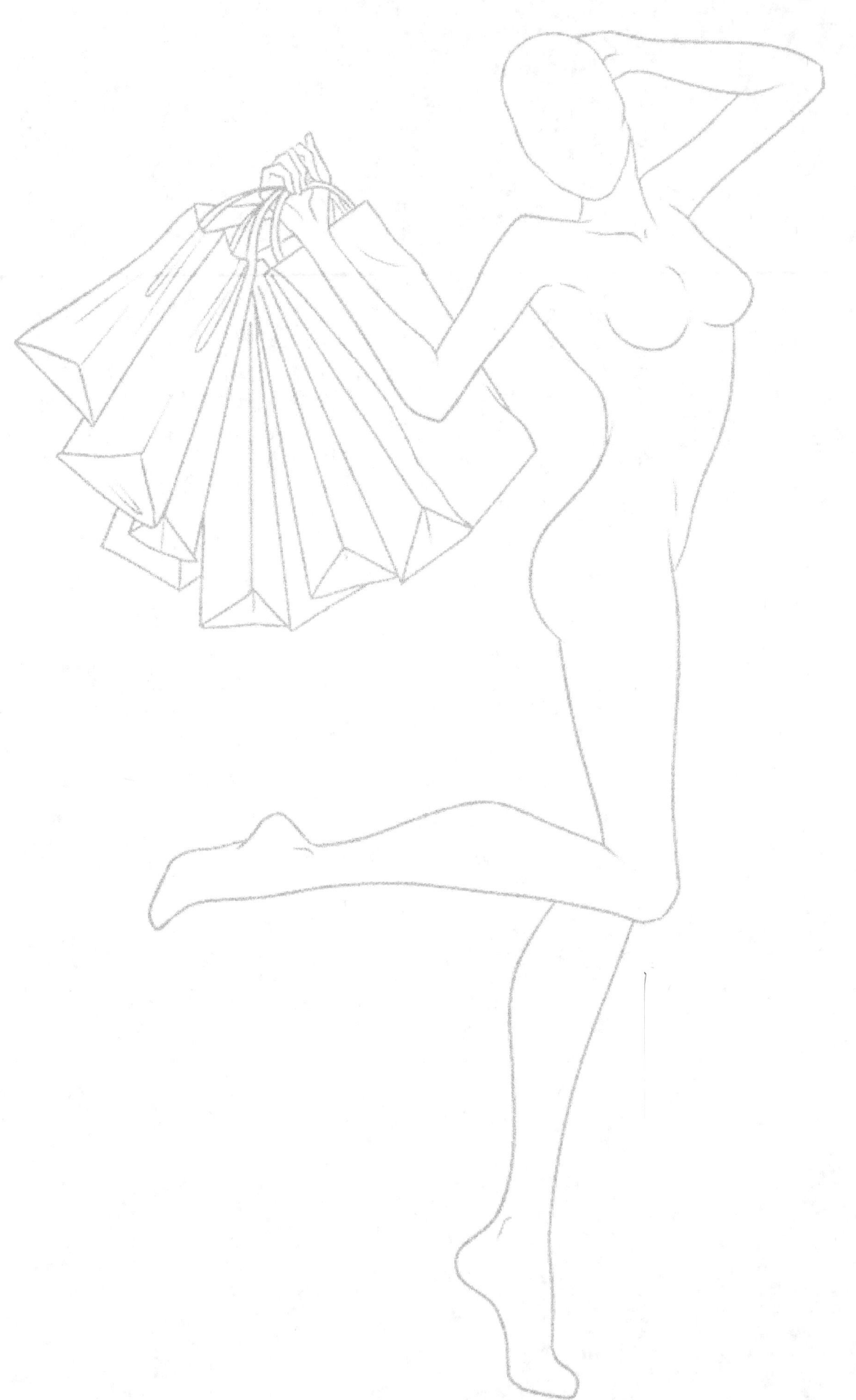

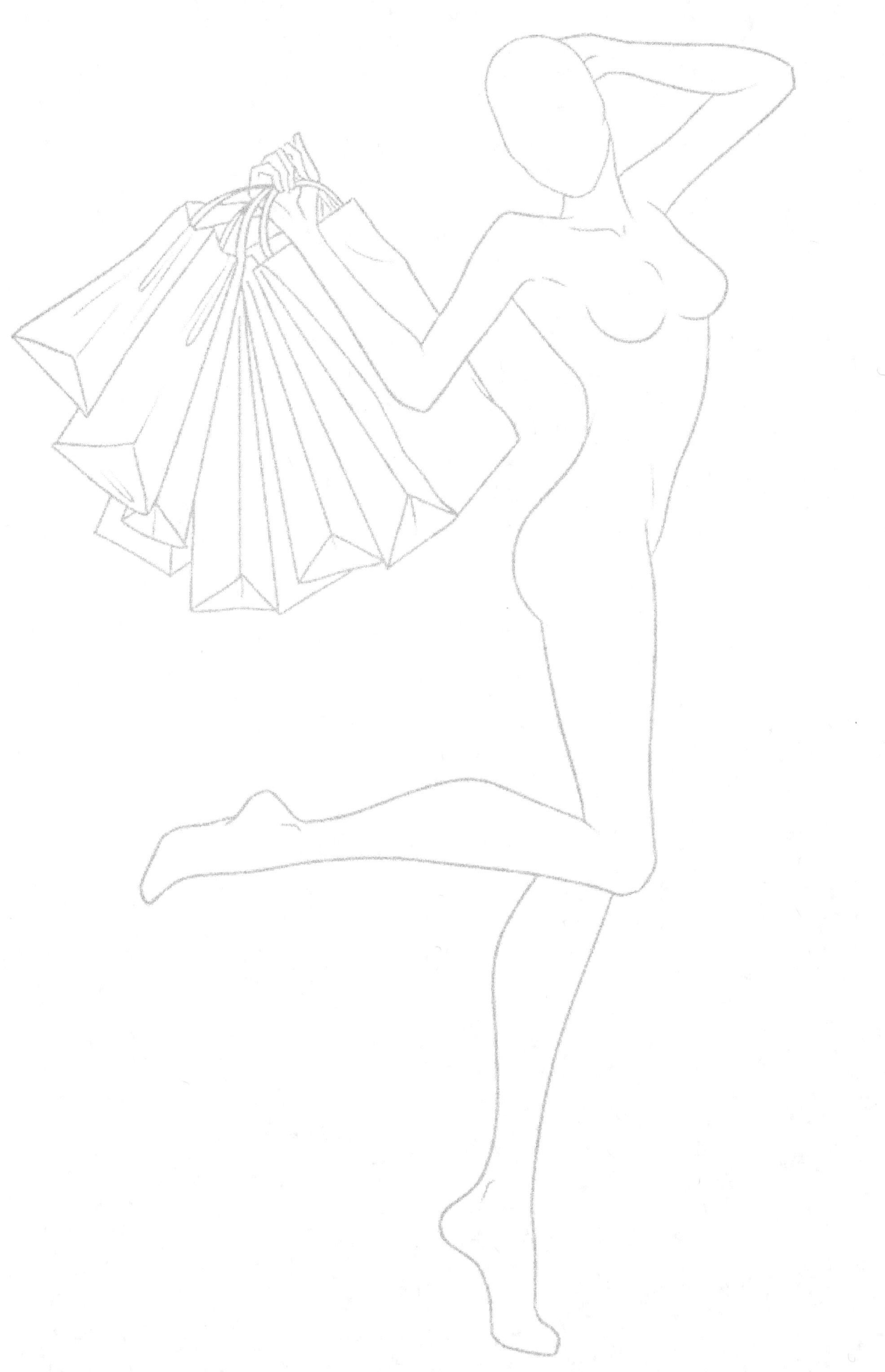

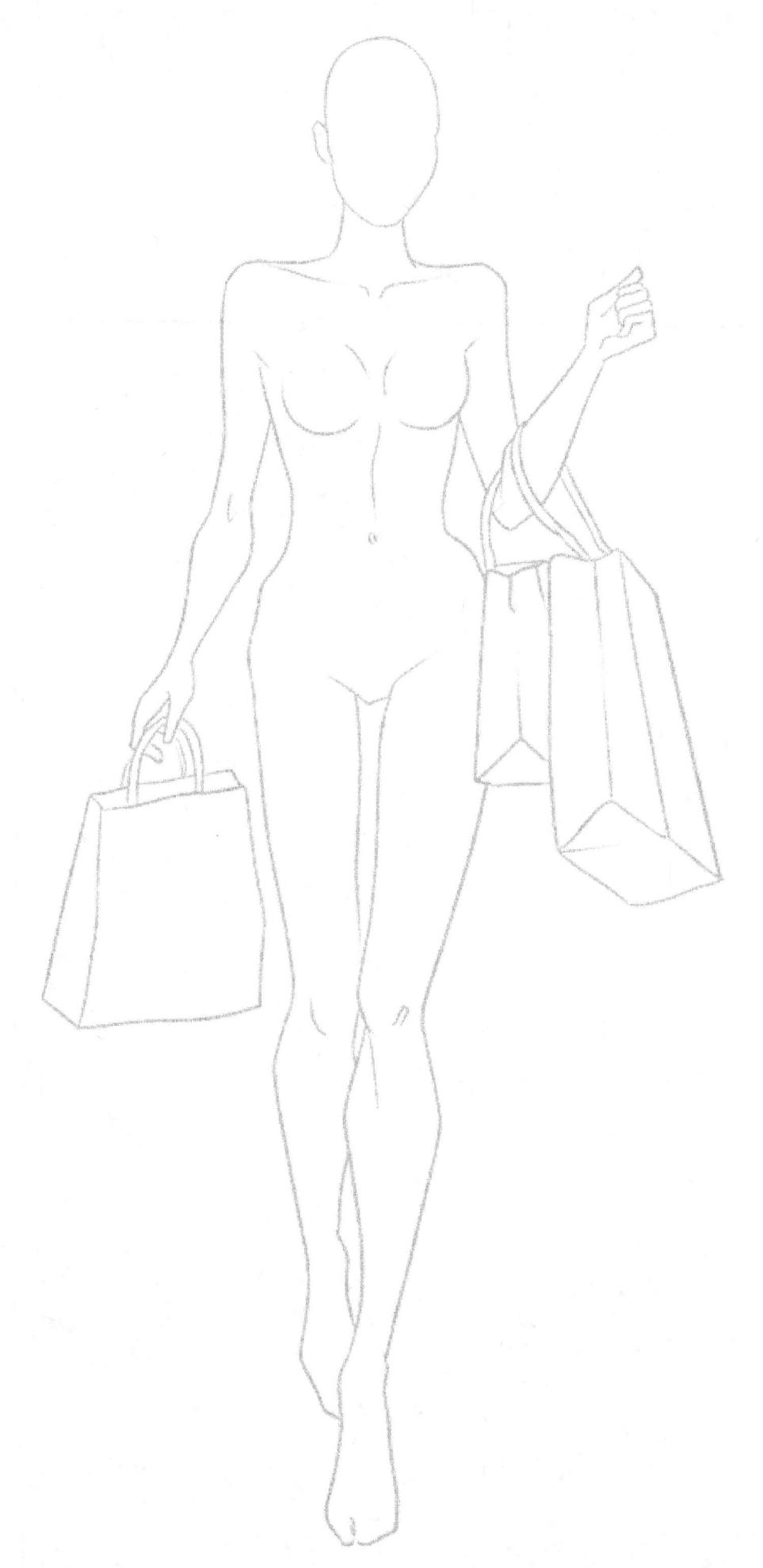

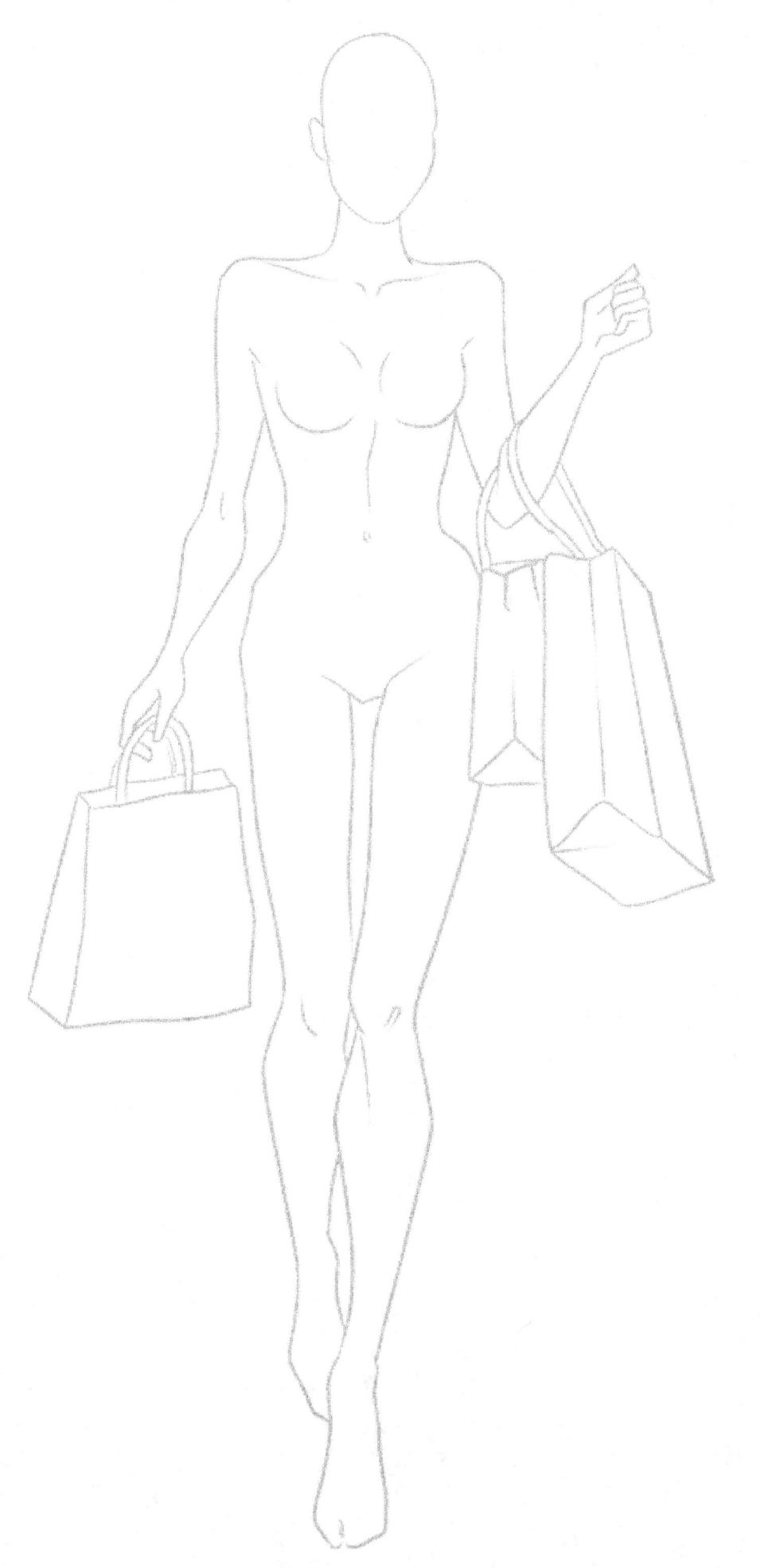

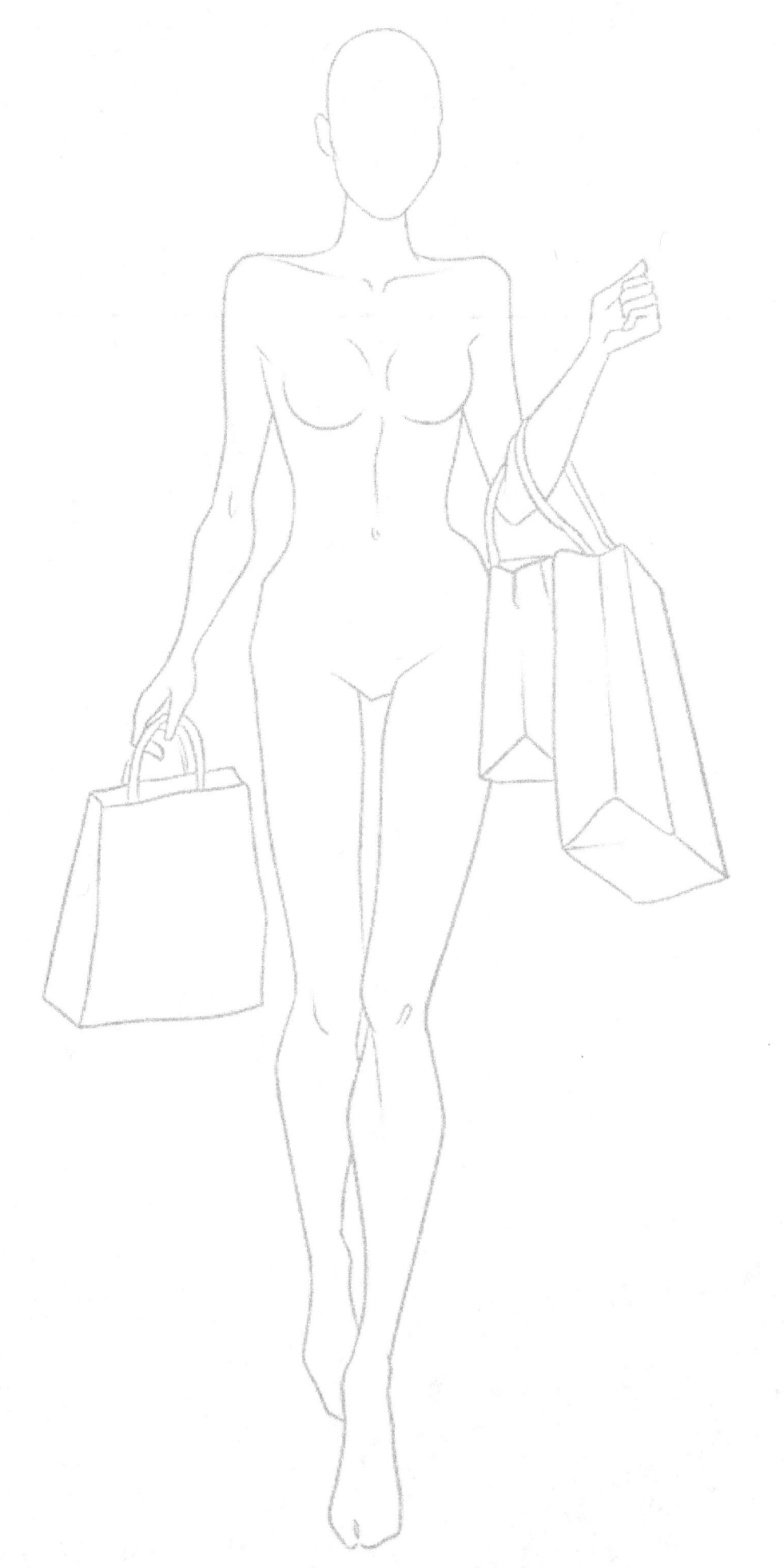

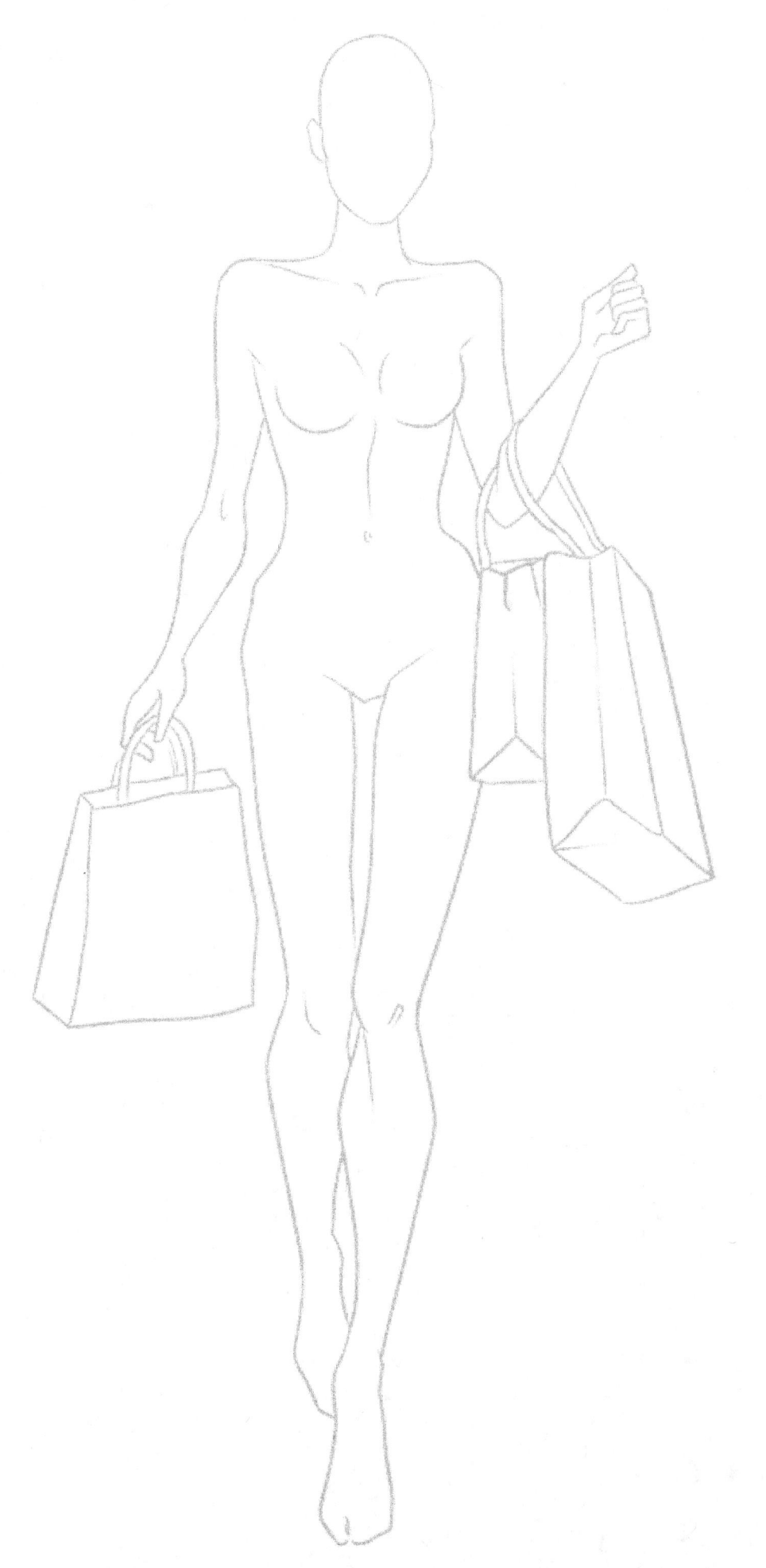

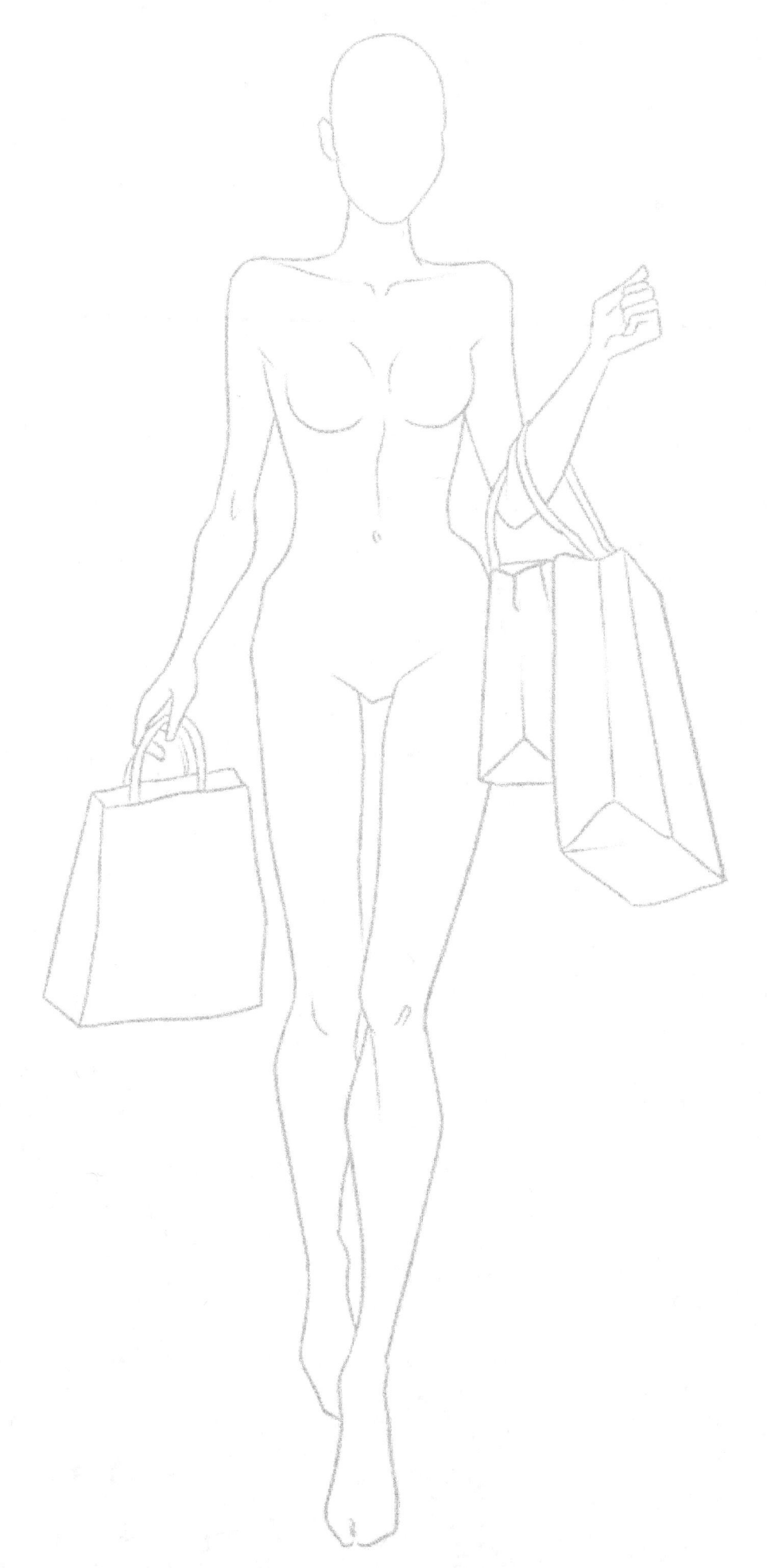

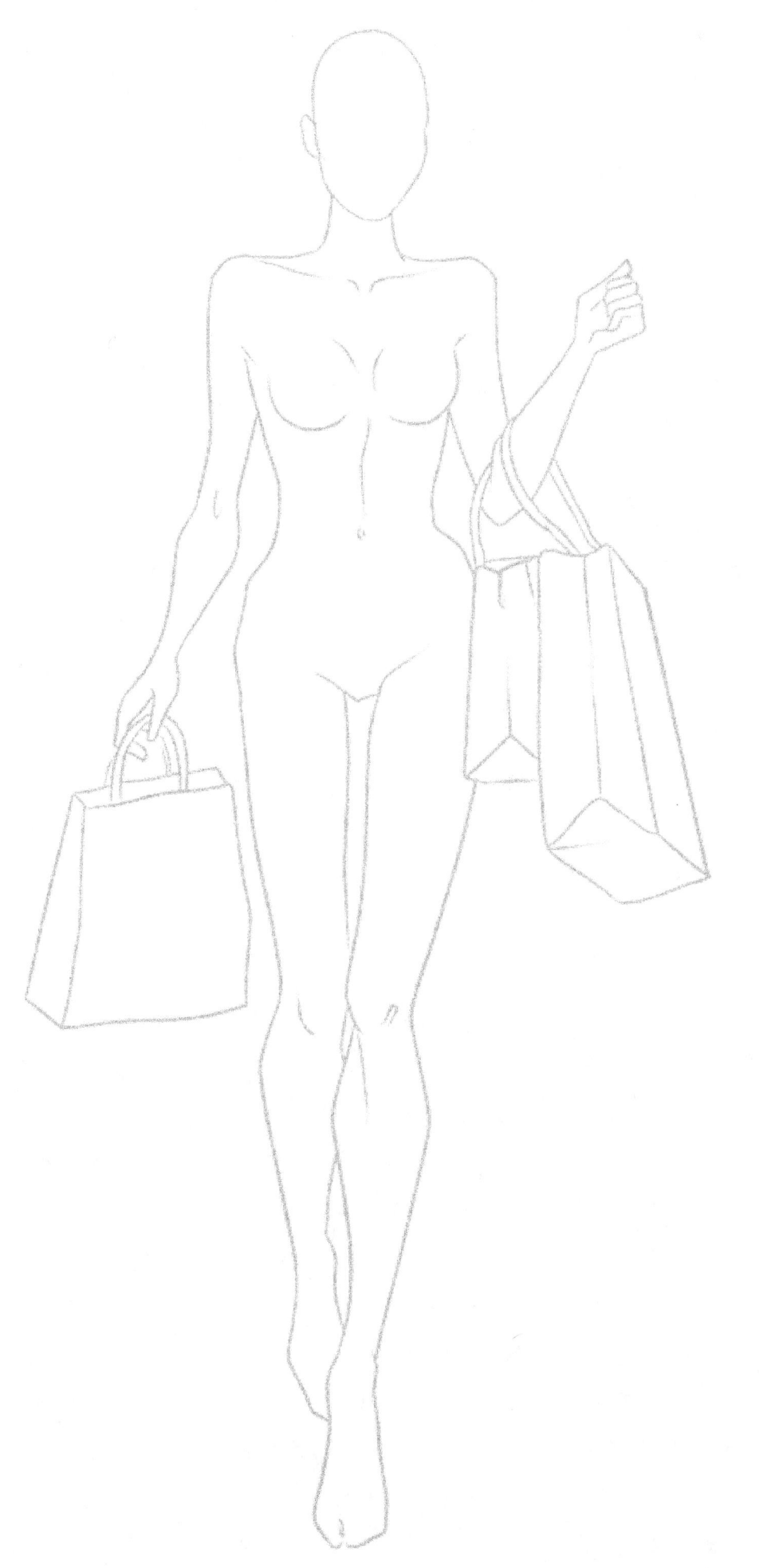

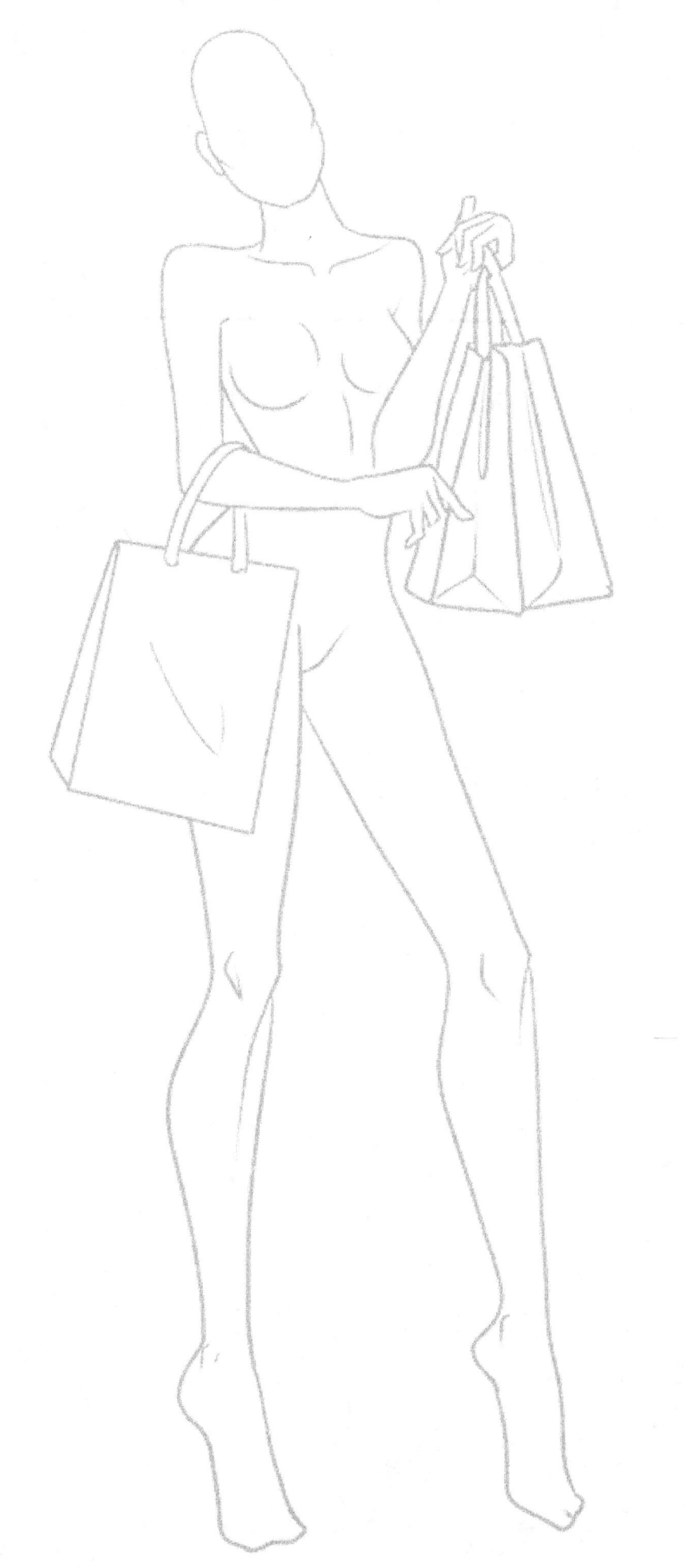

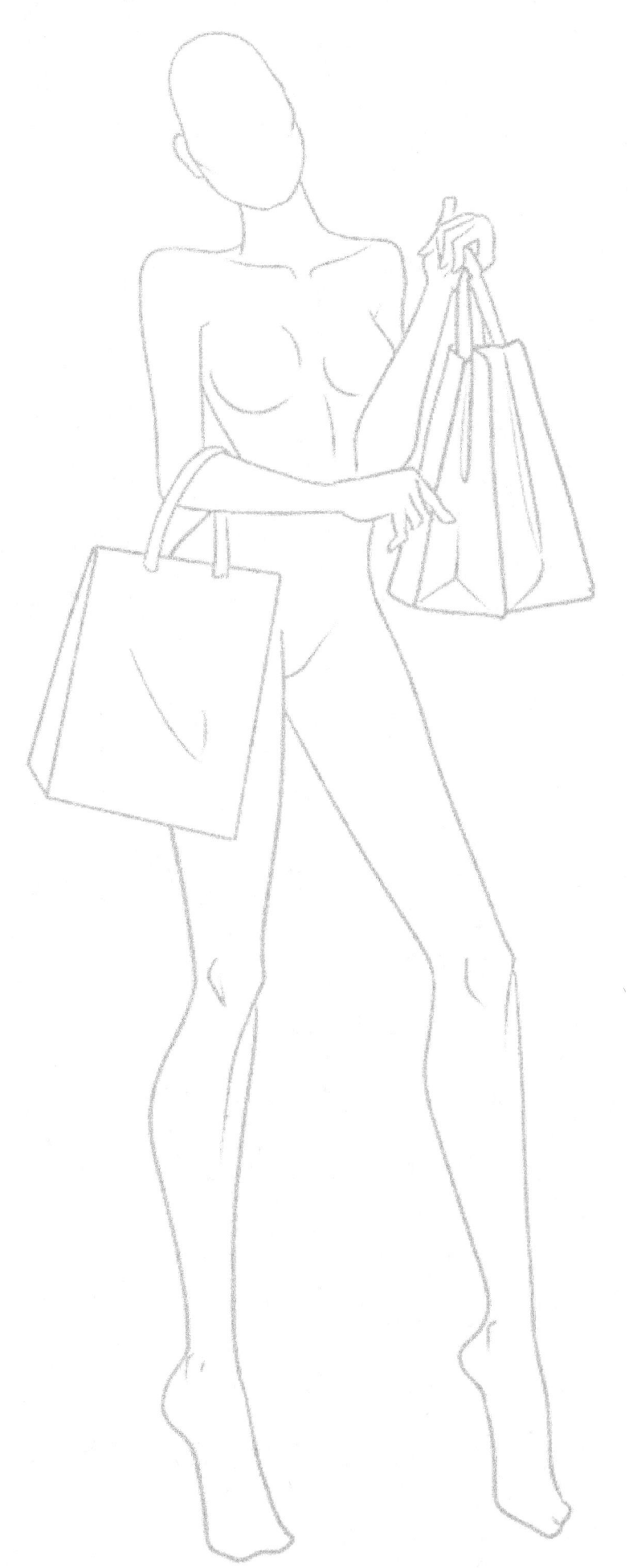

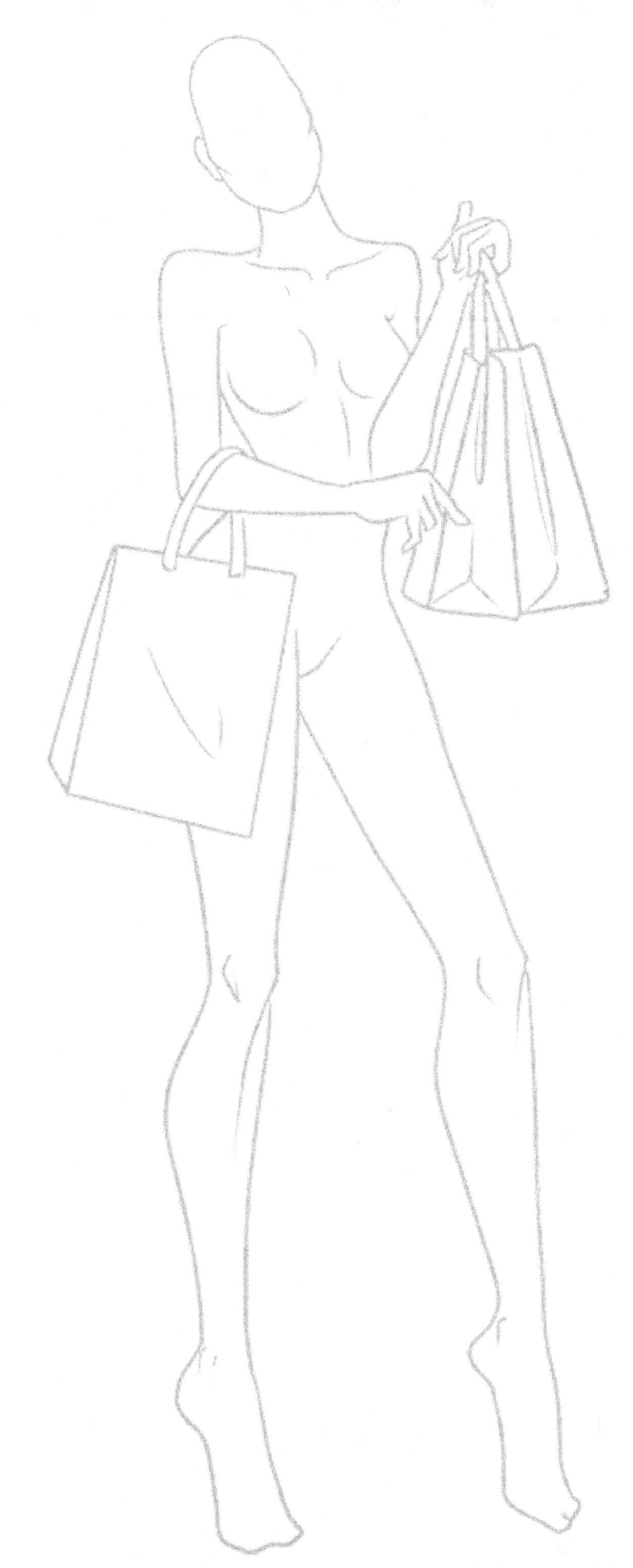

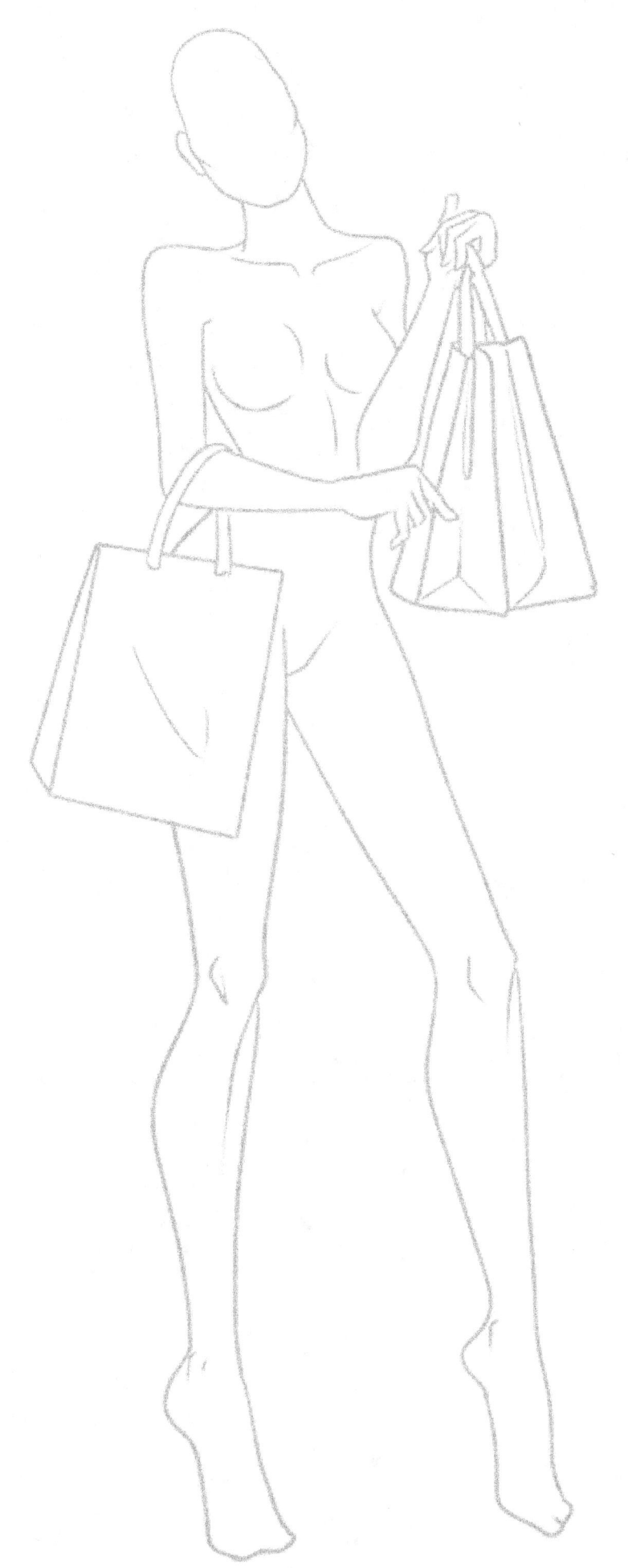

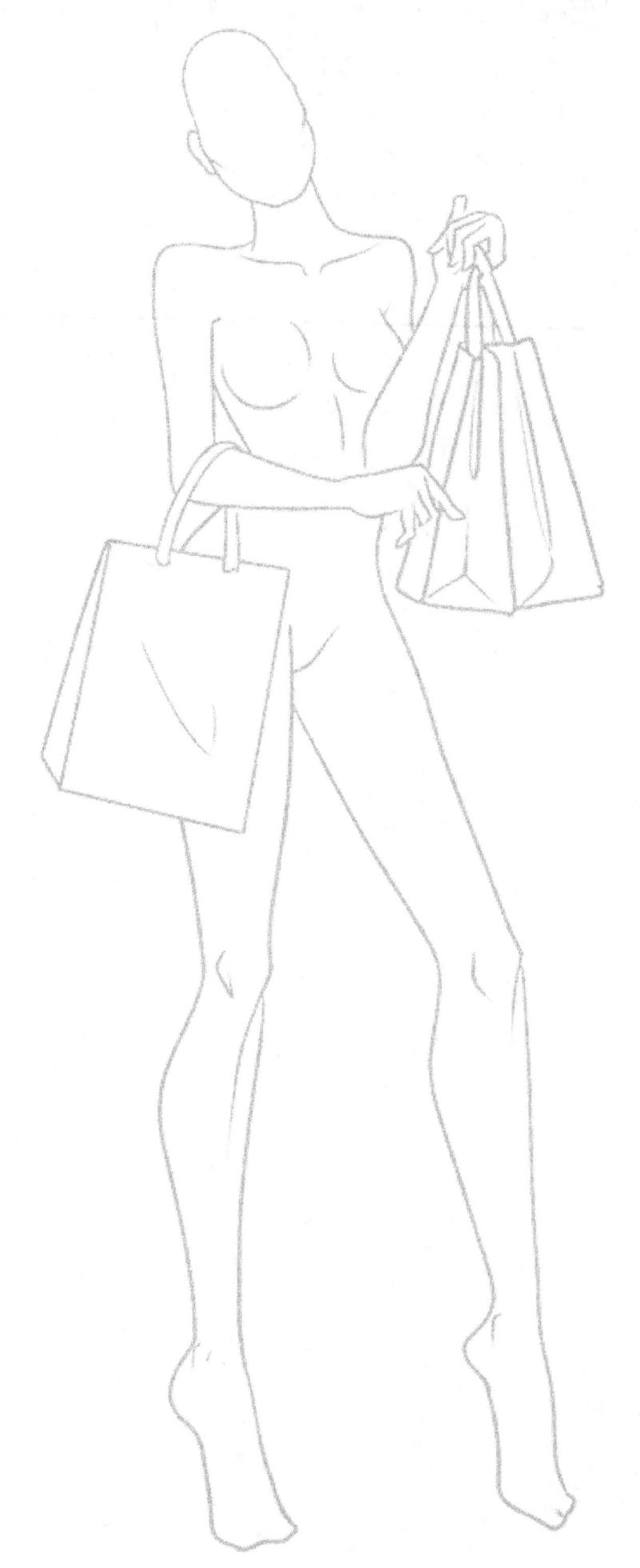

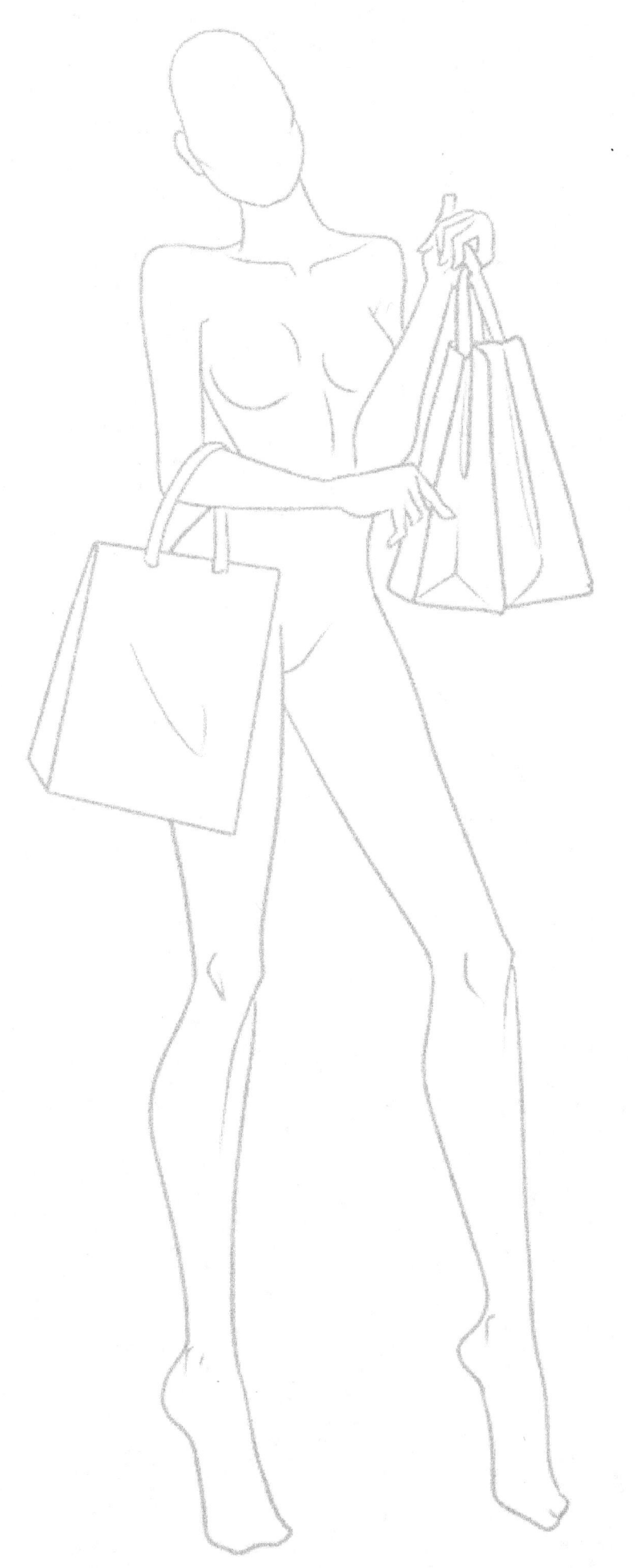

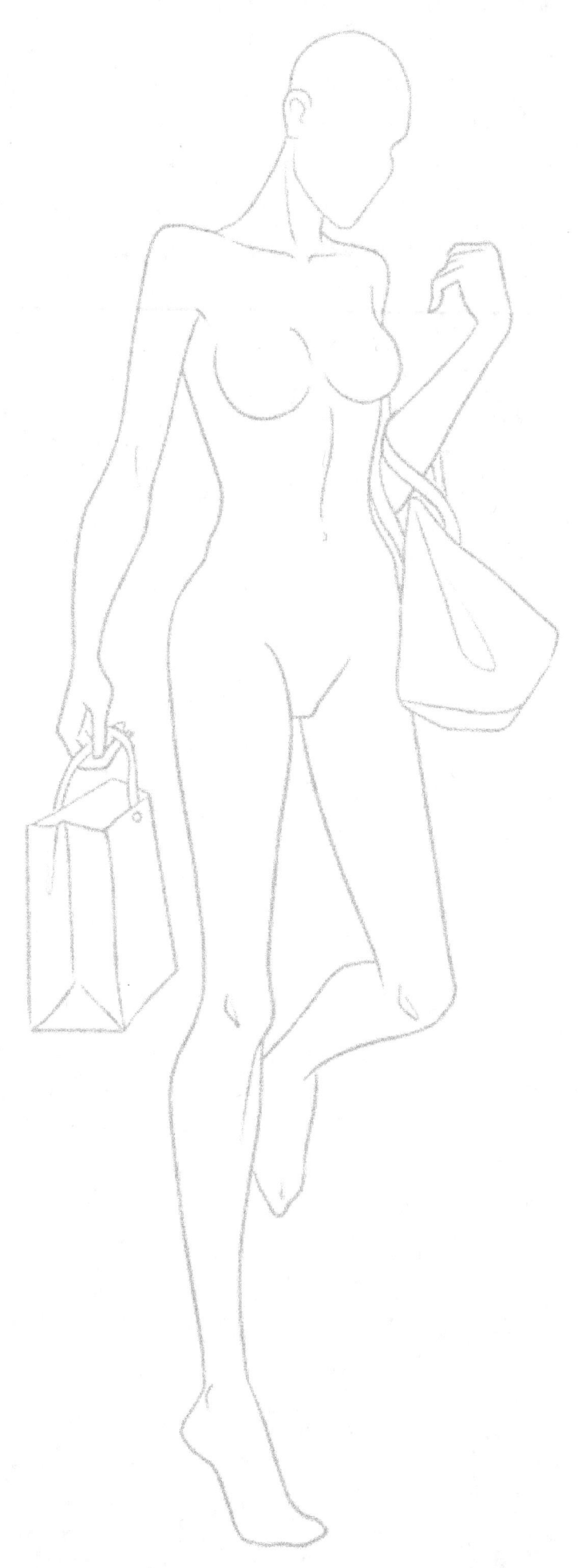

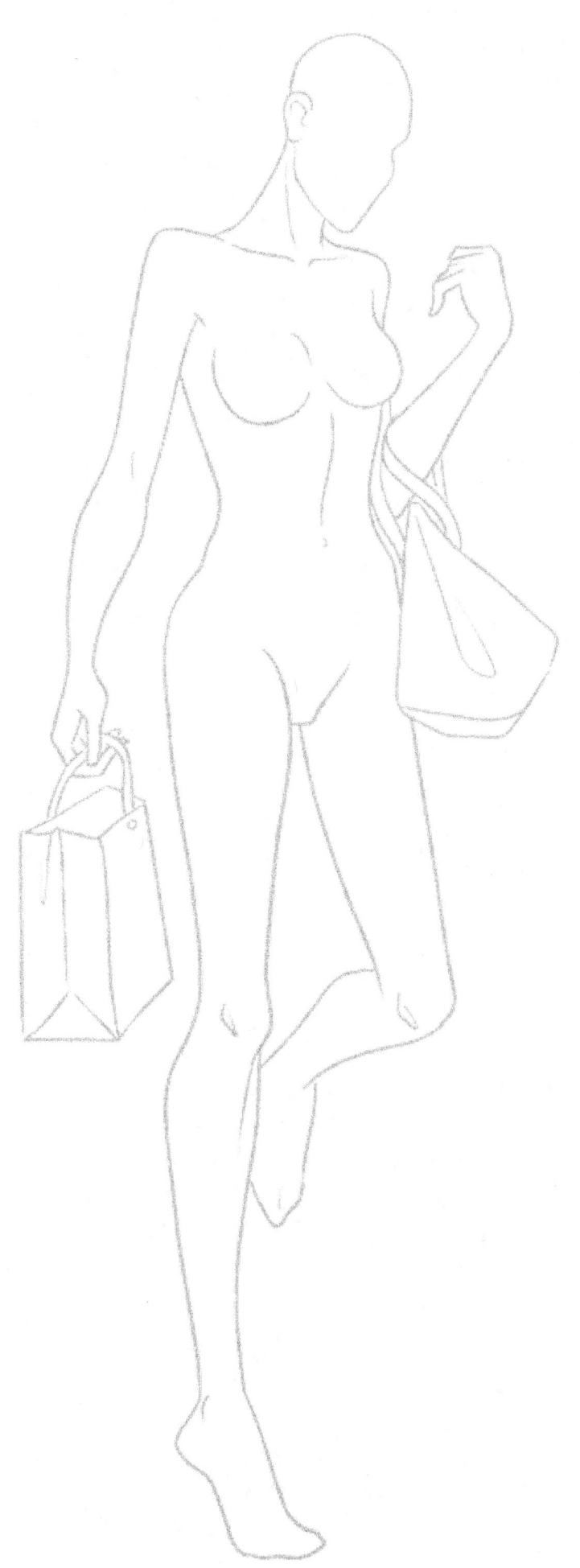

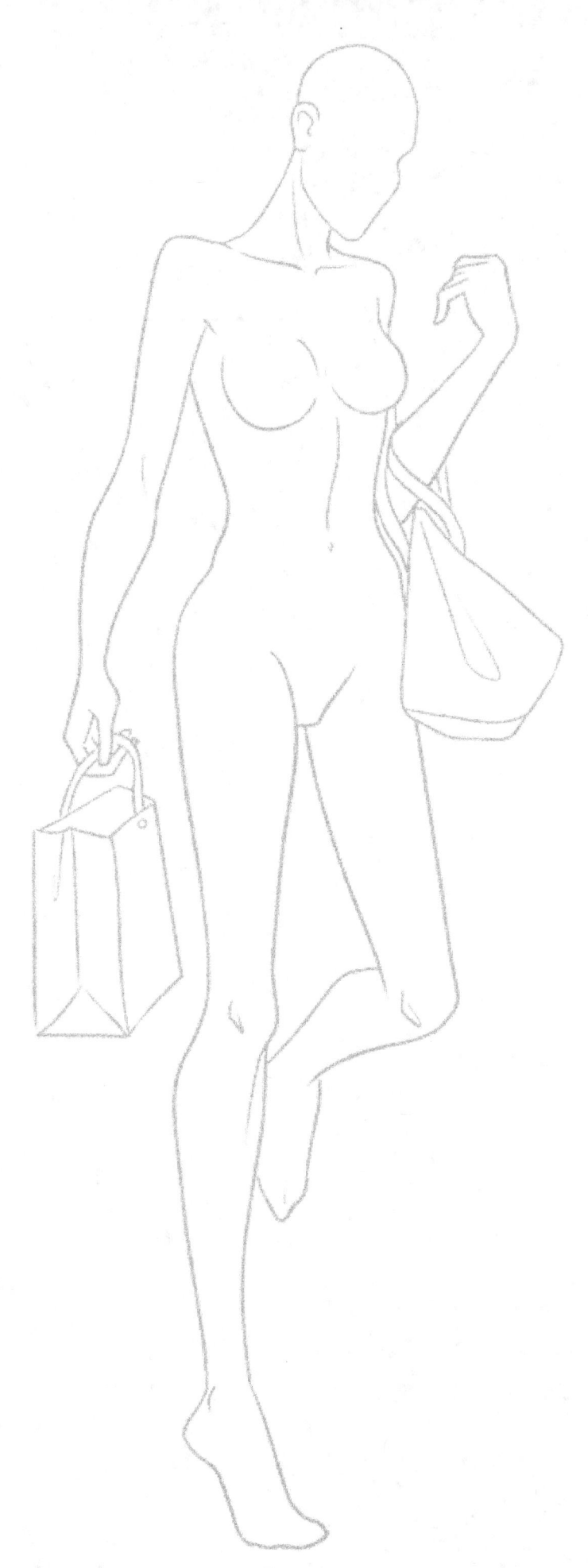

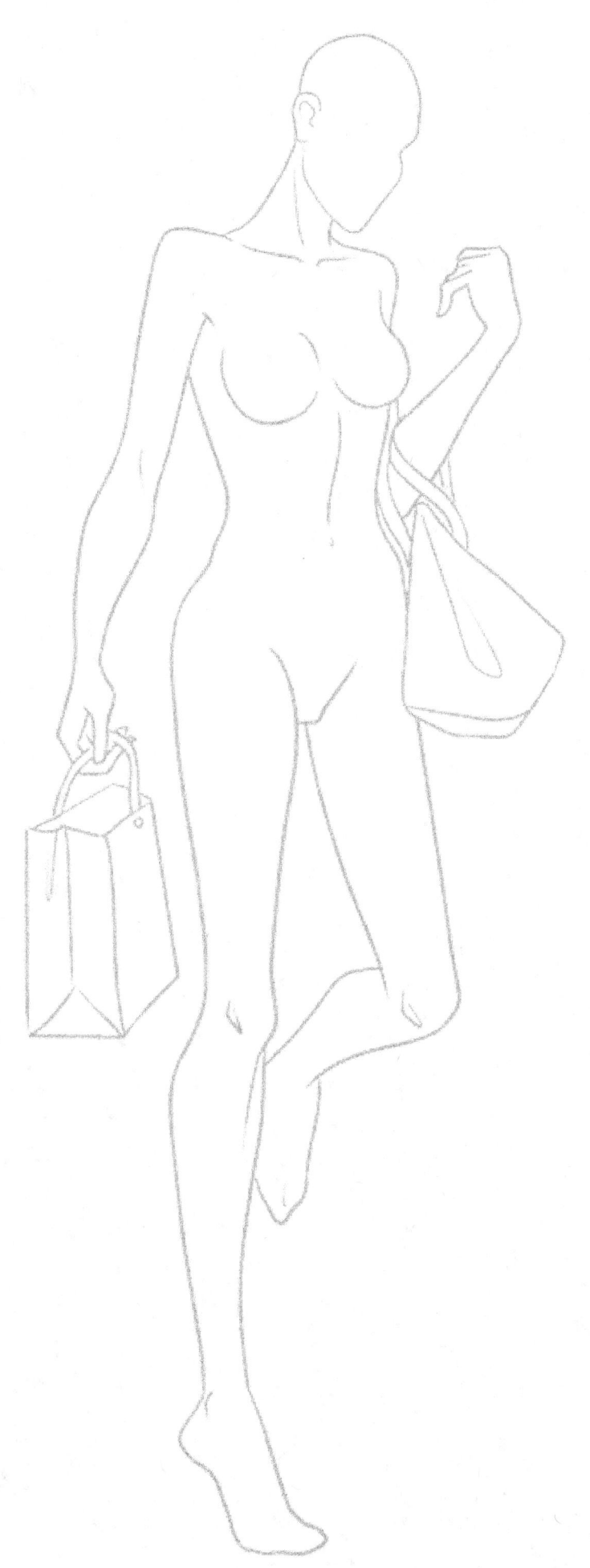

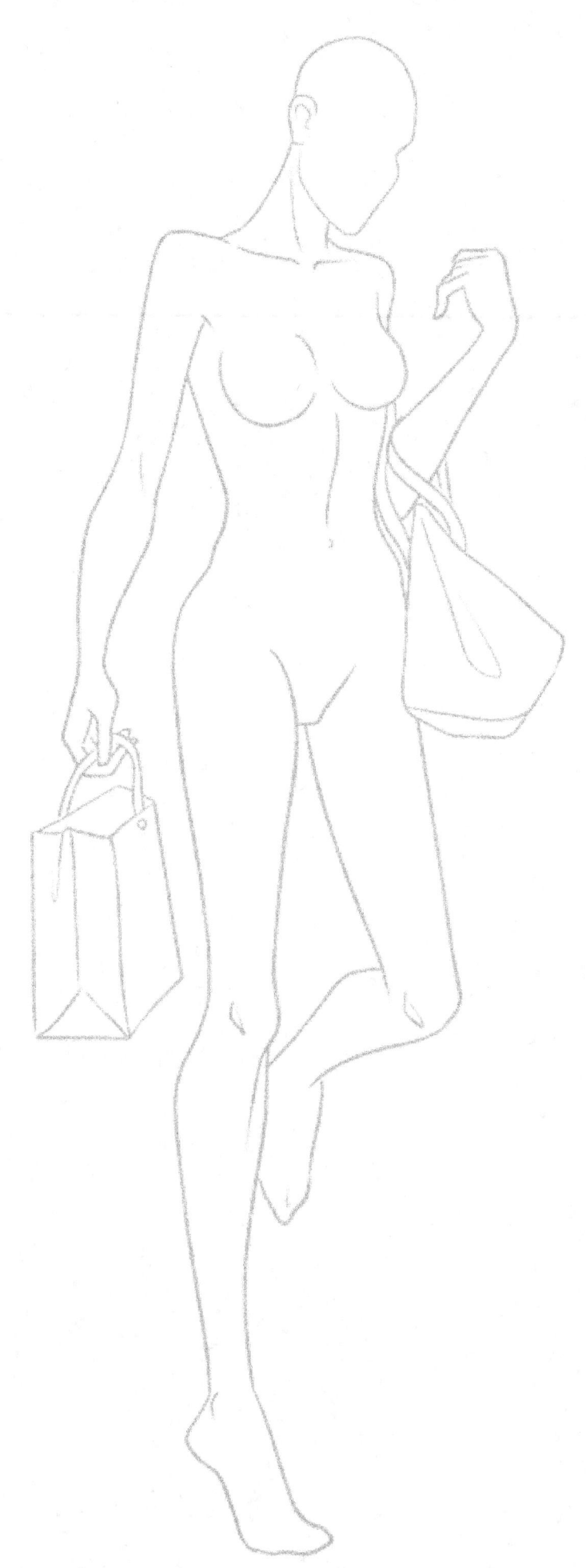

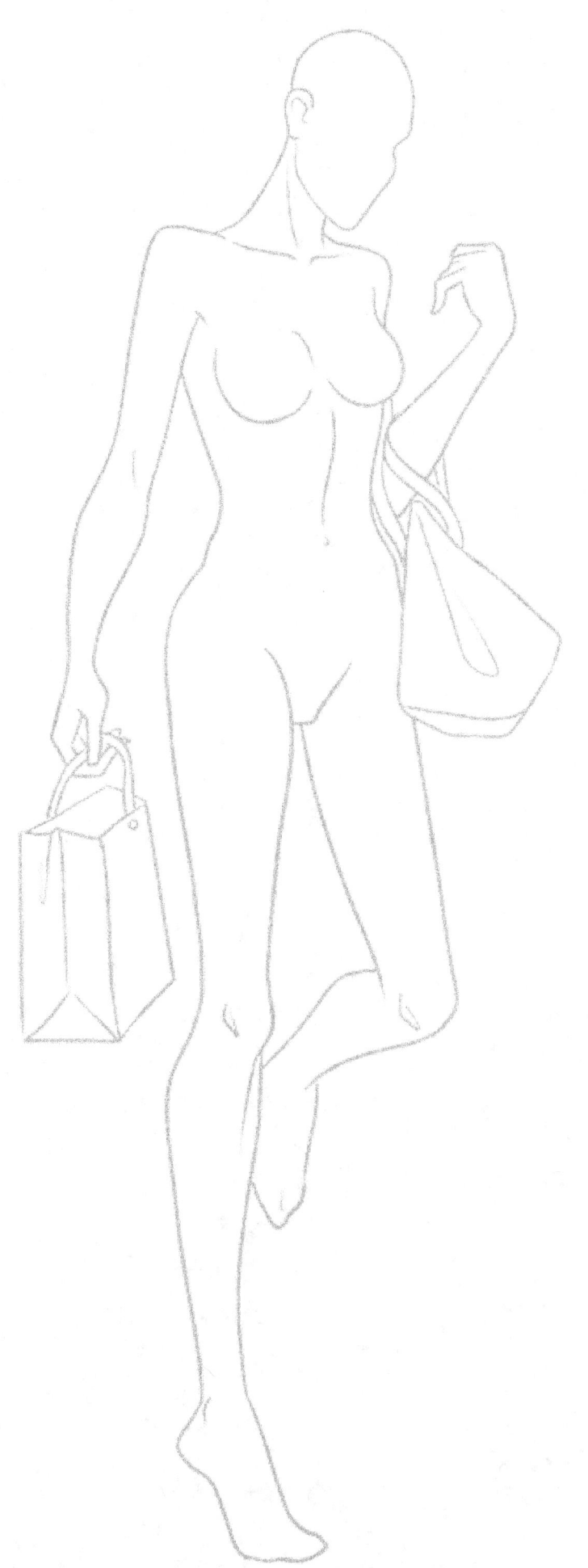

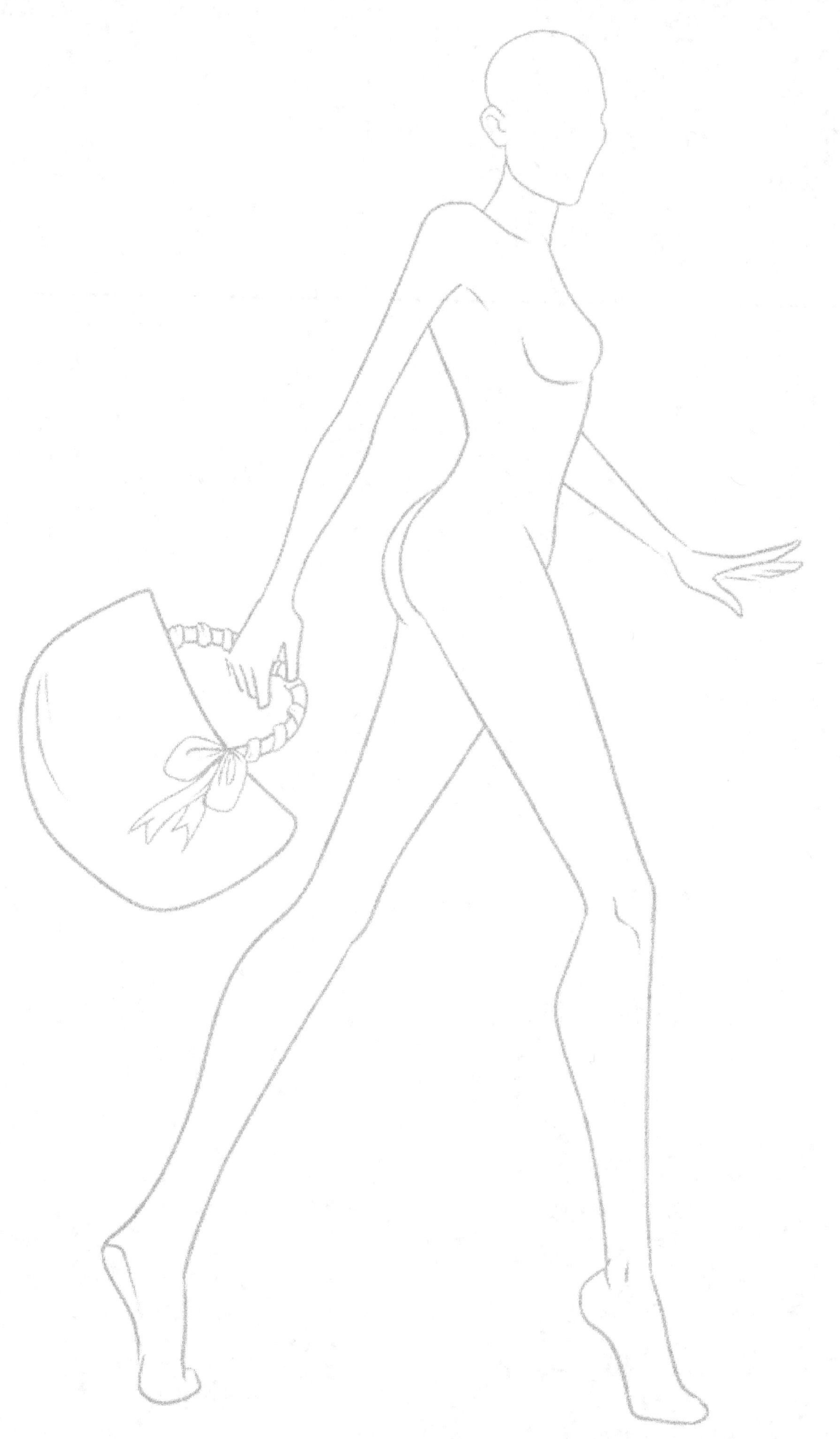

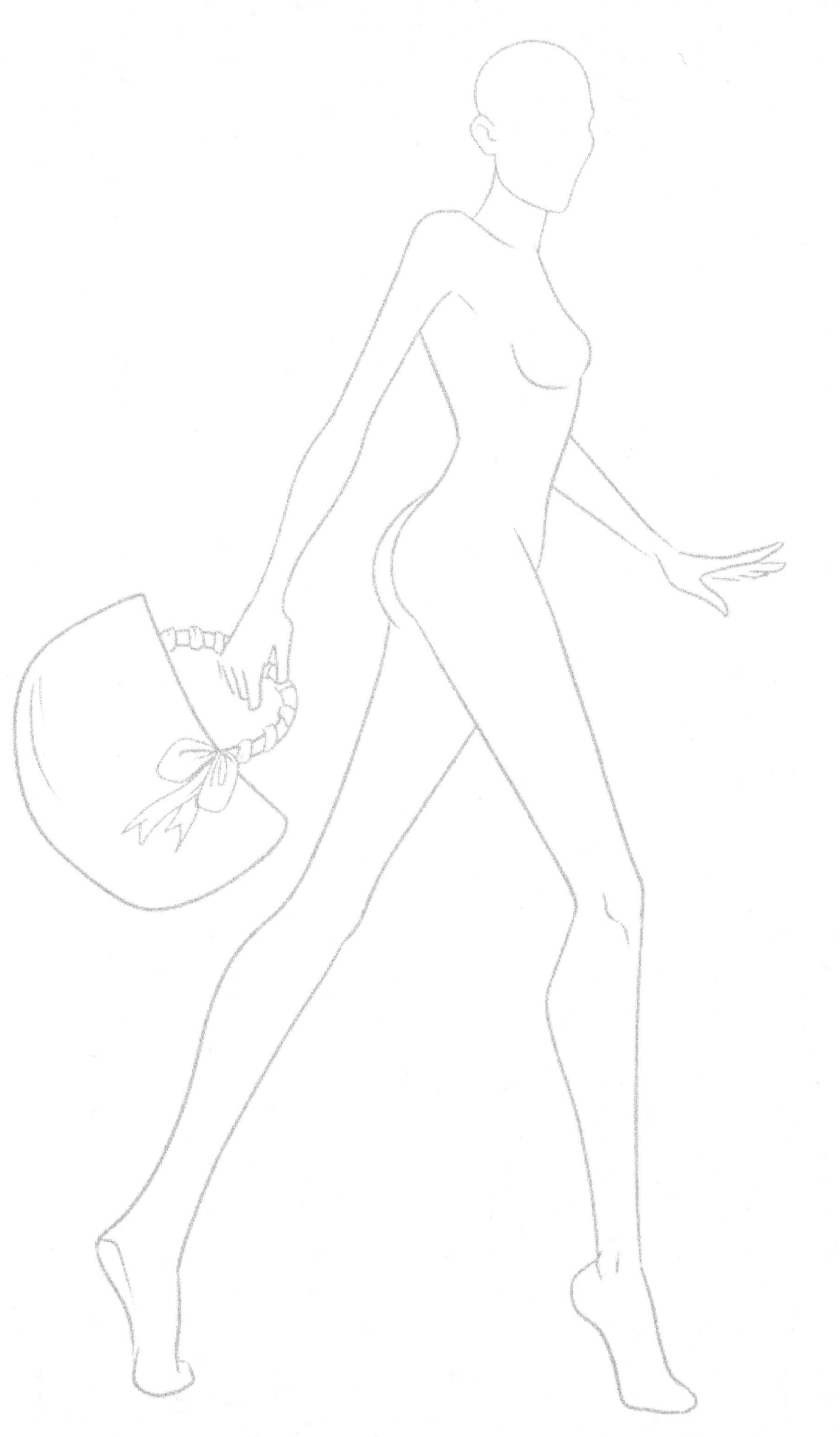

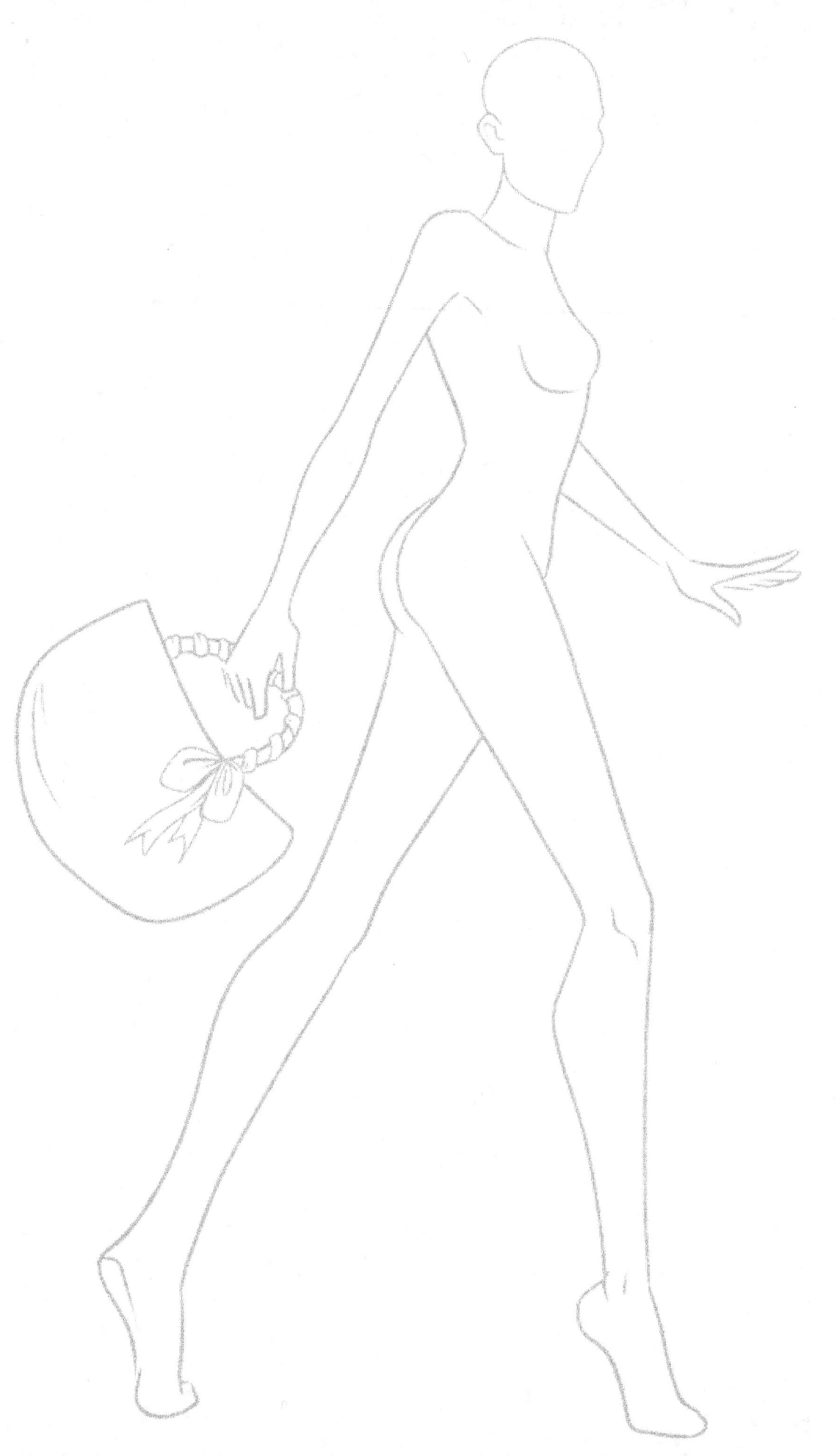

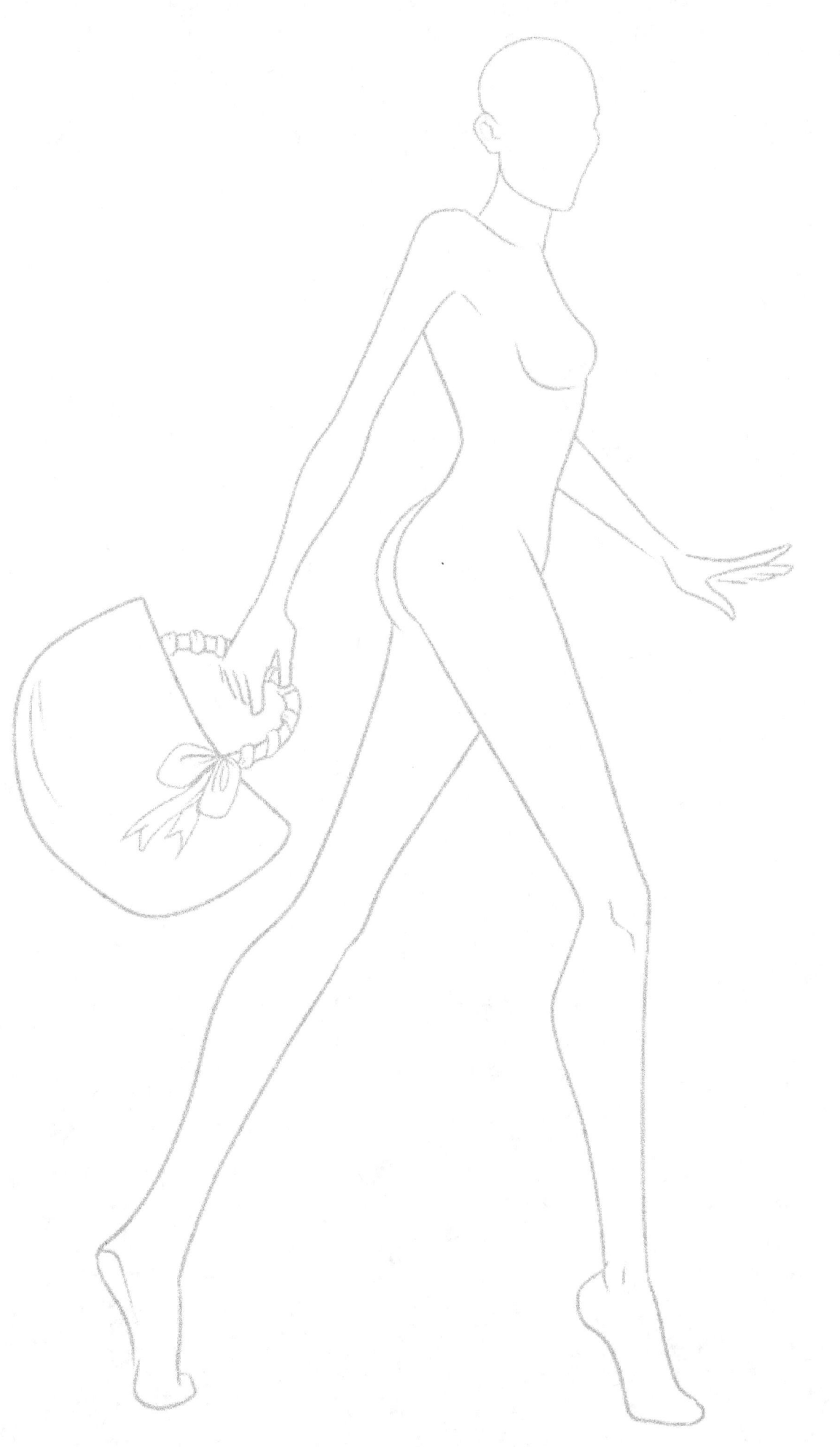

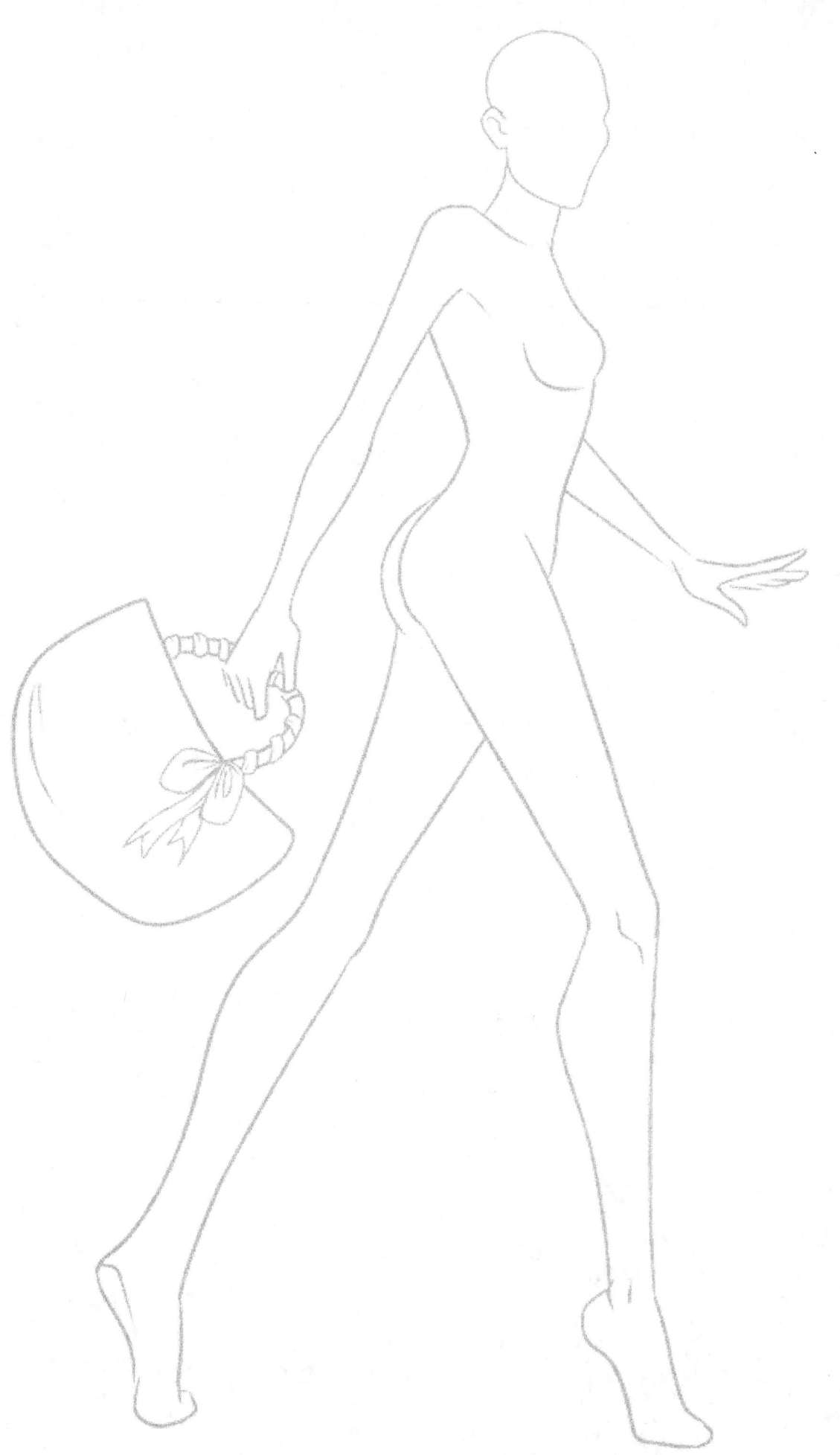

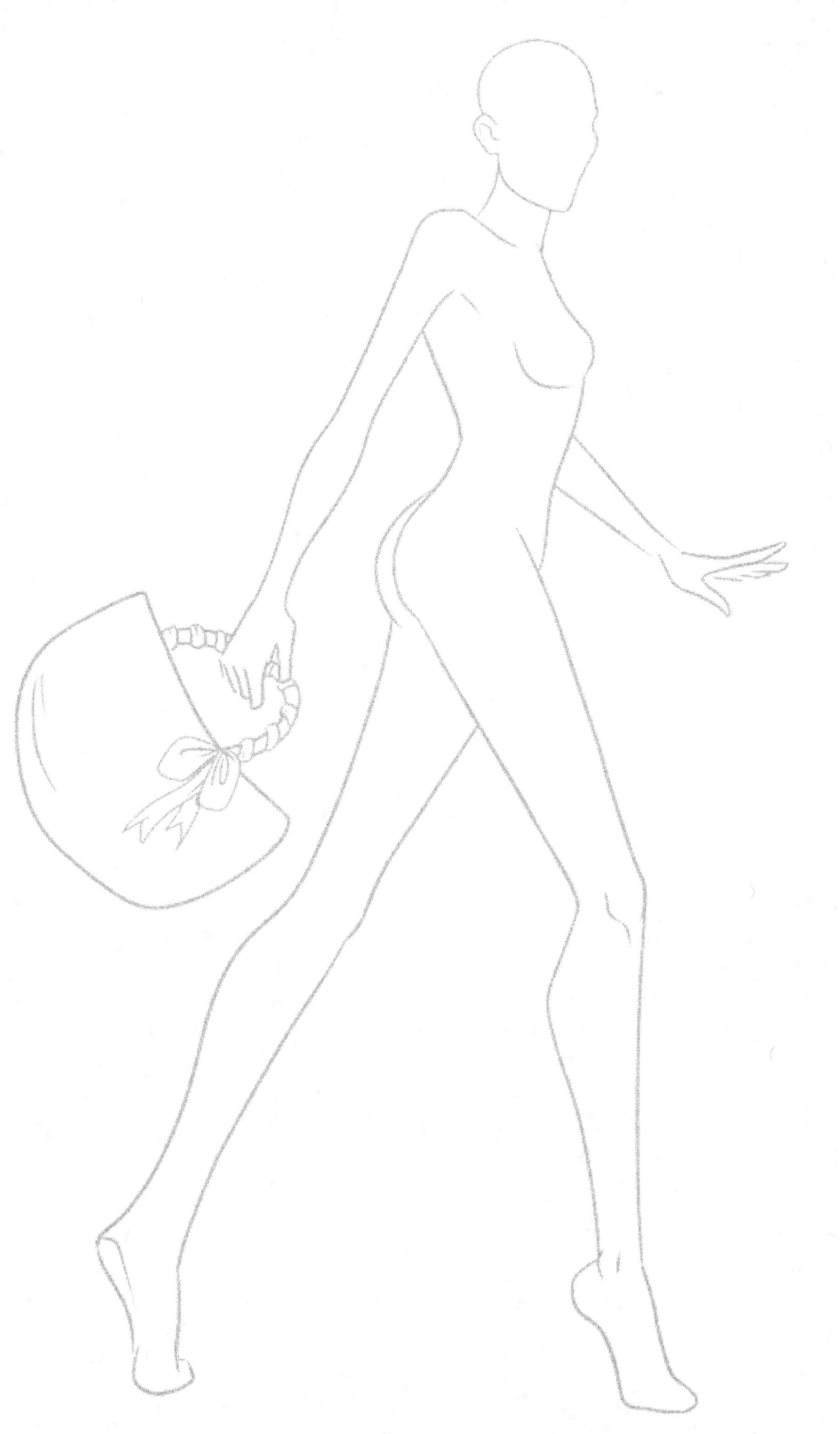

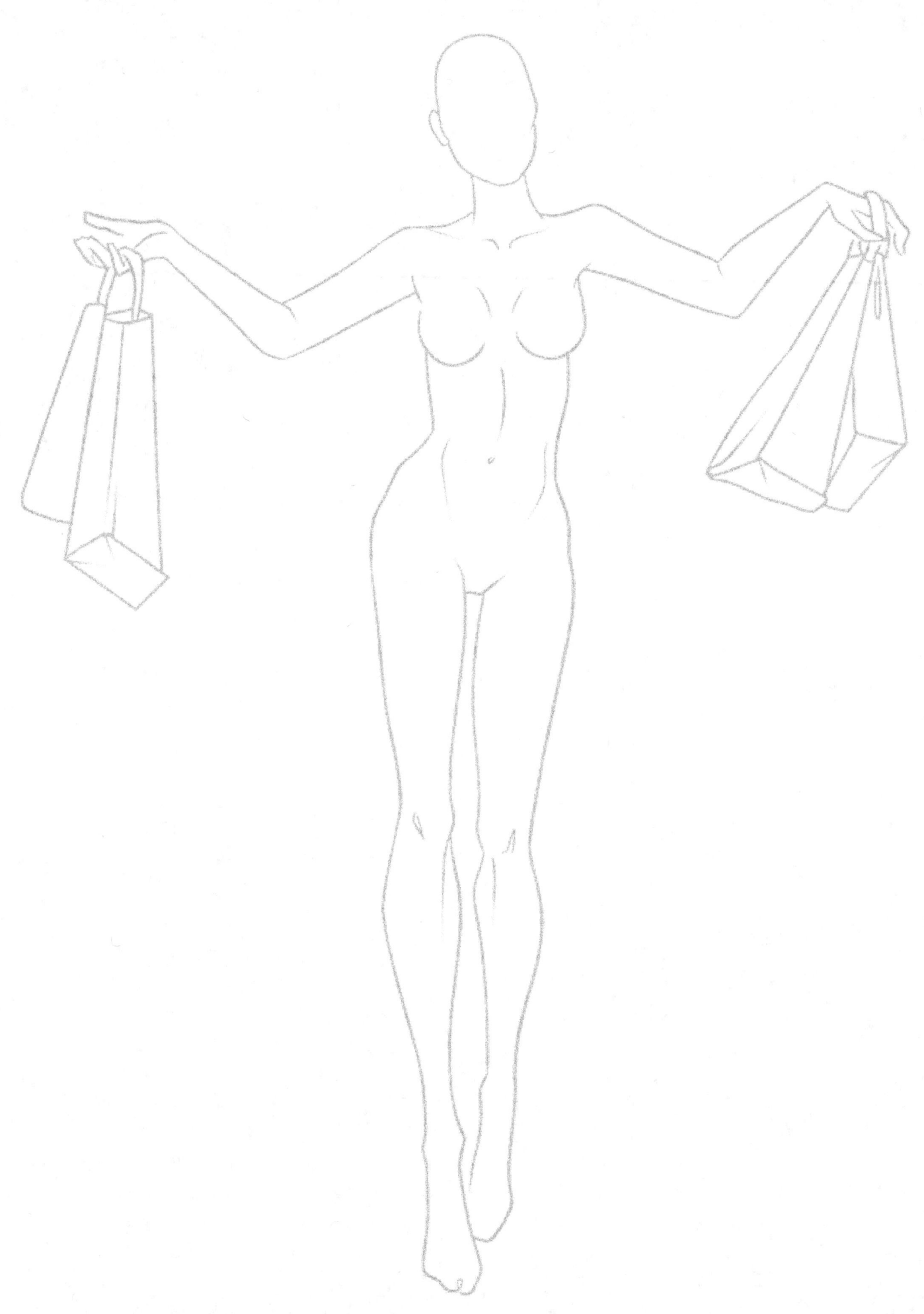

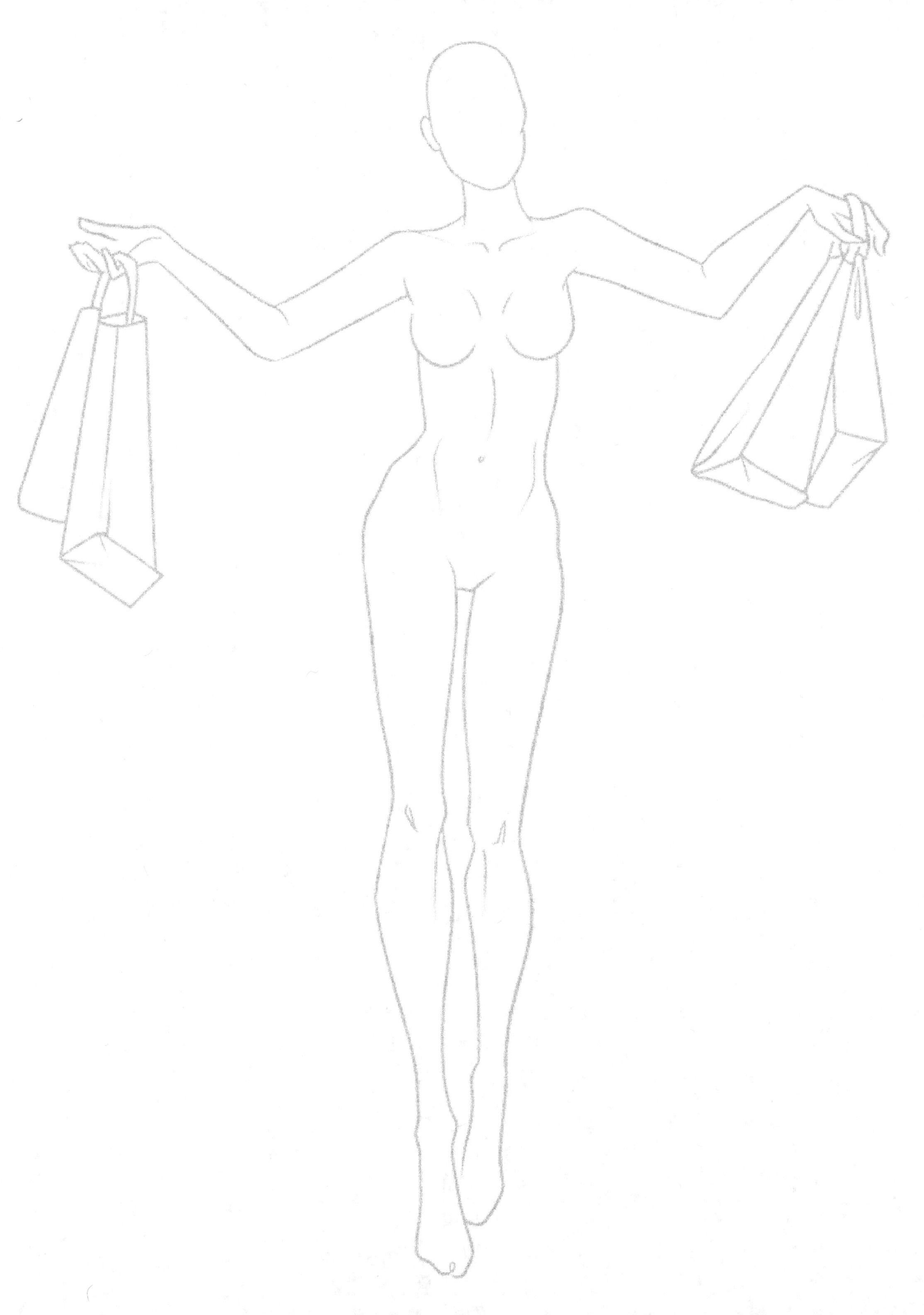

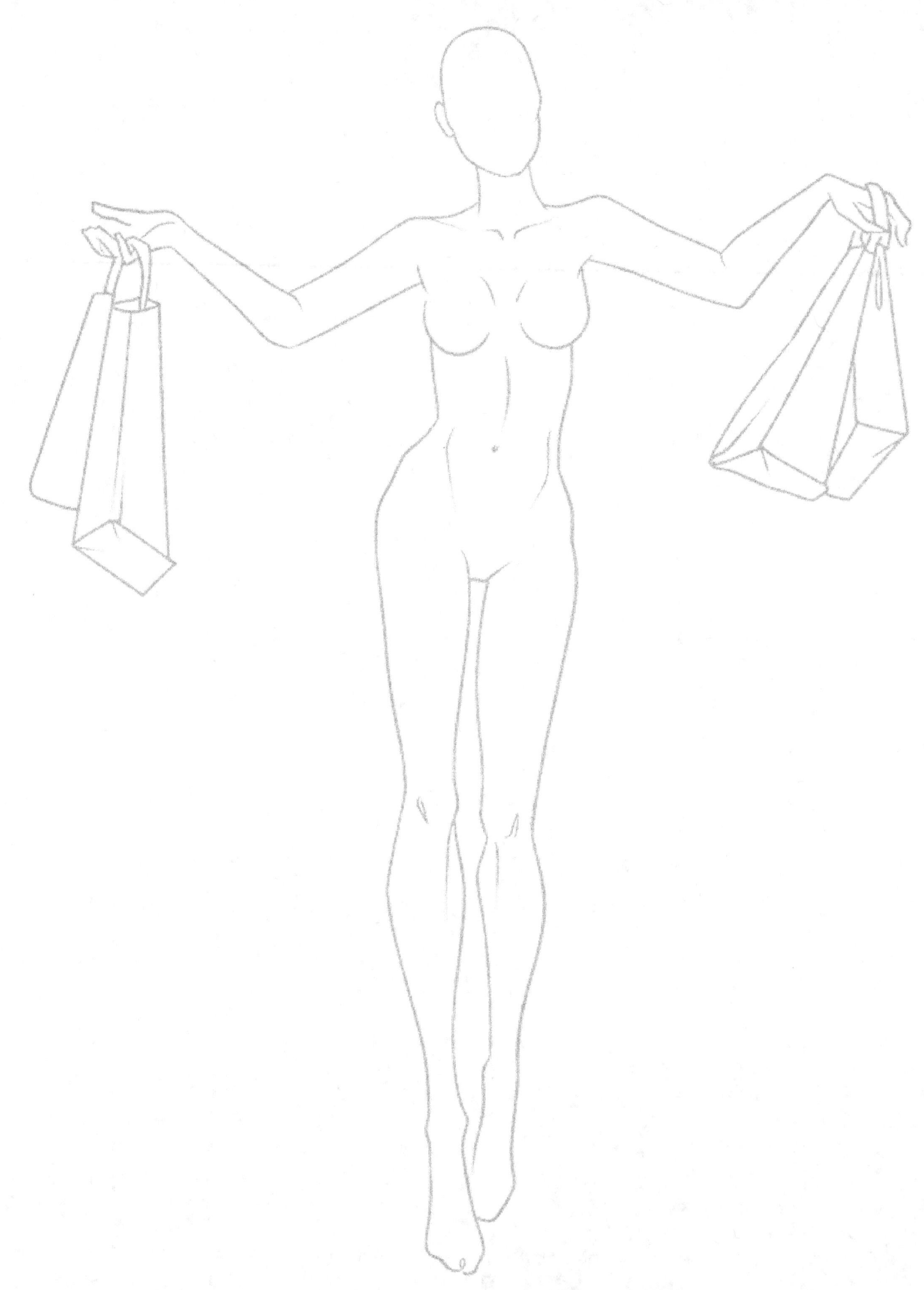

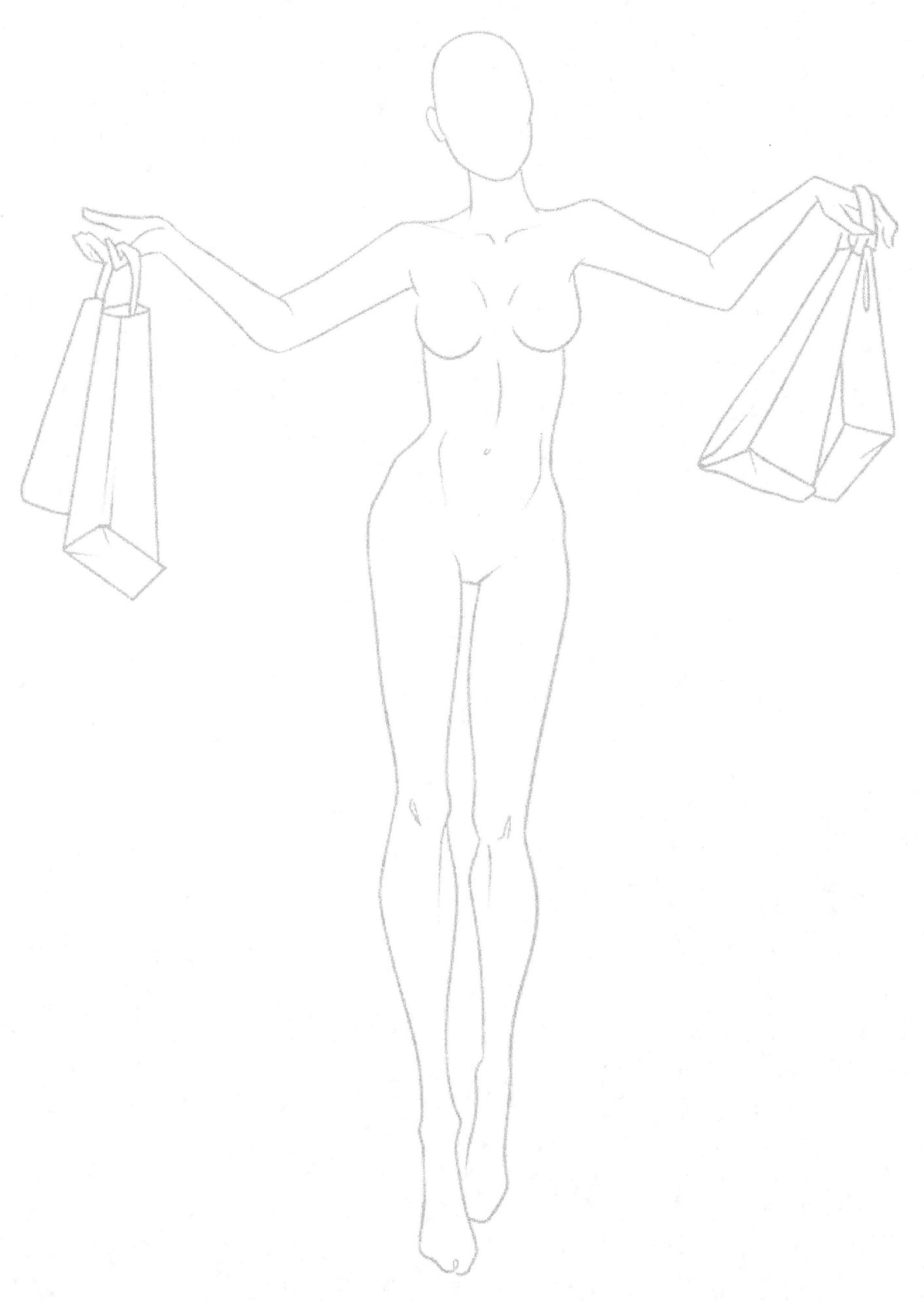

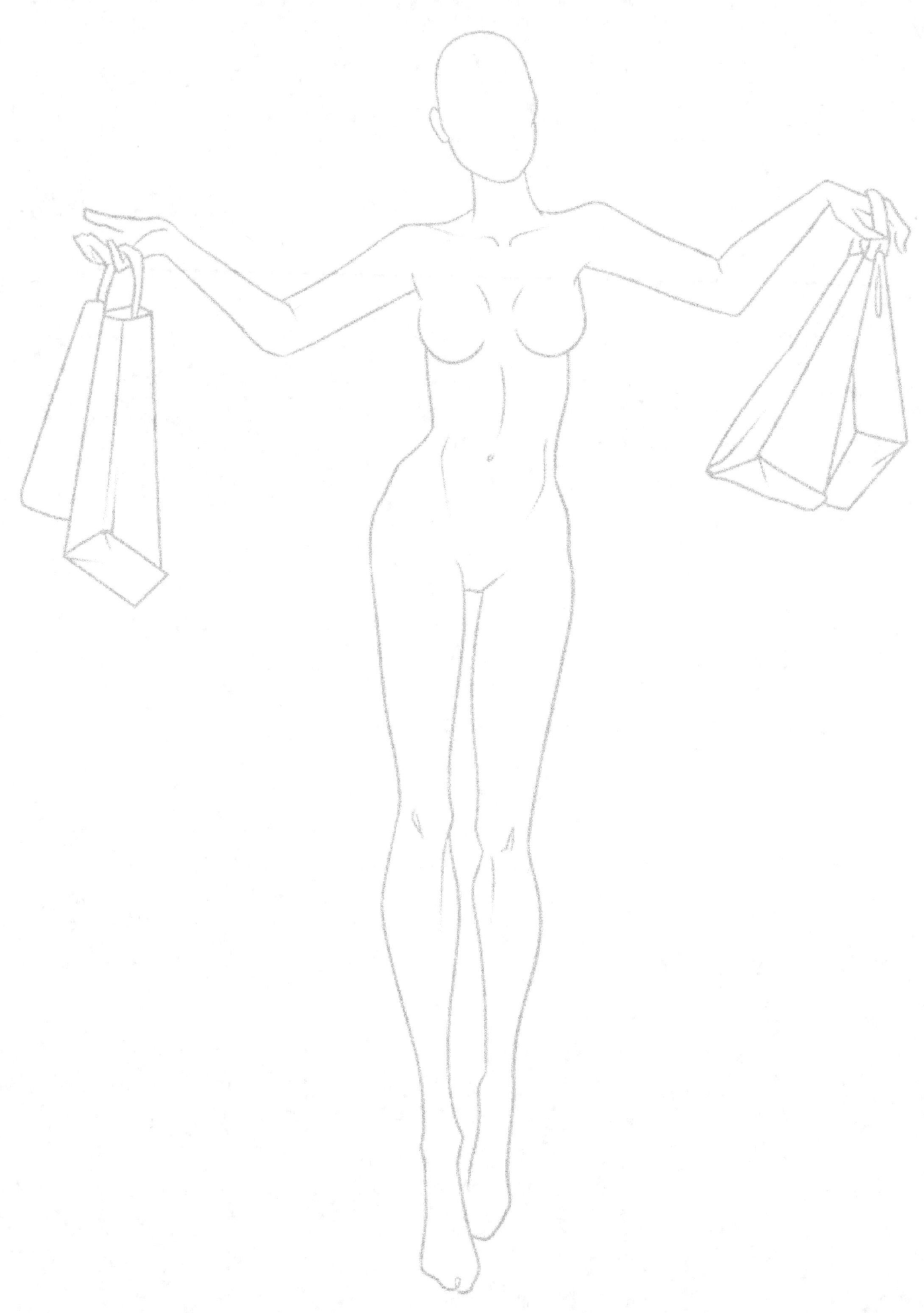

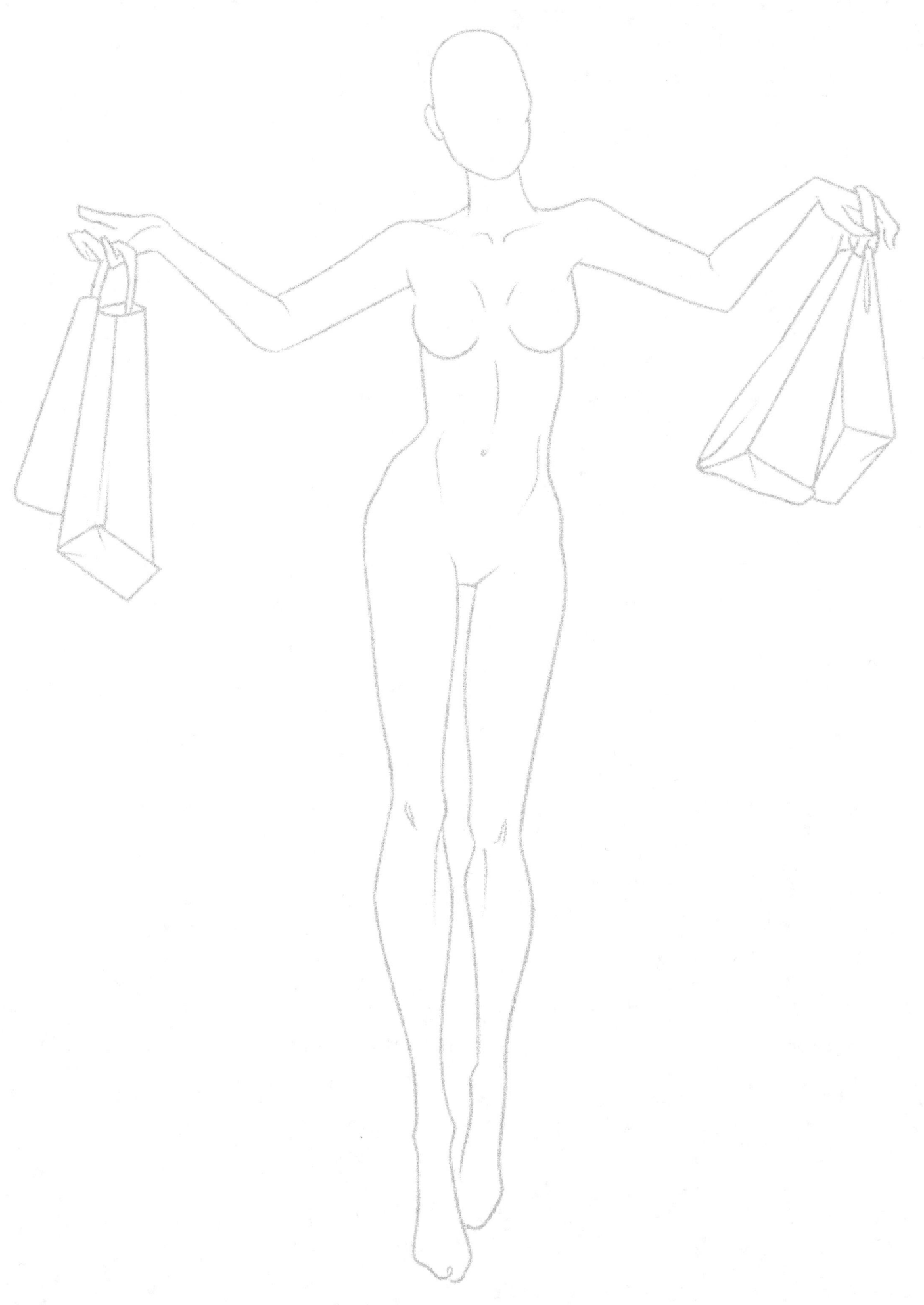

DASHED LINE FIGURE TEMPLATES

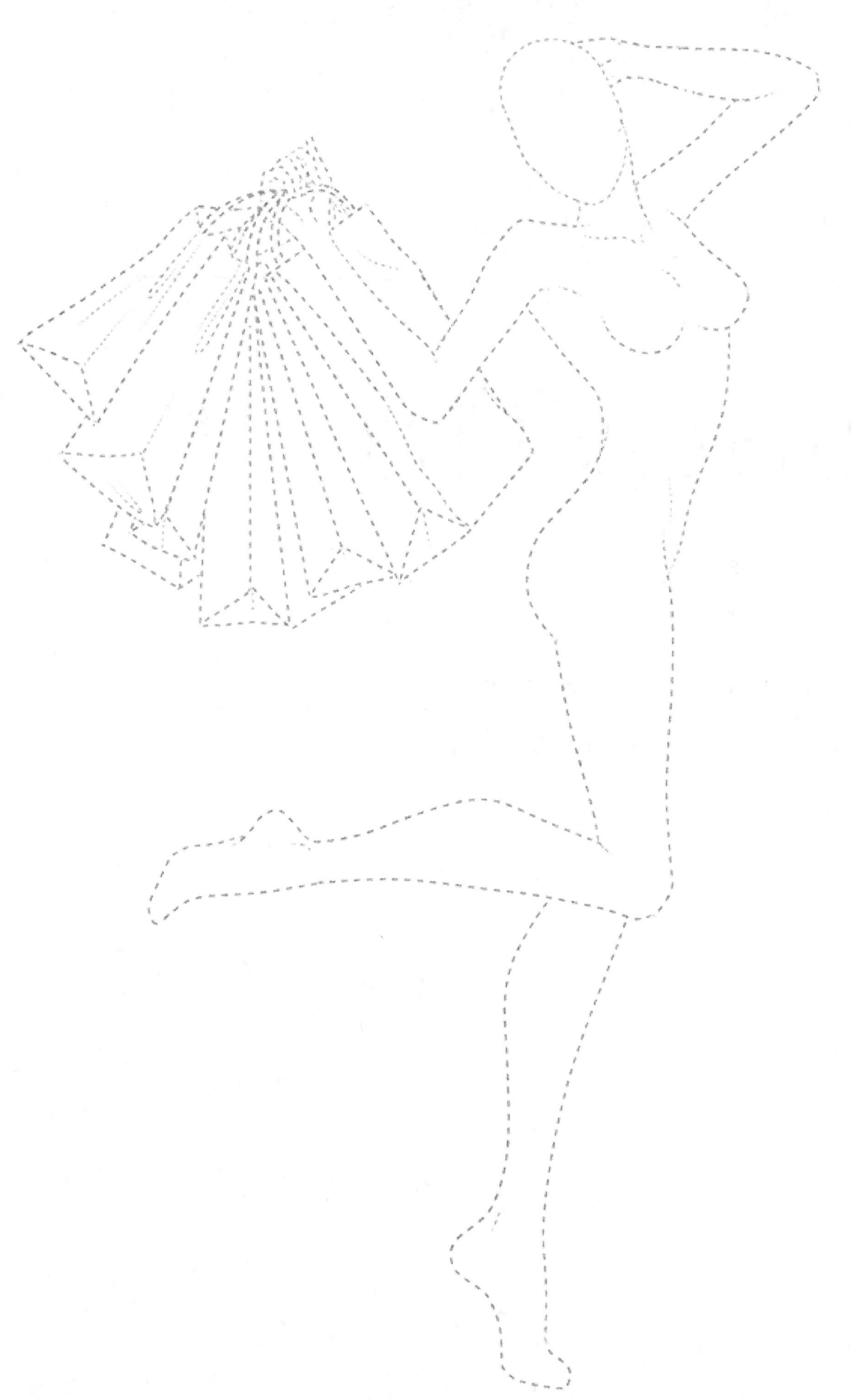

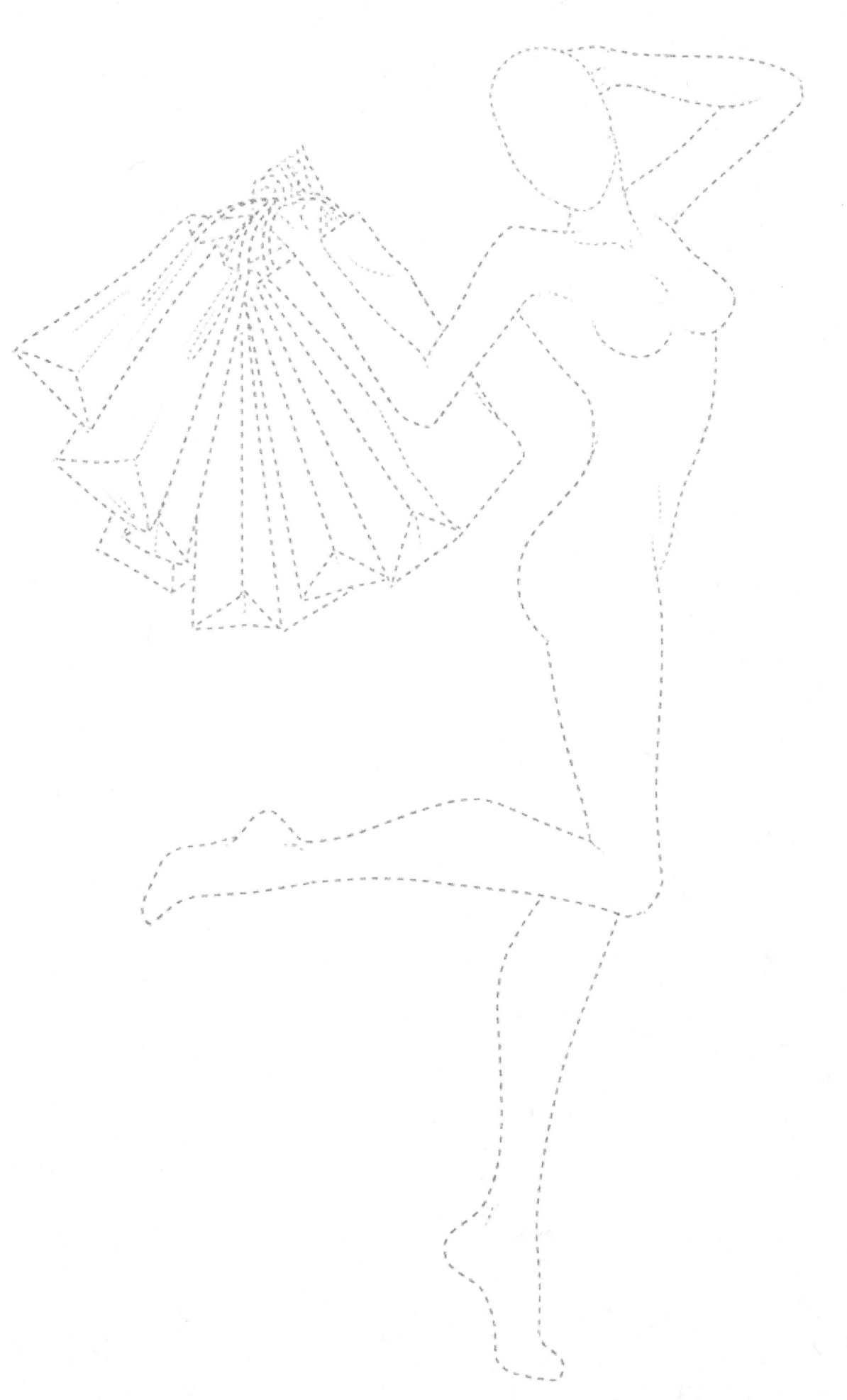

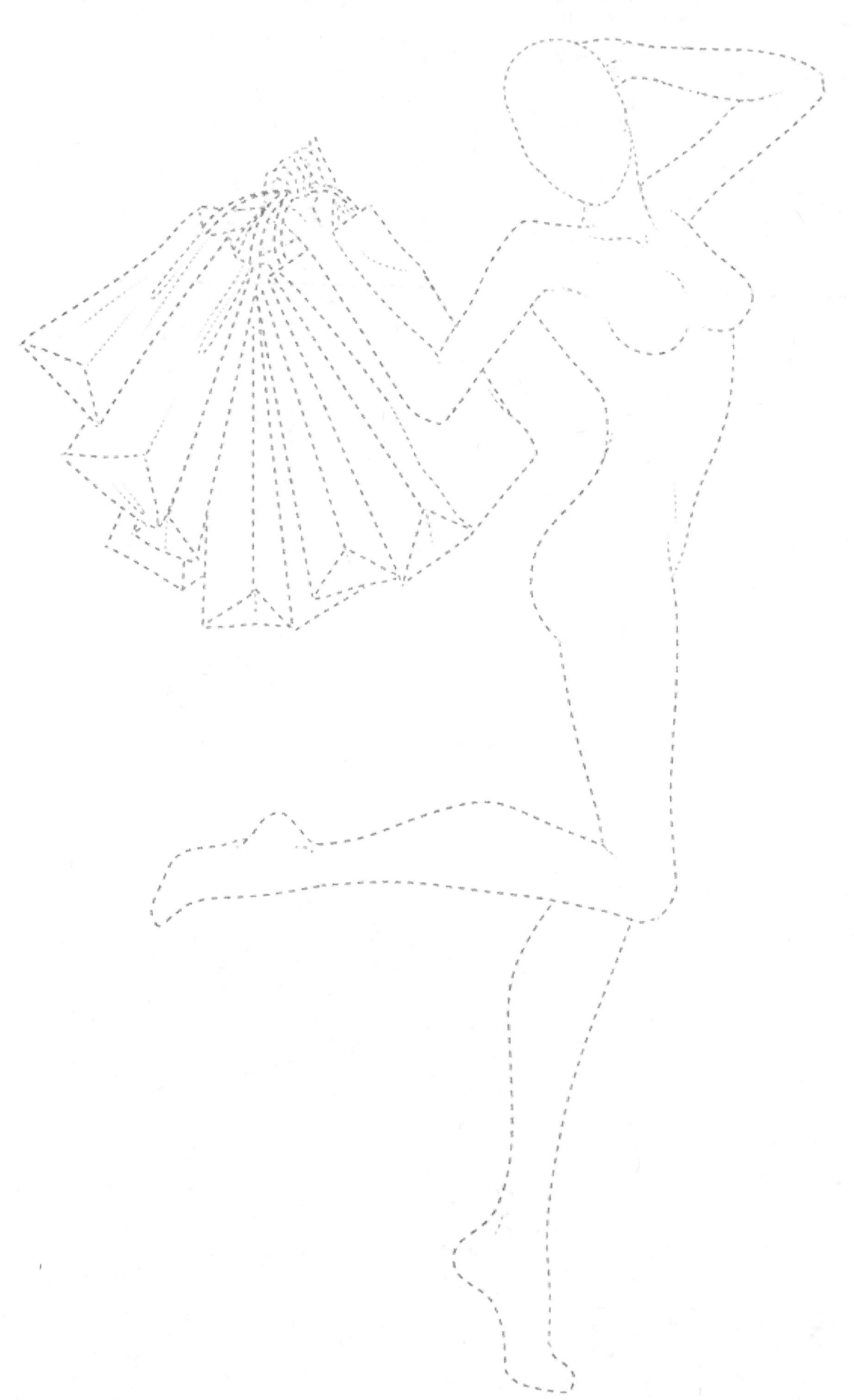

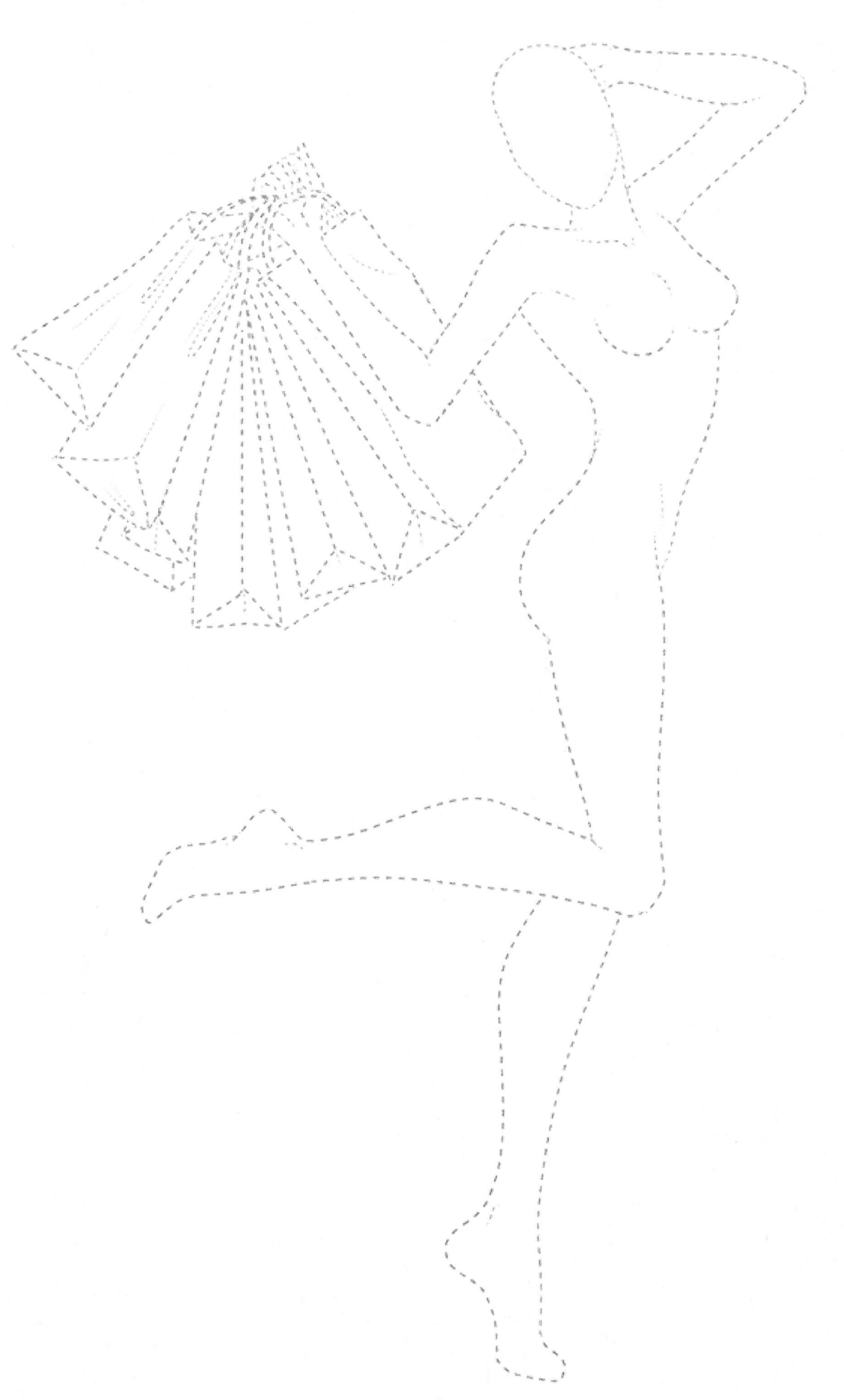

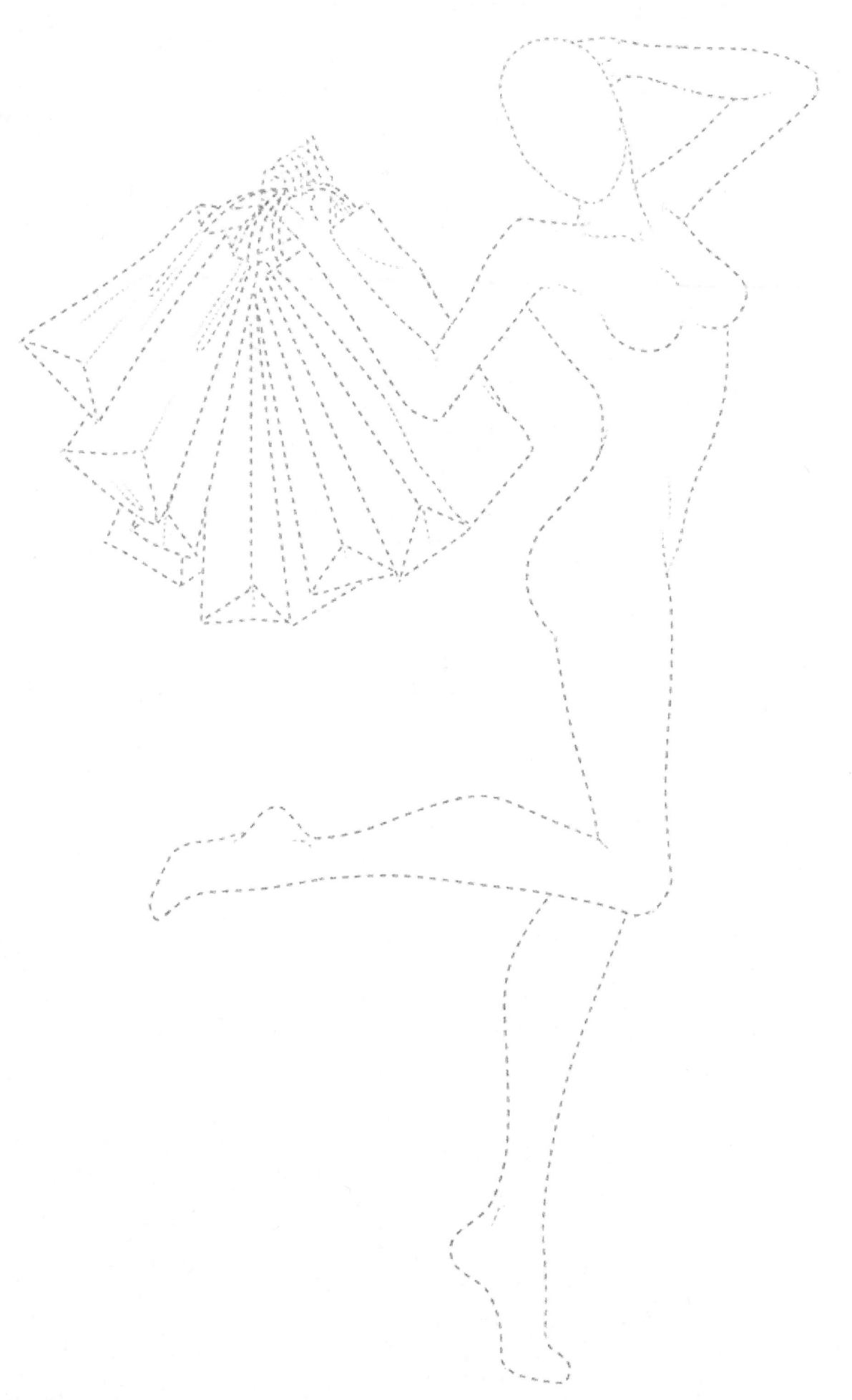

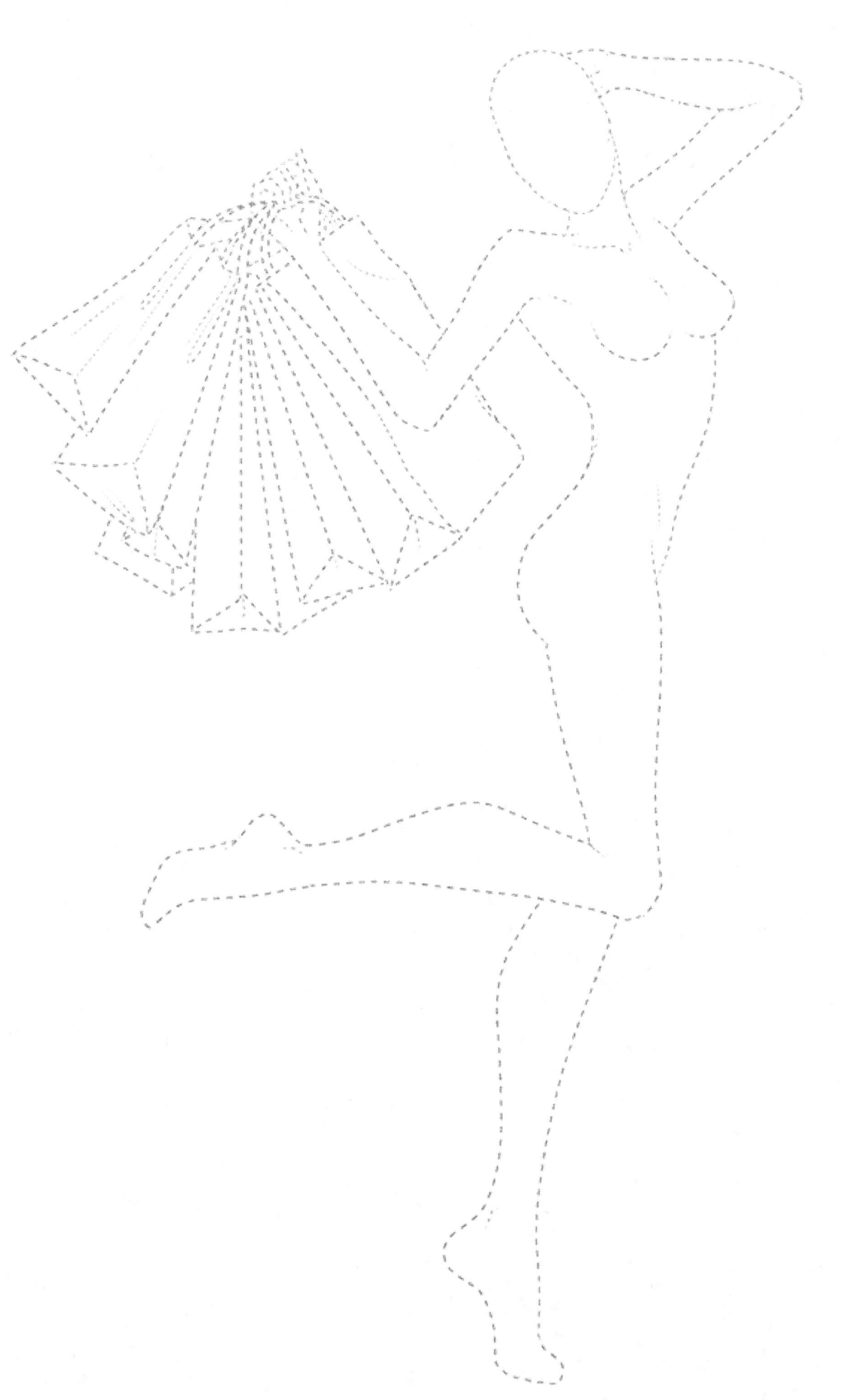

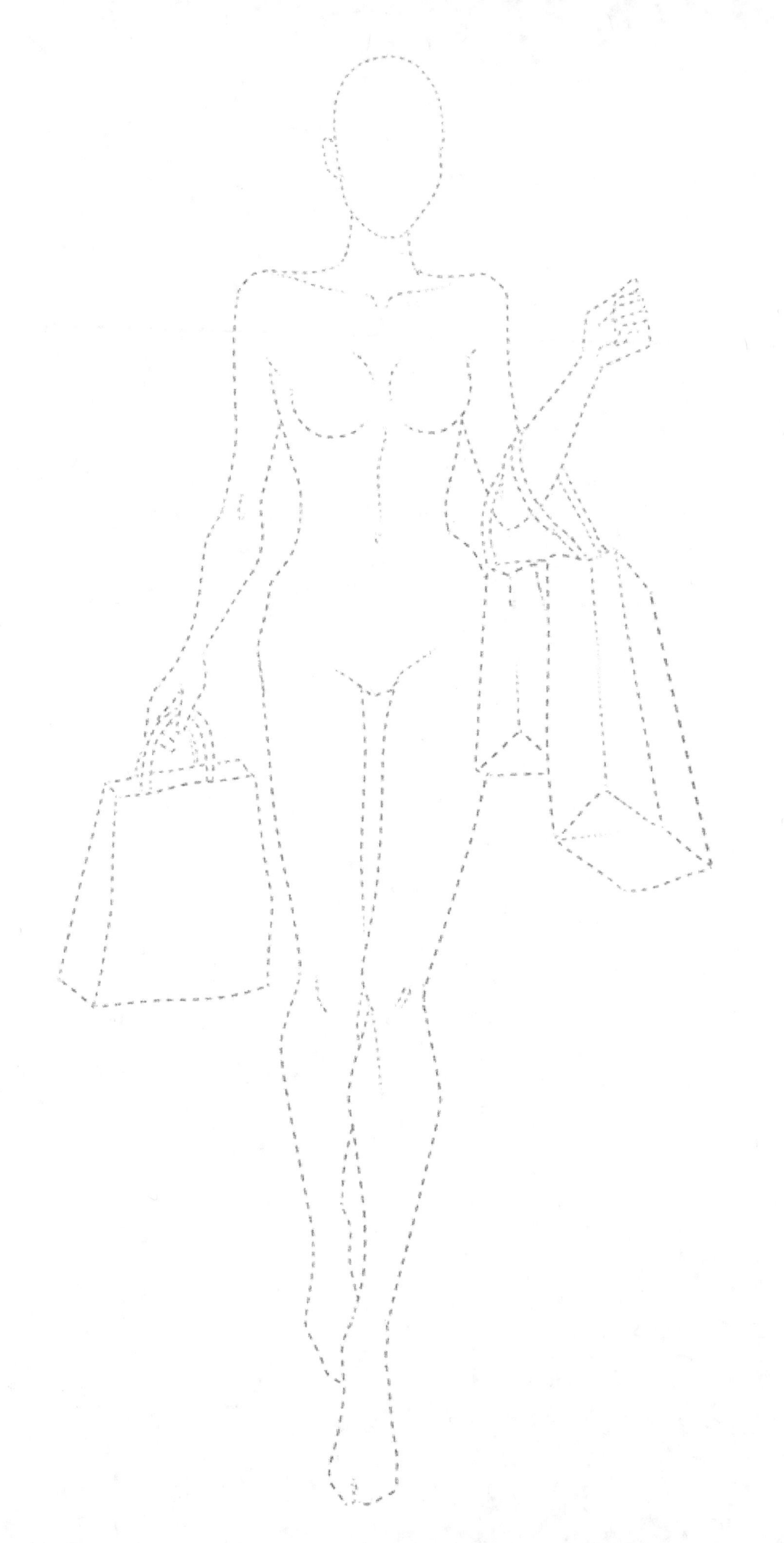

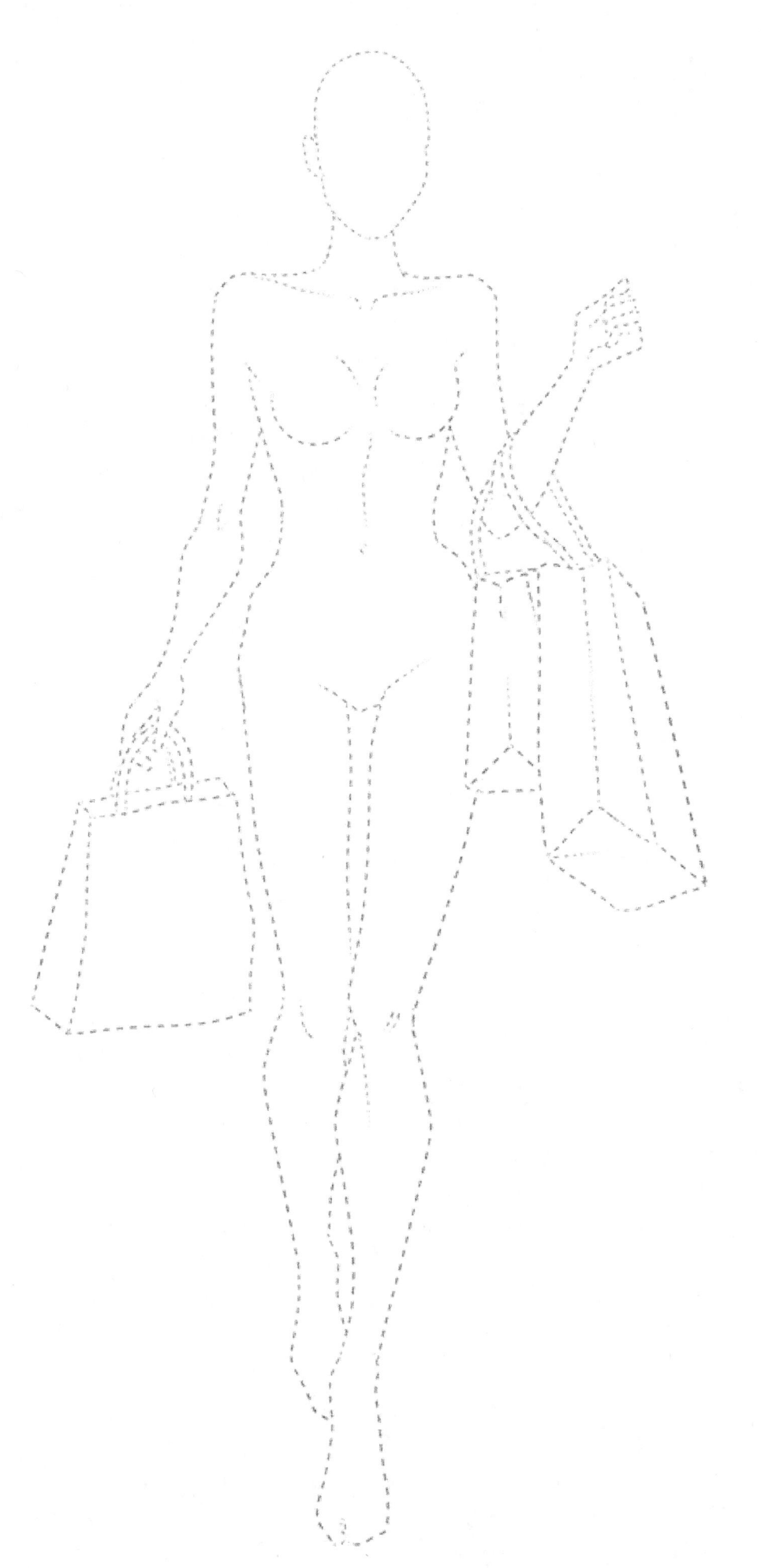

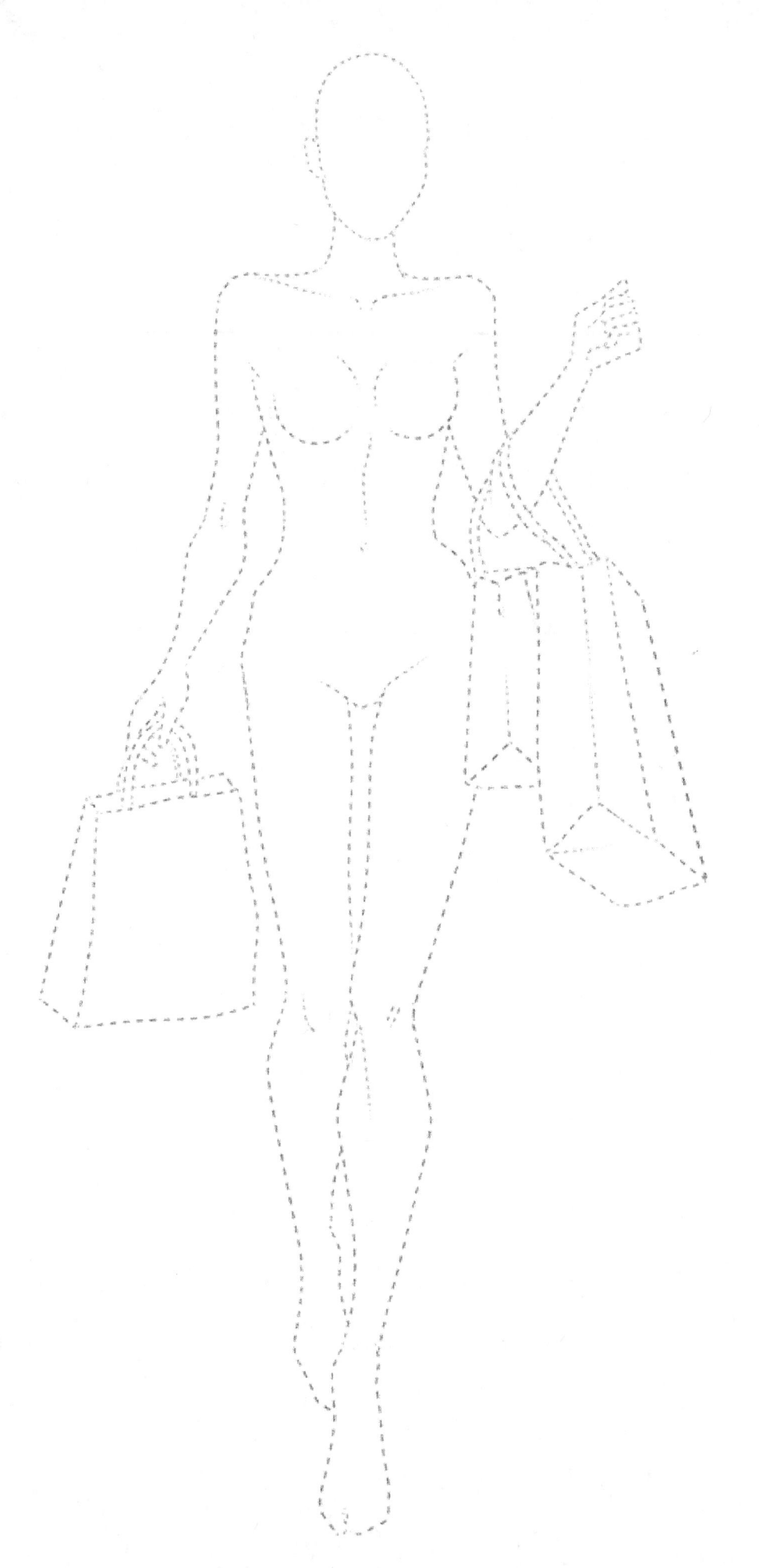

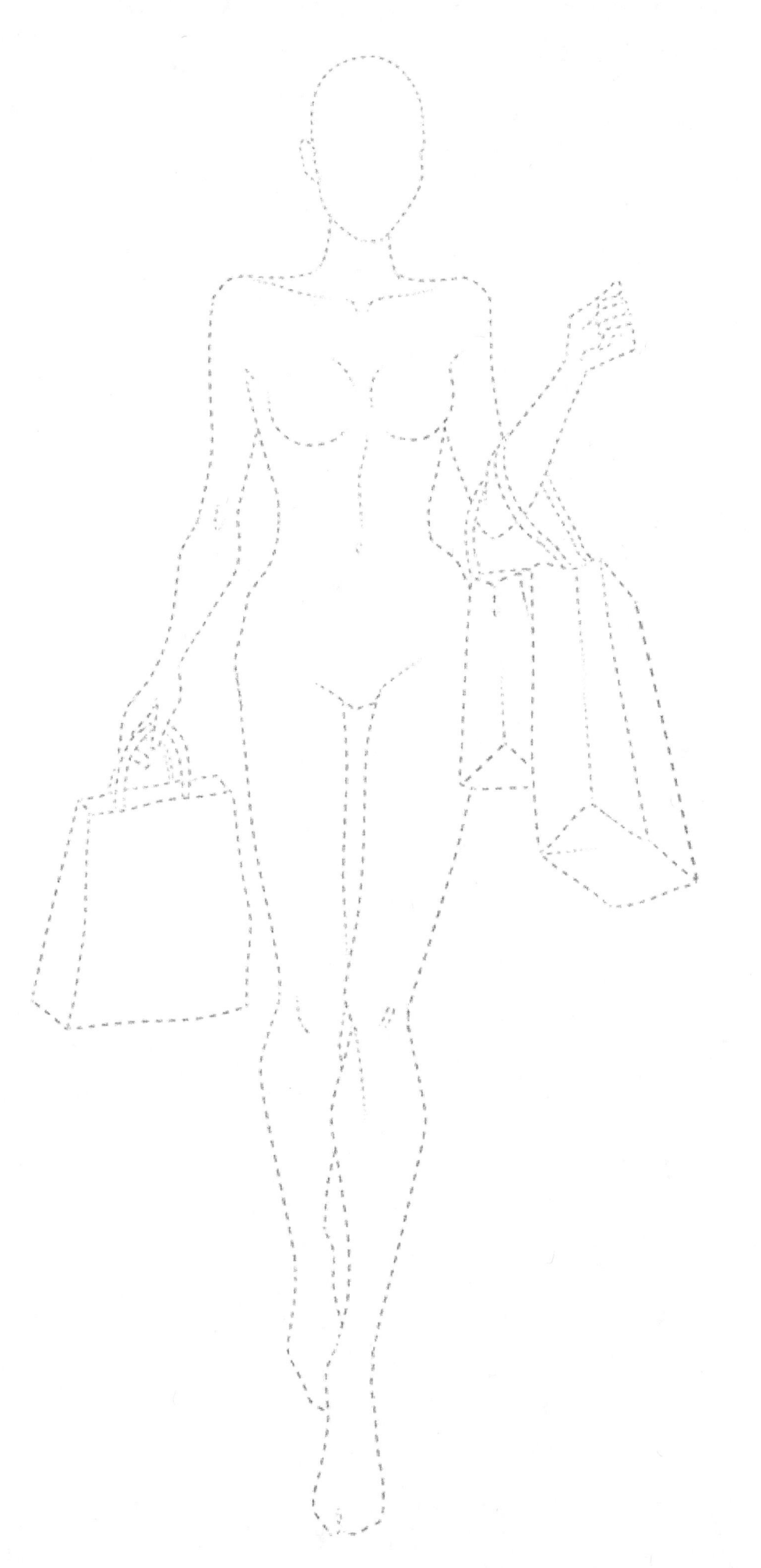

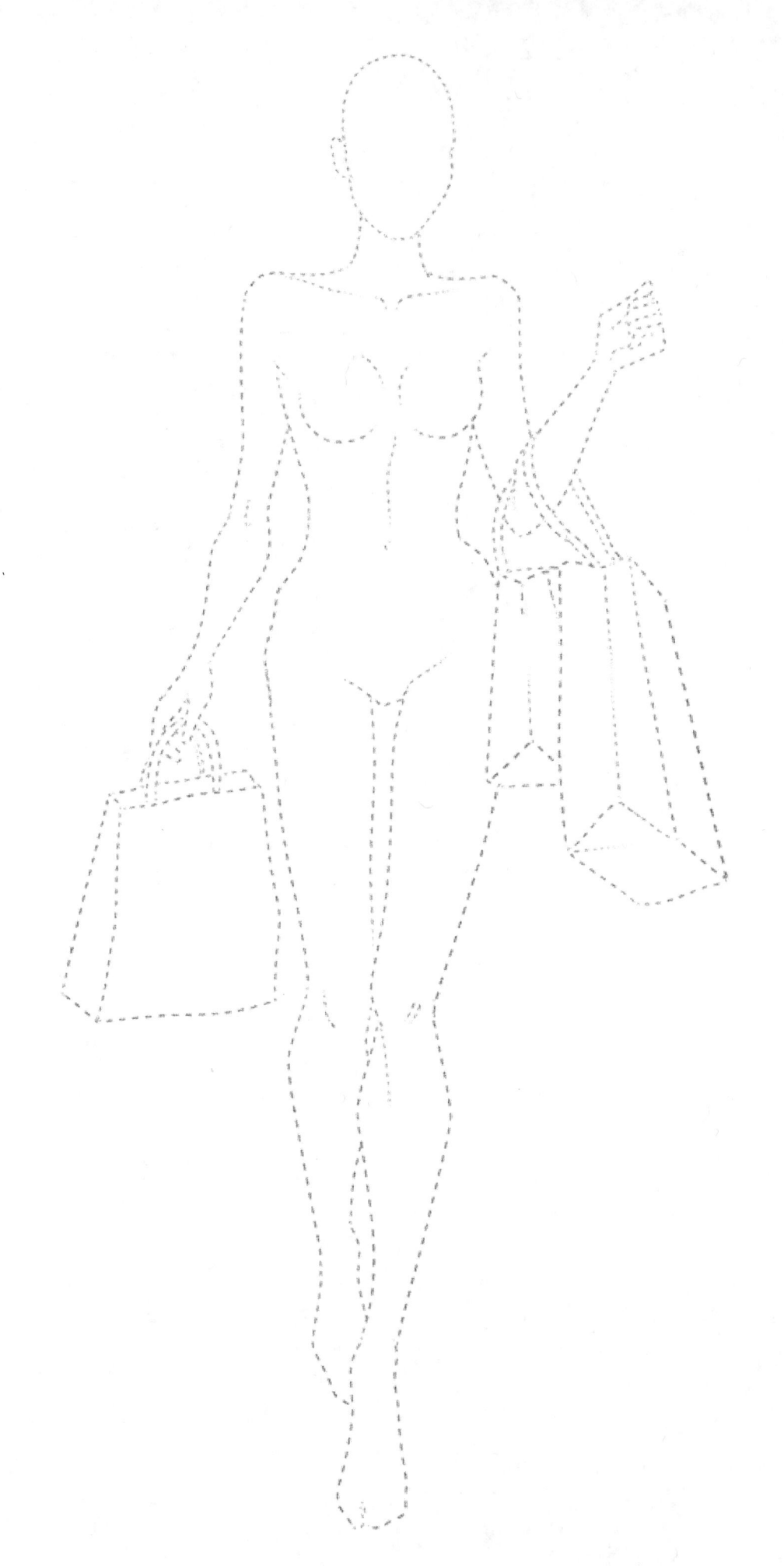

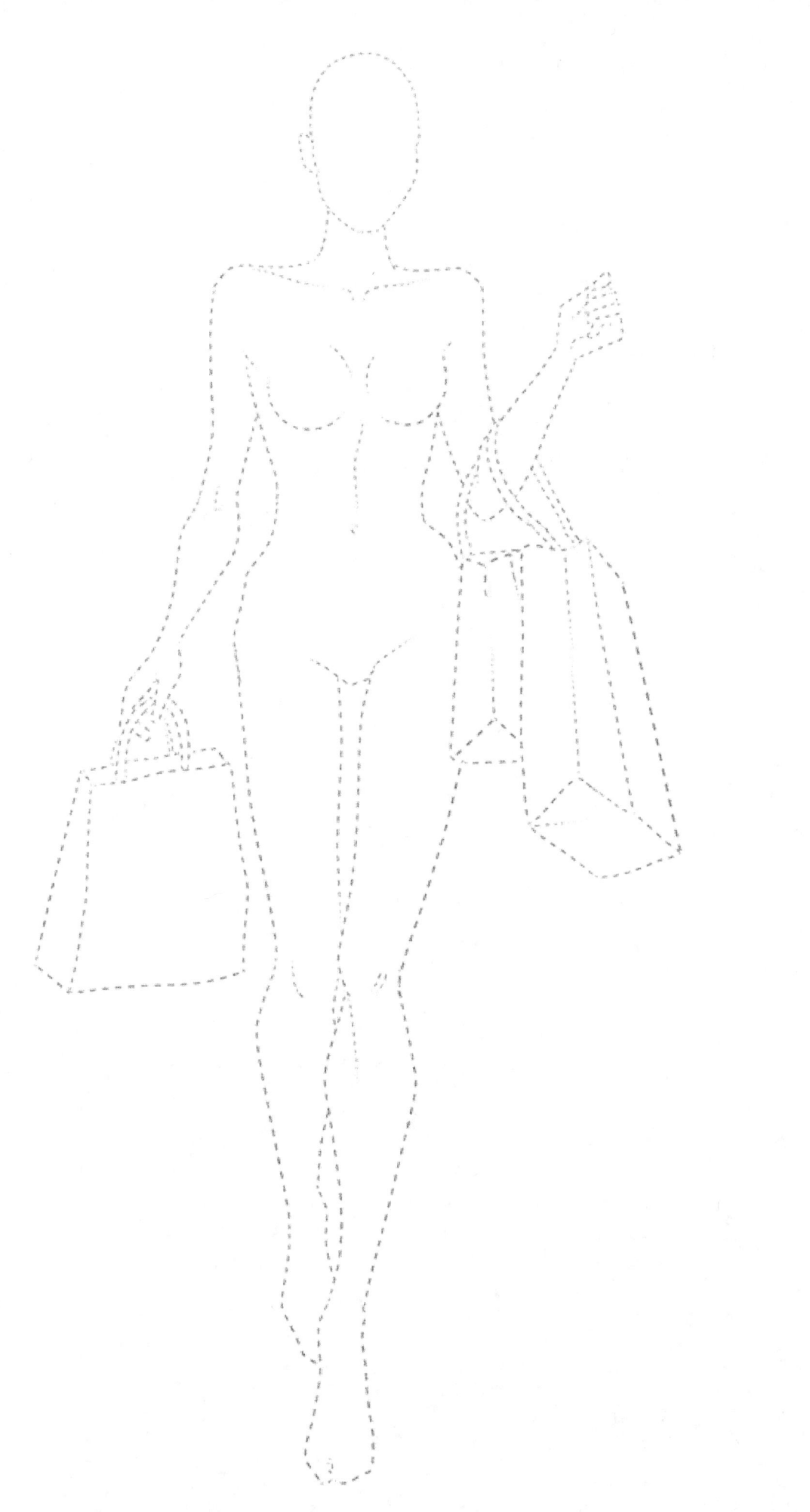

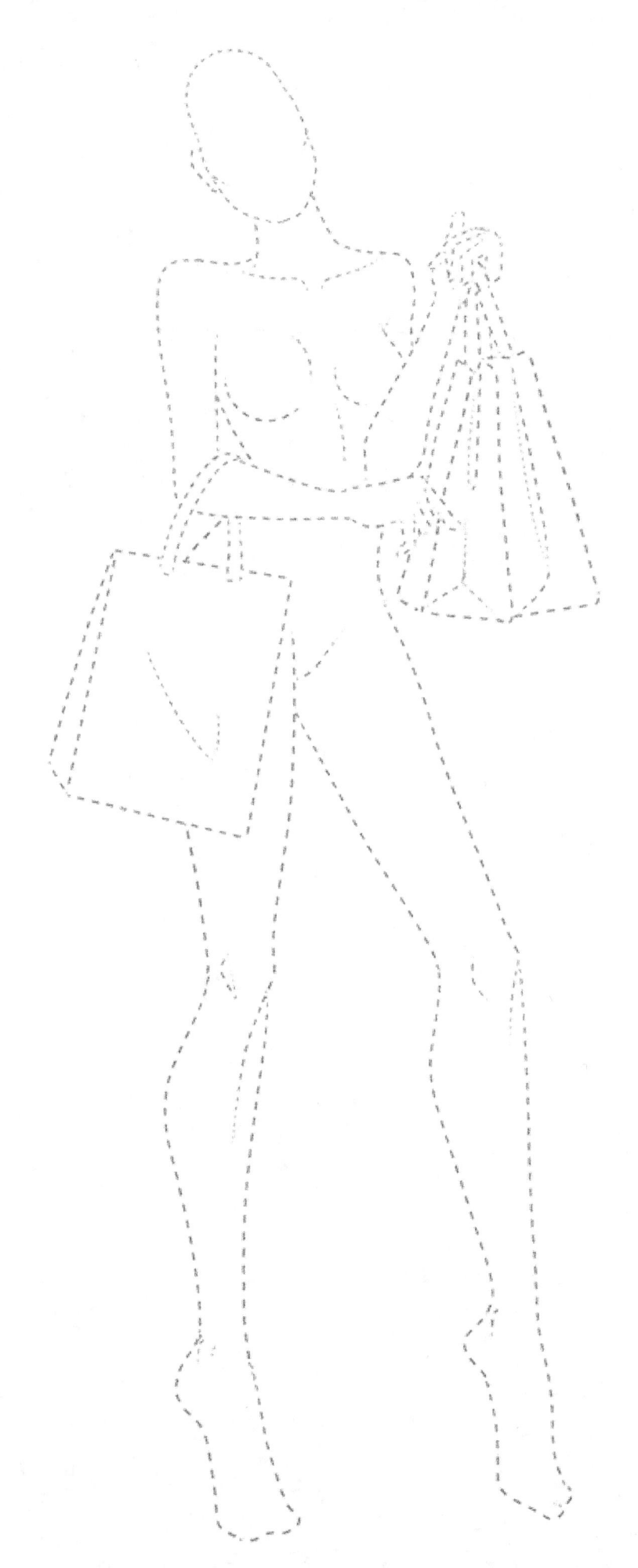

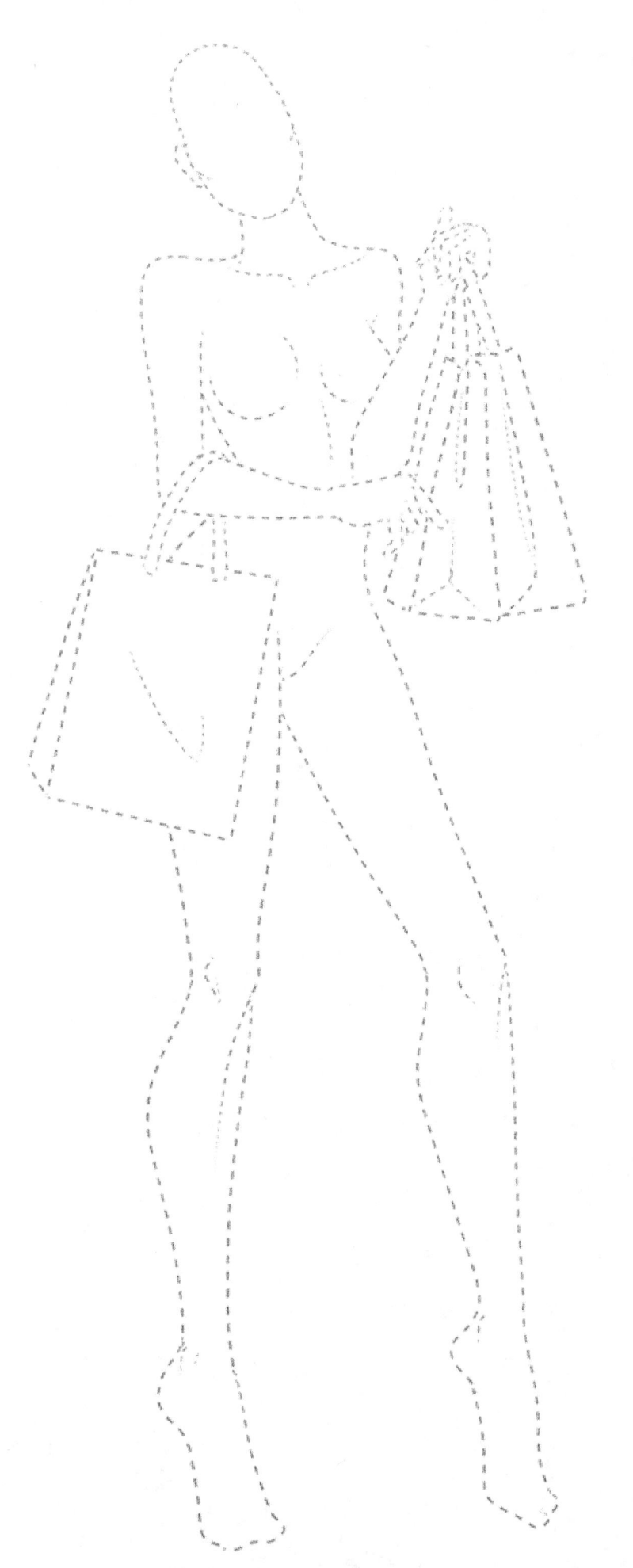

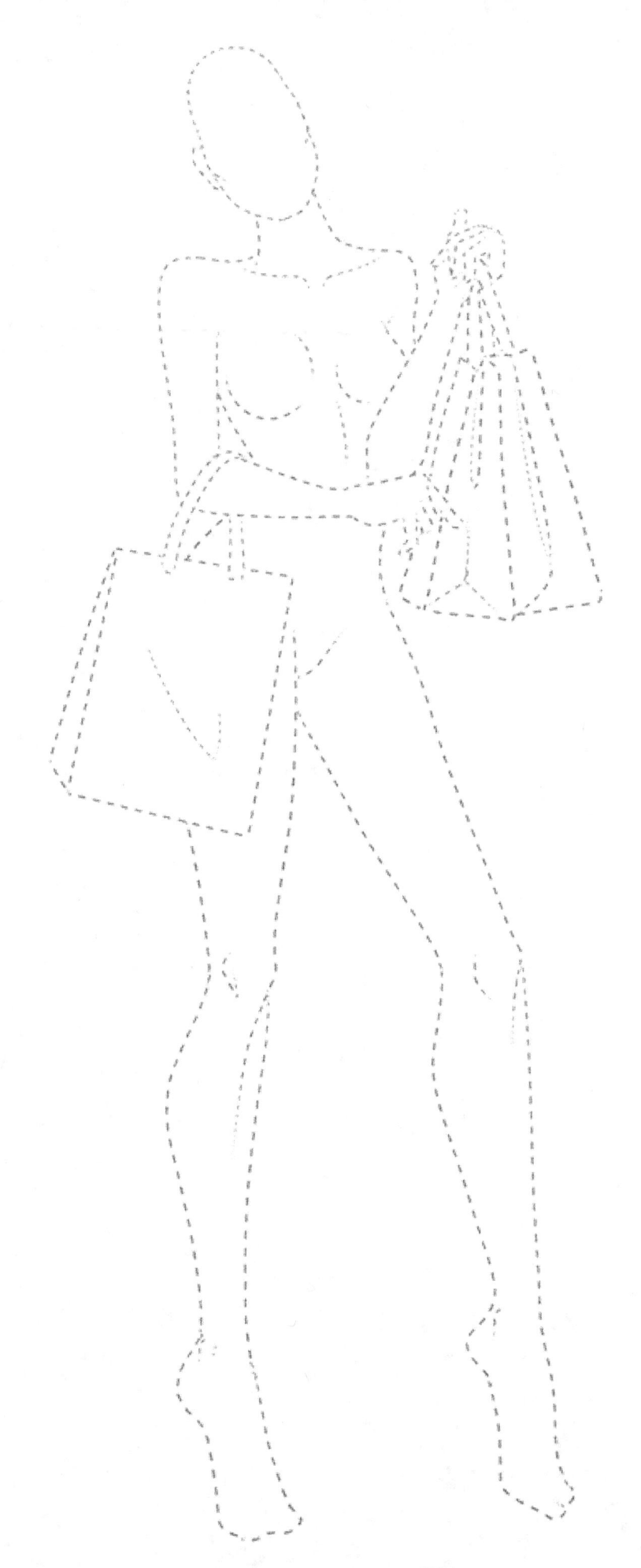

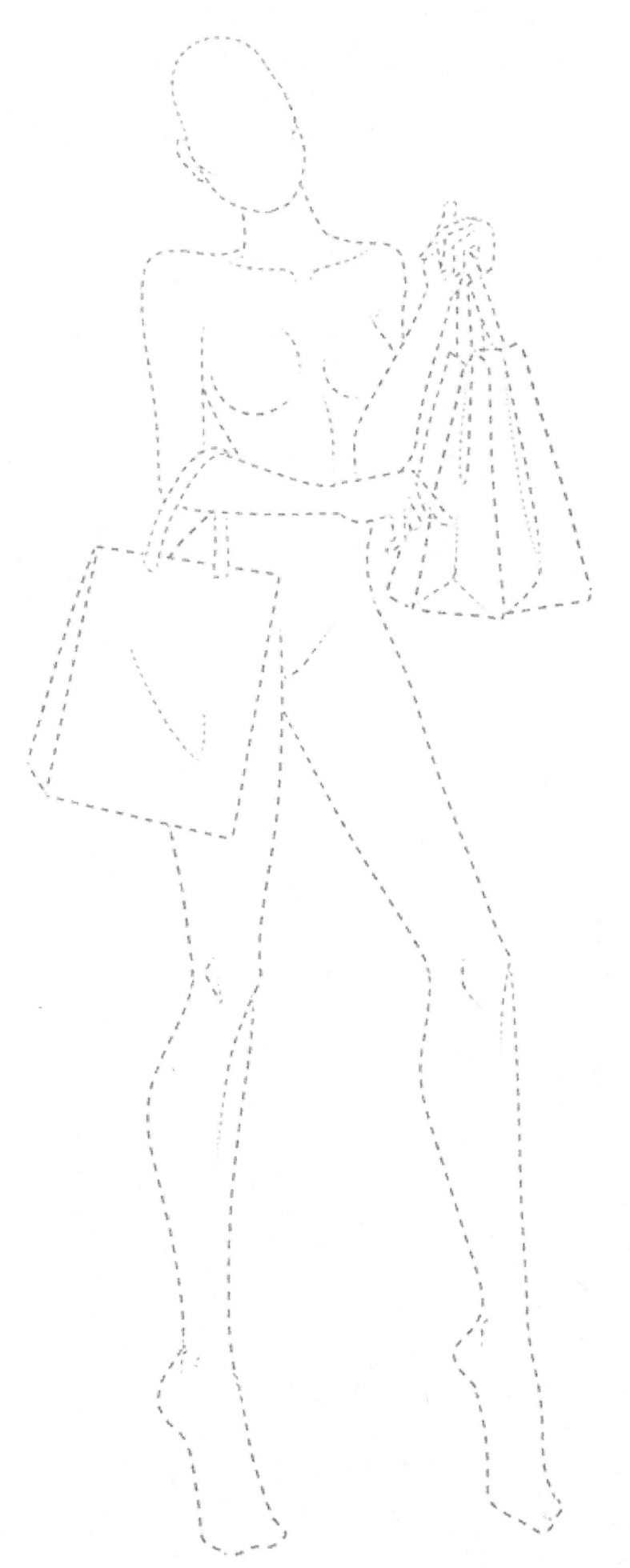

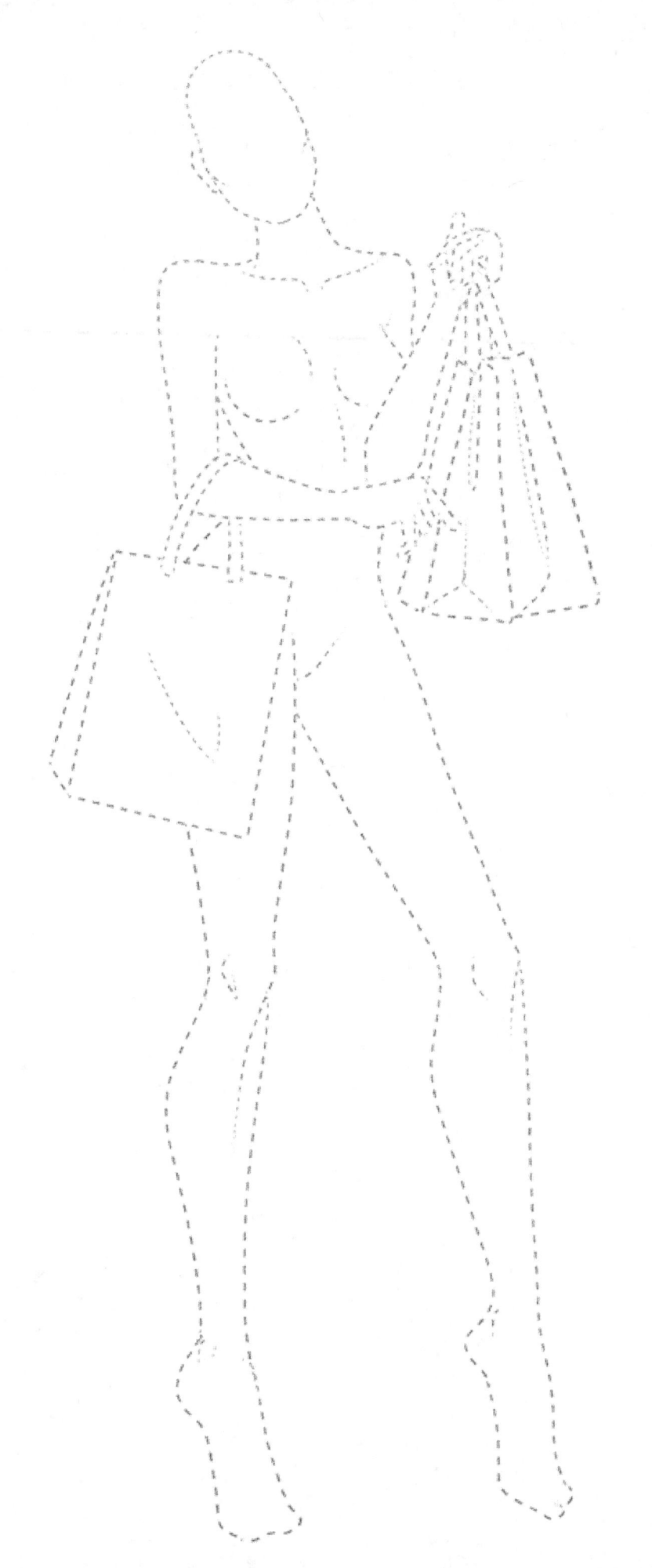

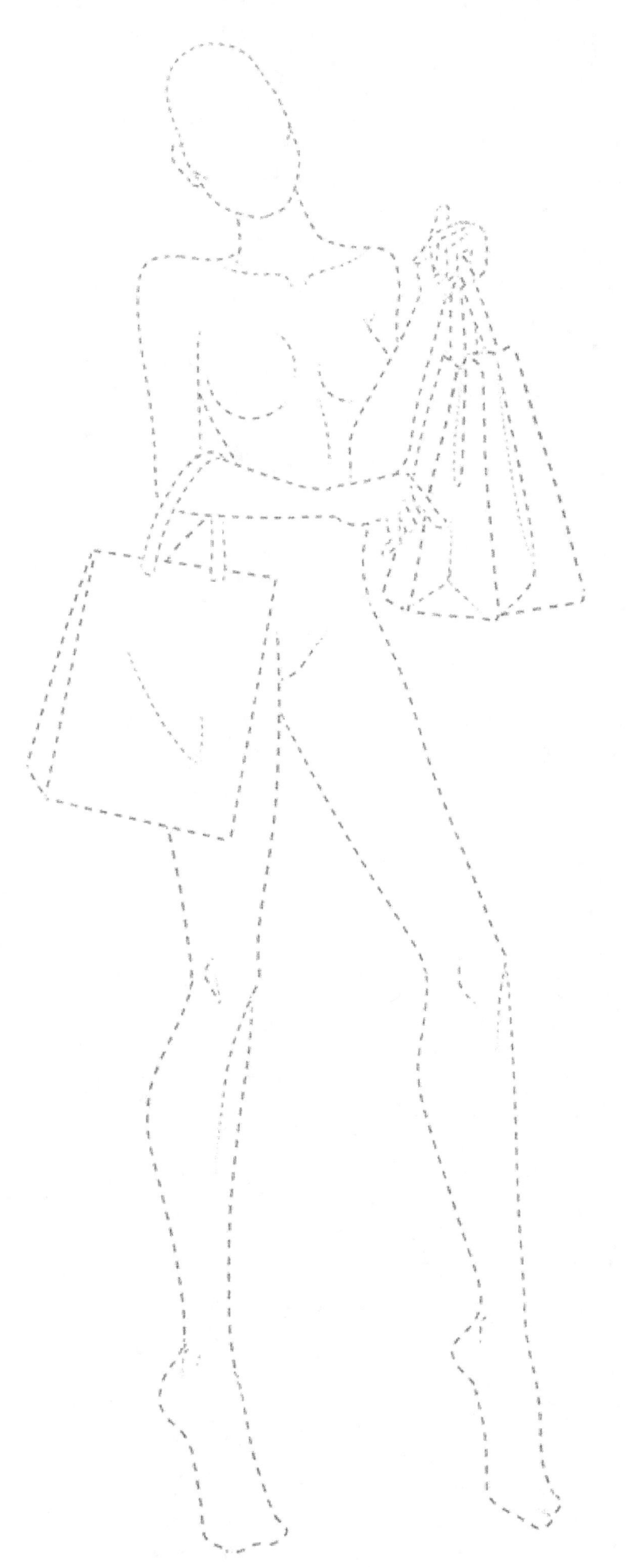

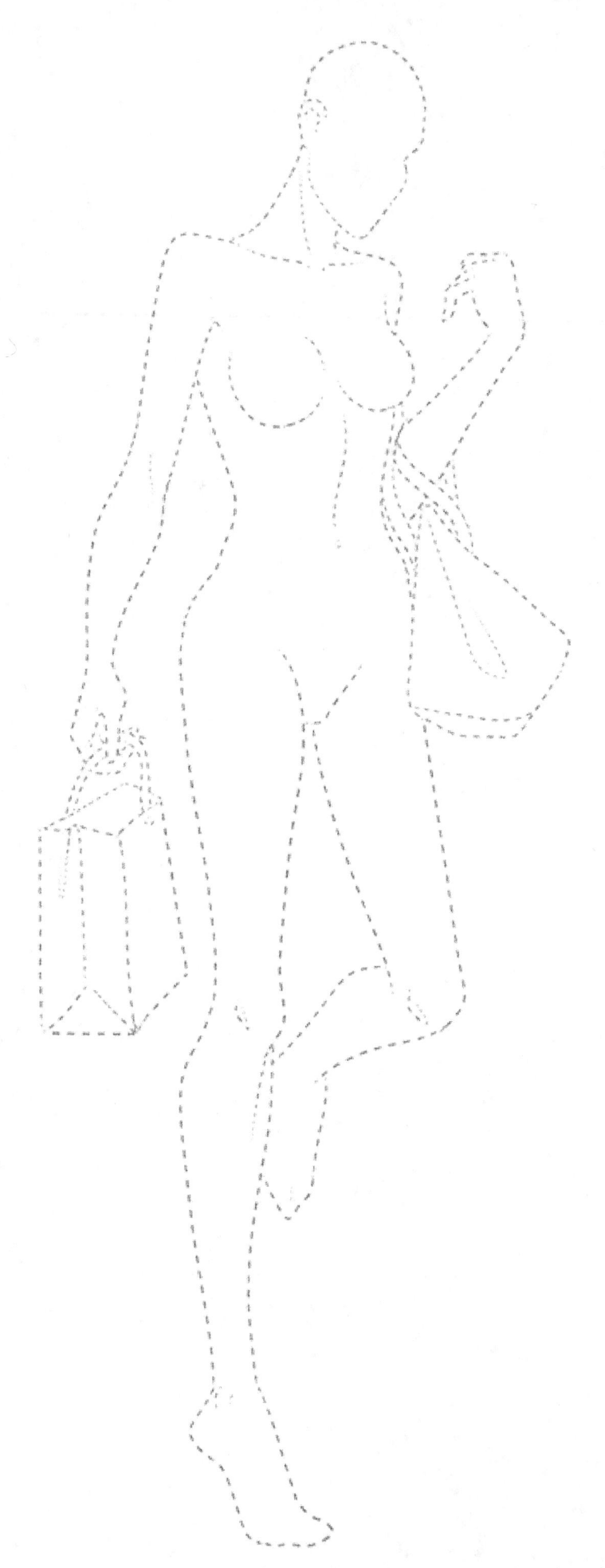

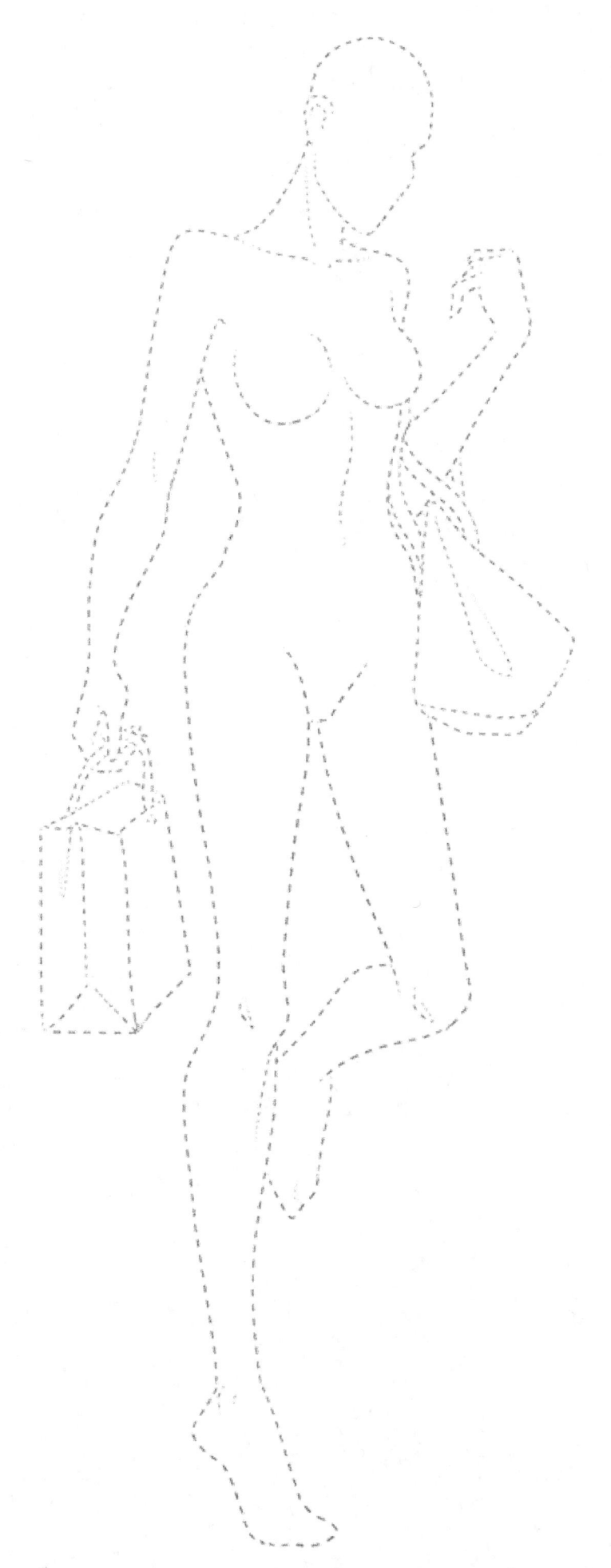

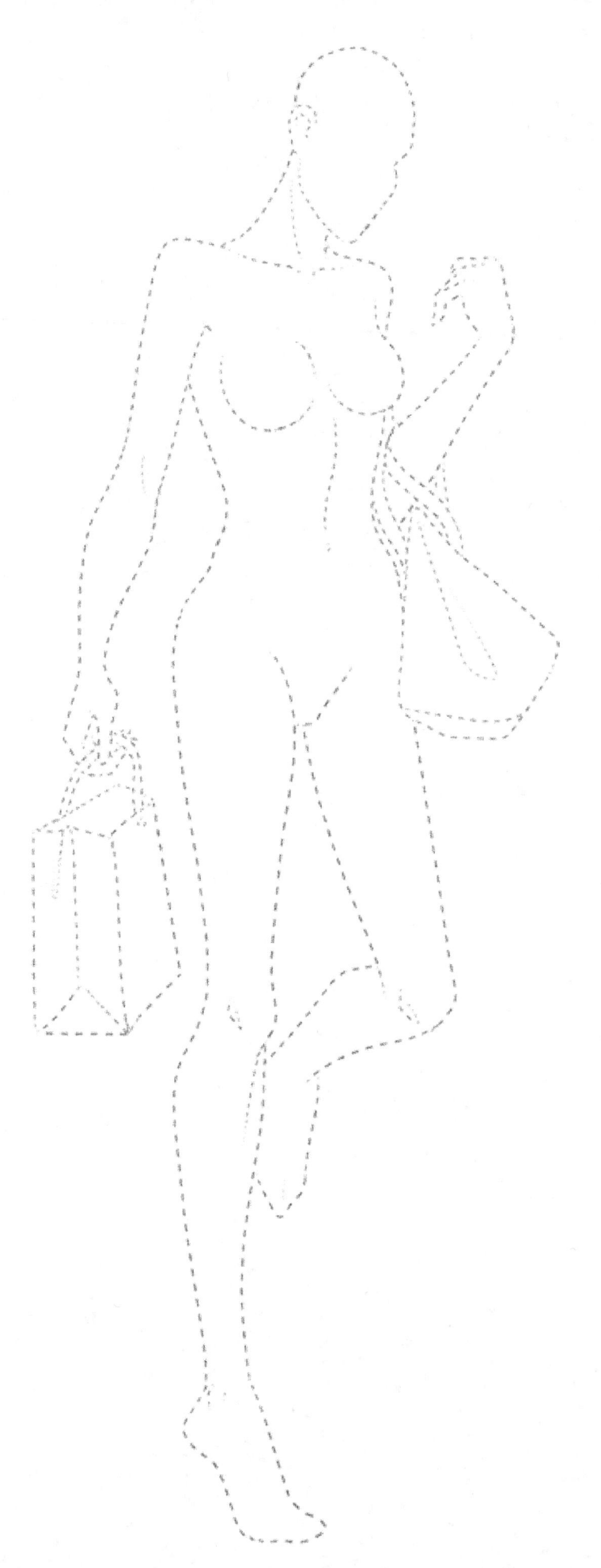

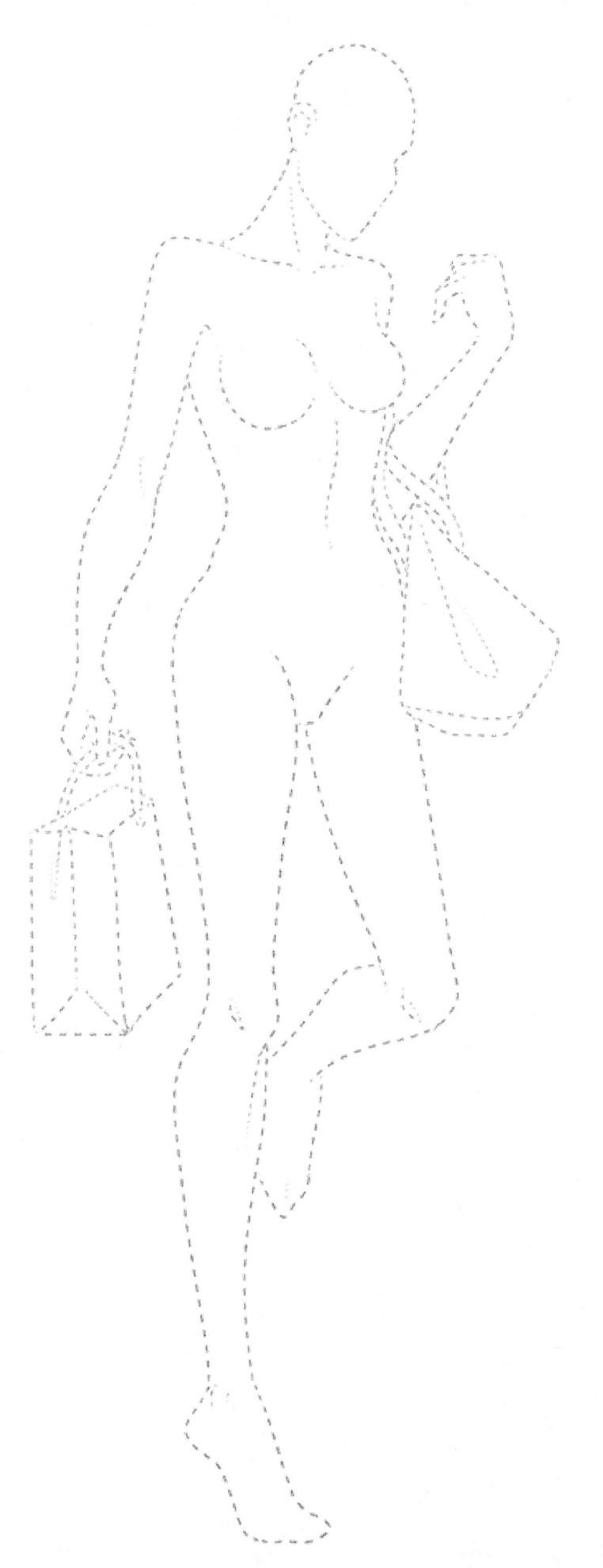

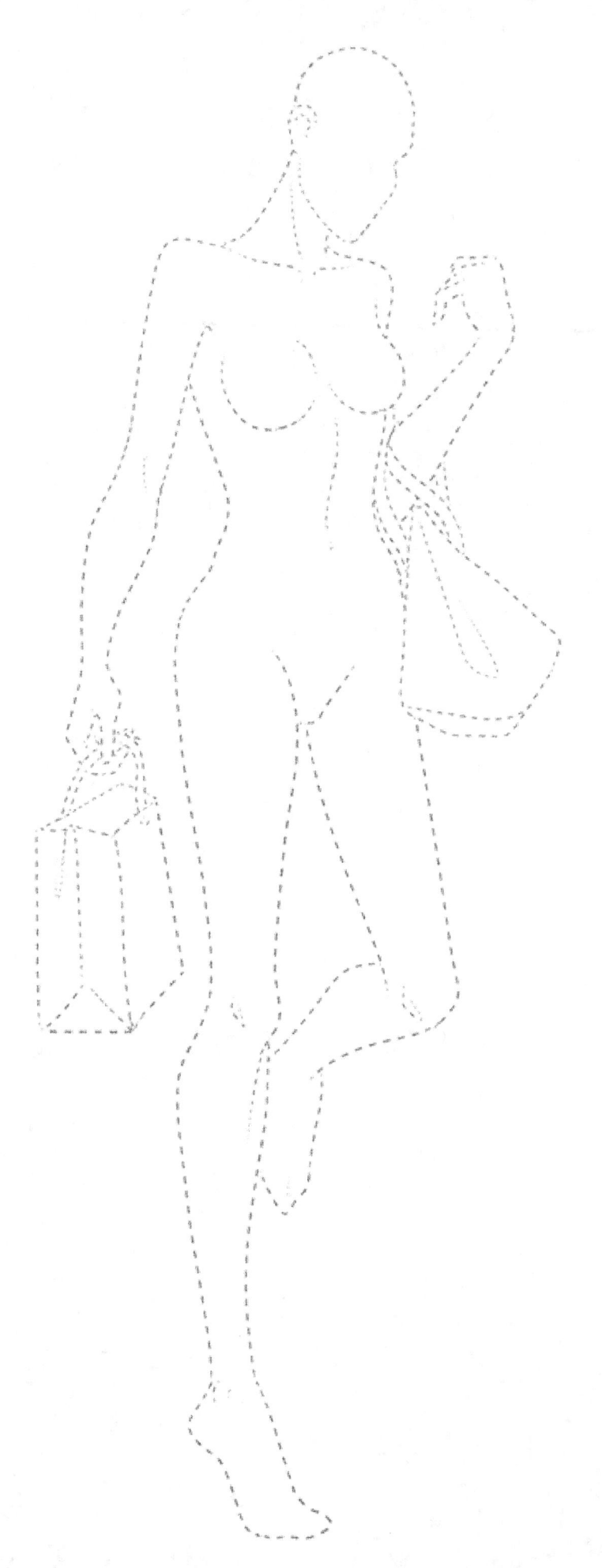

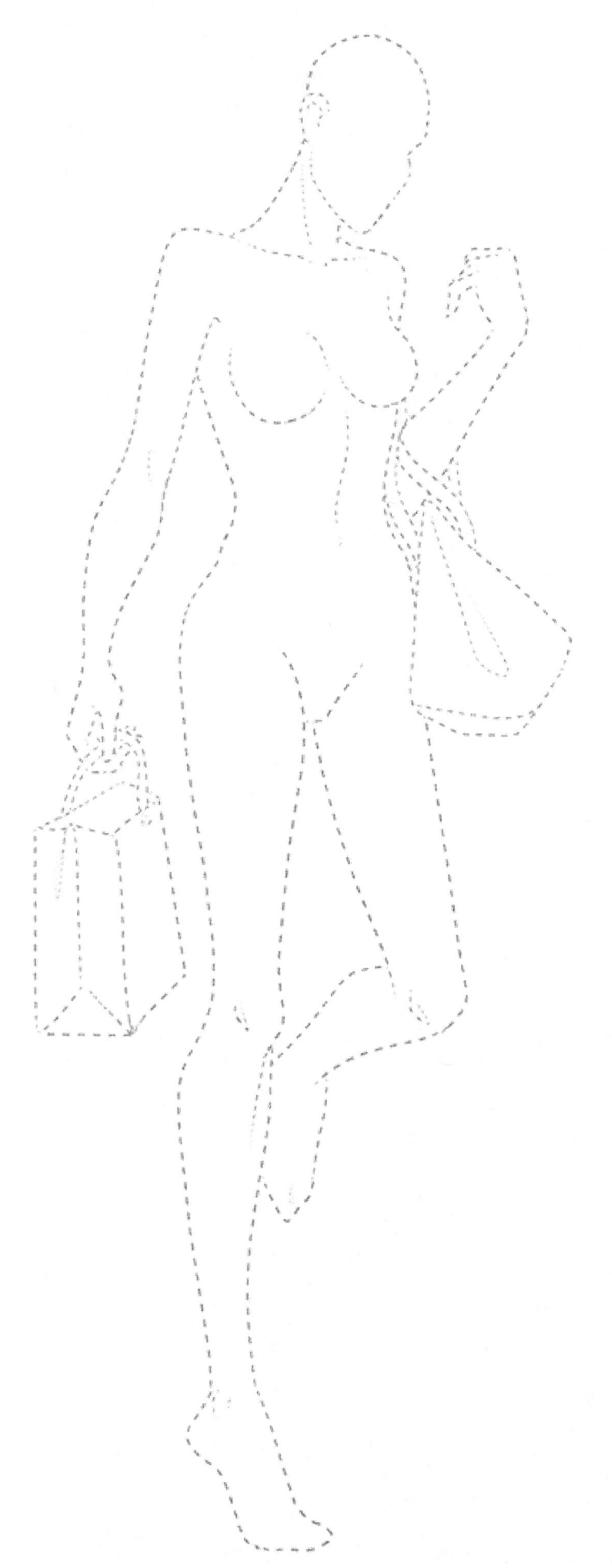

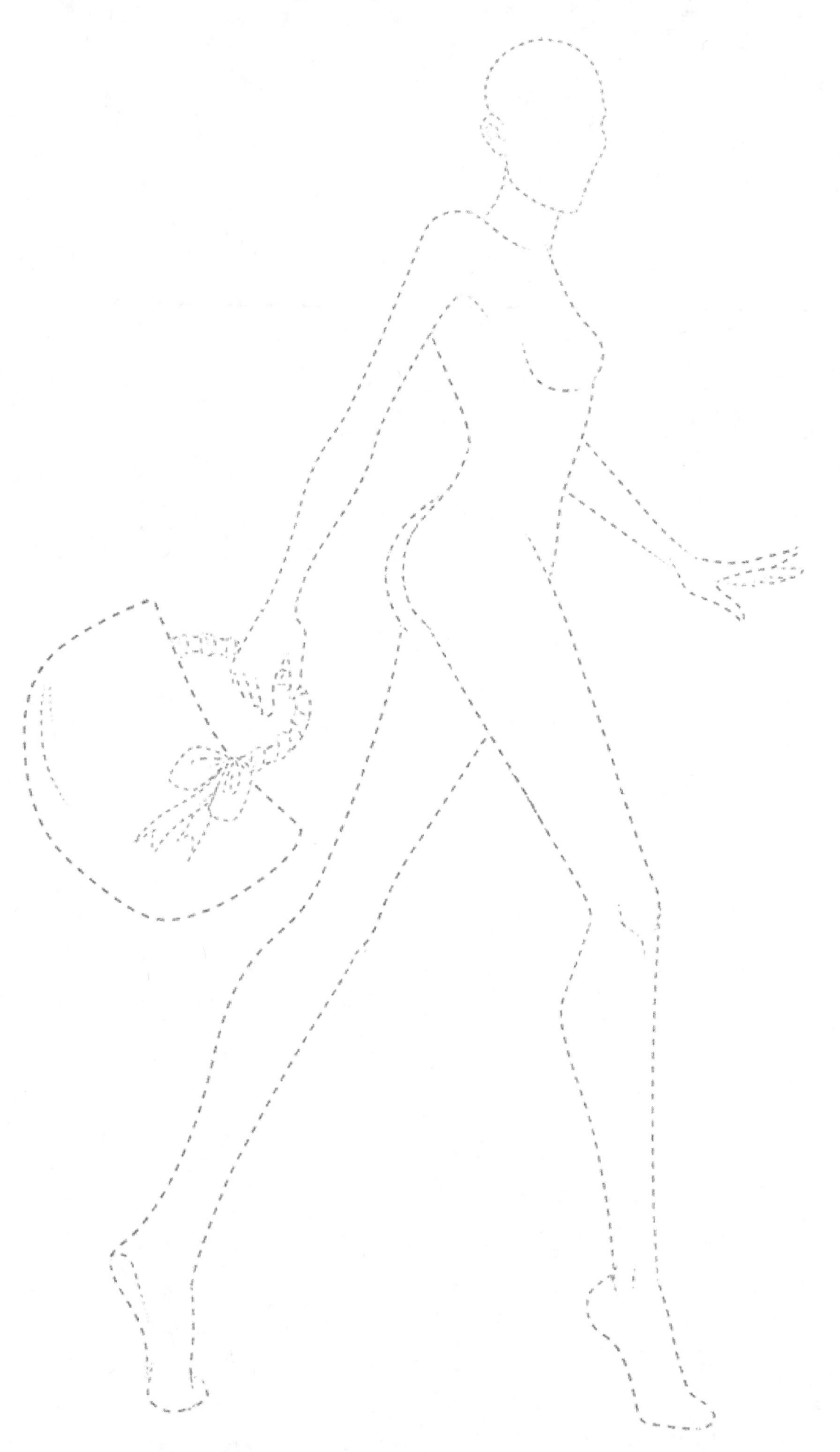

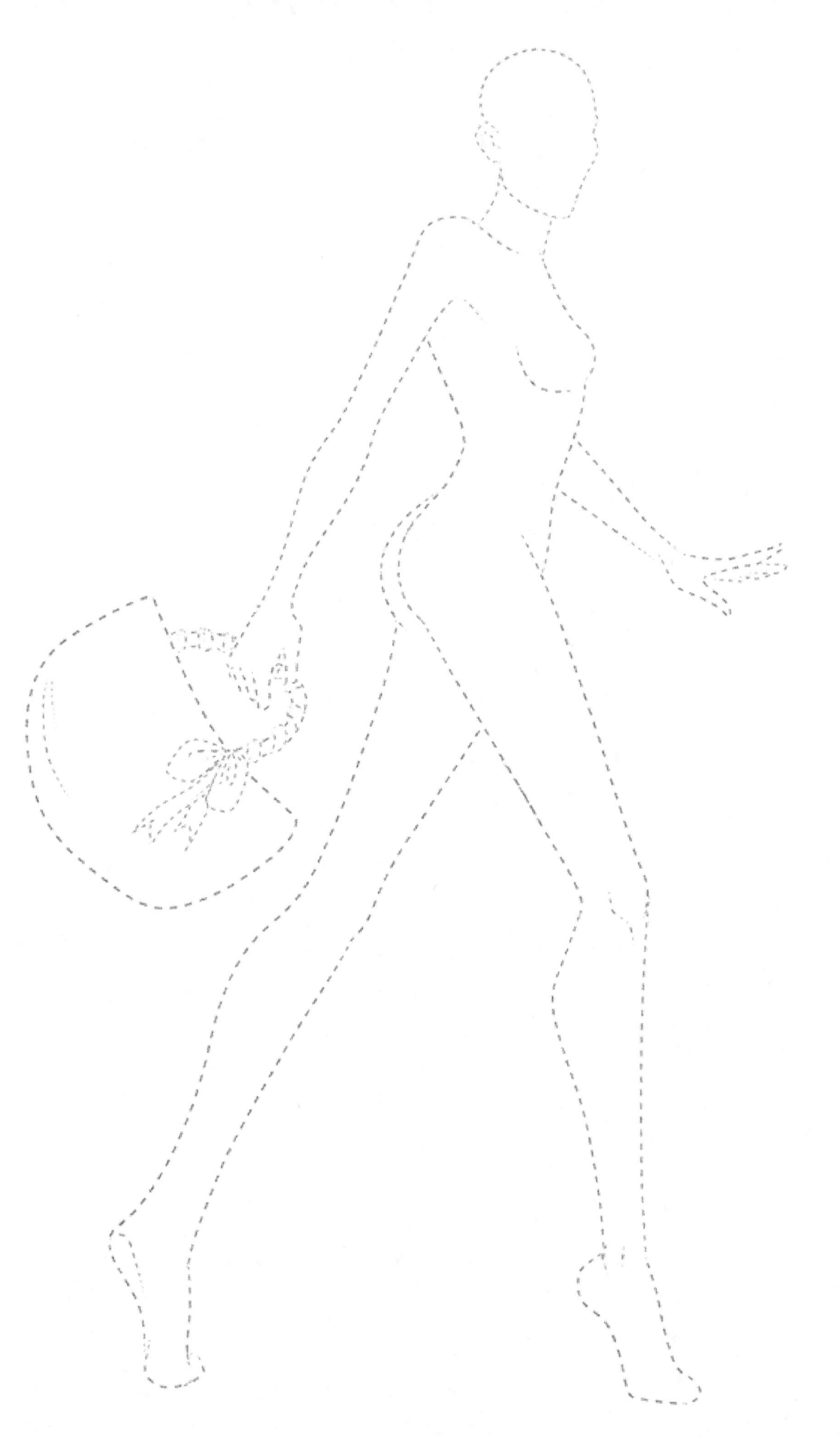

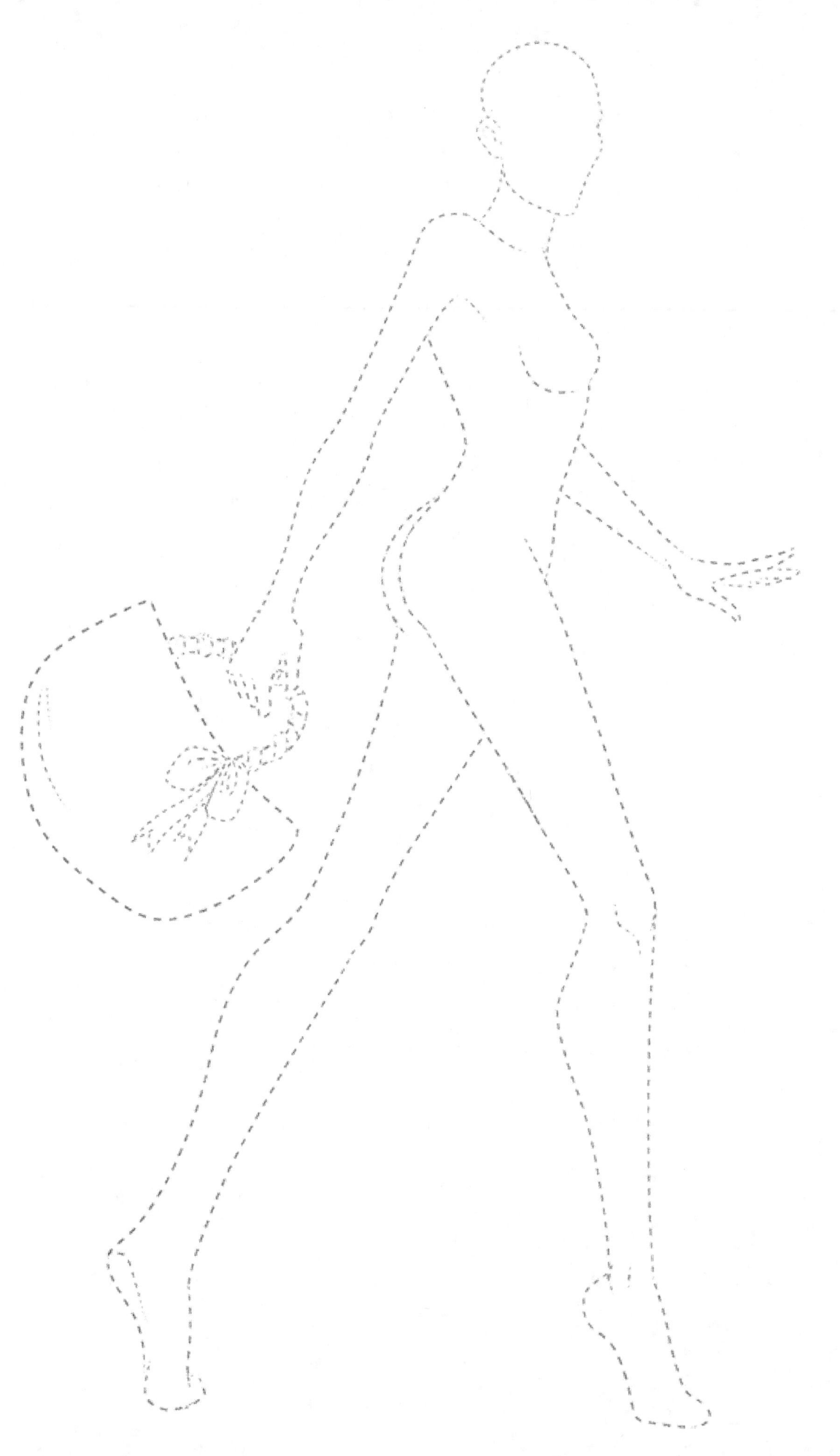

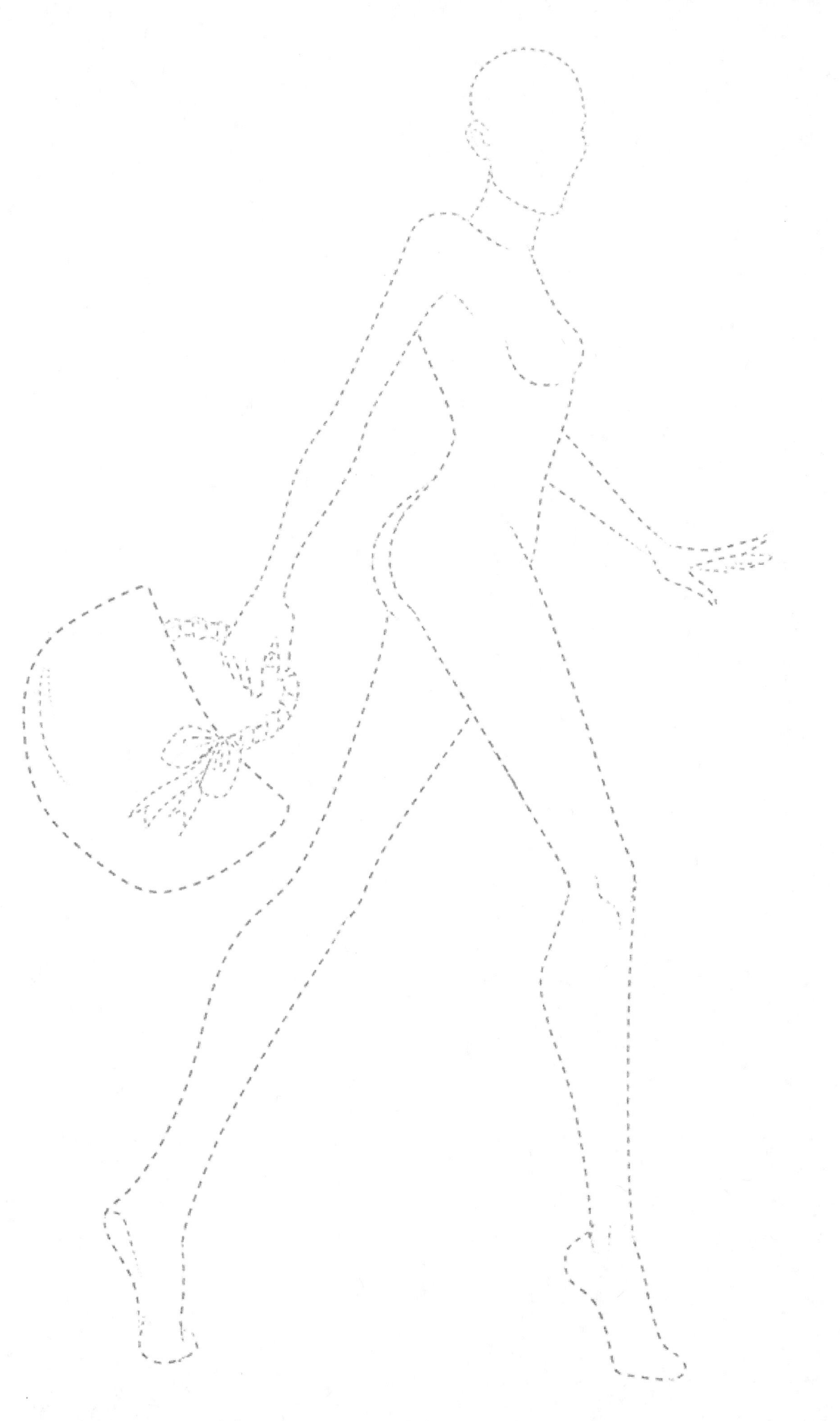

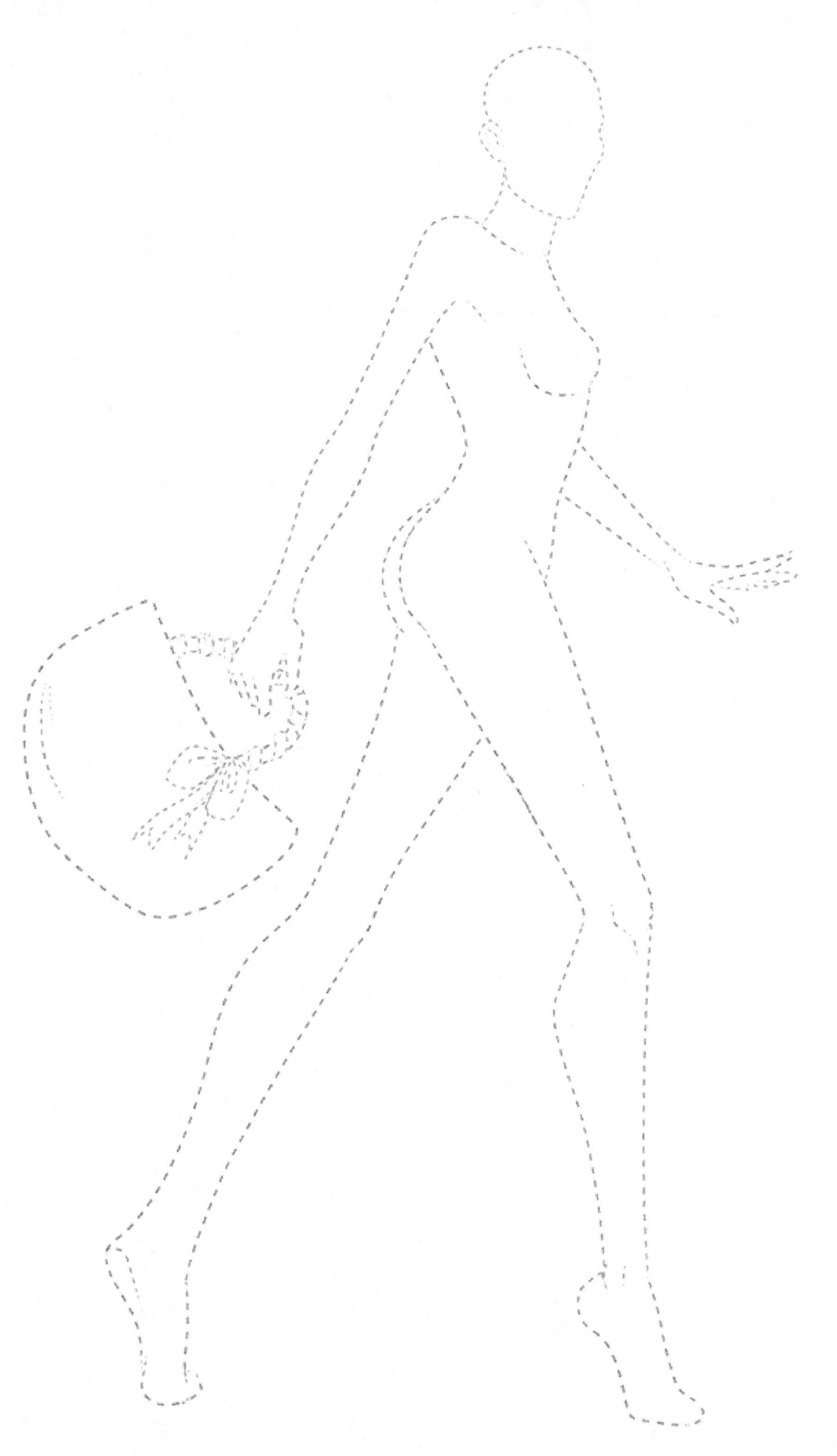

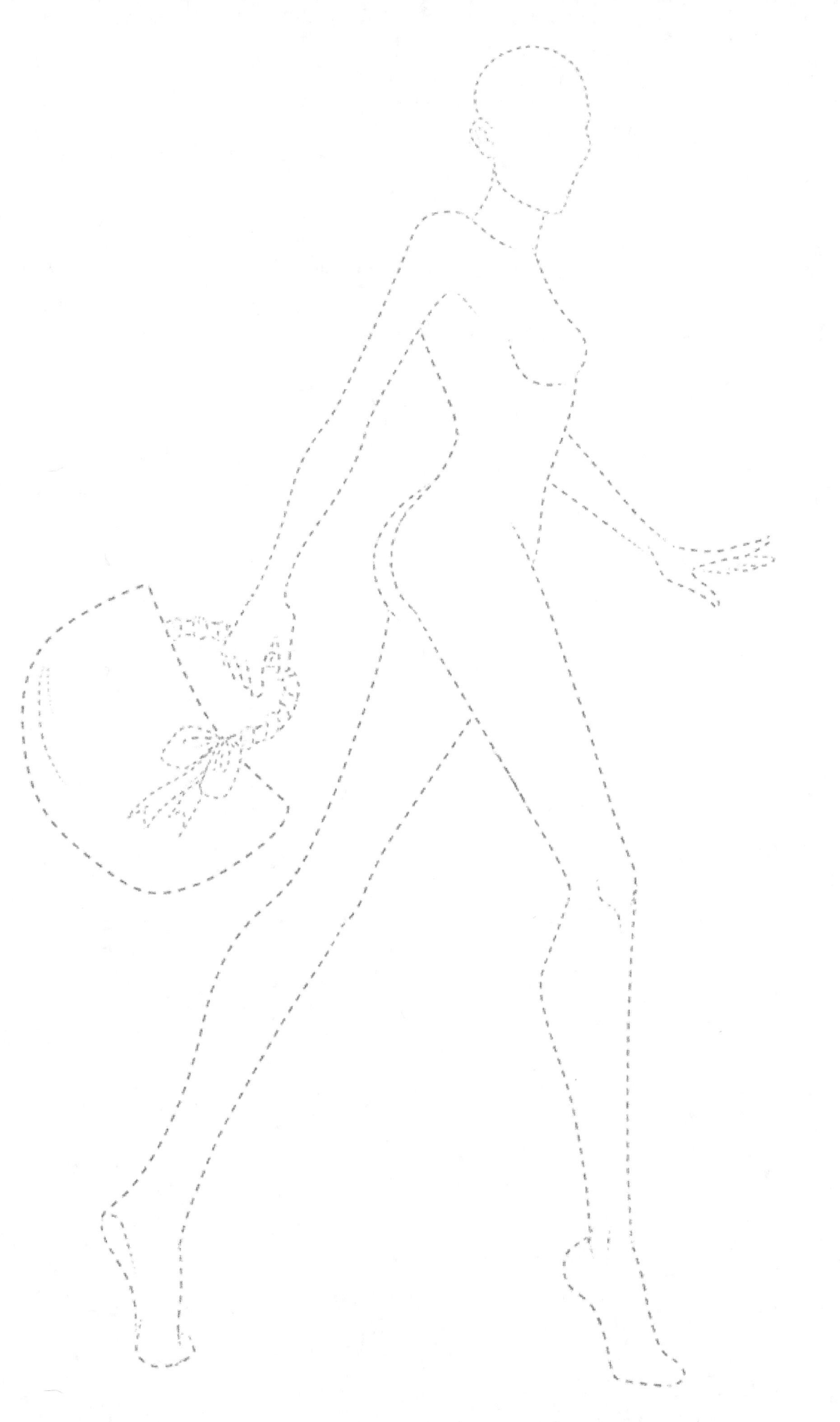

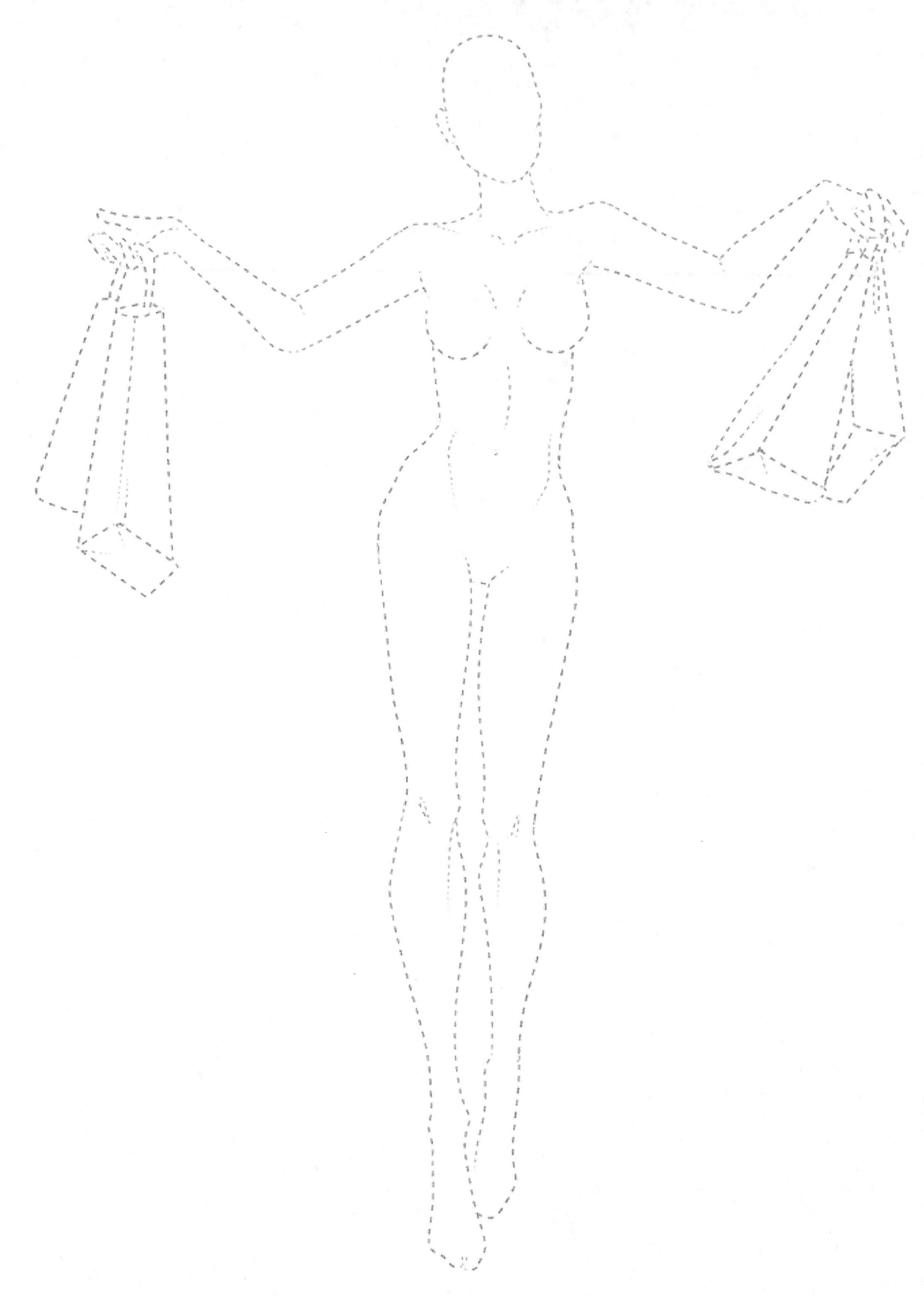

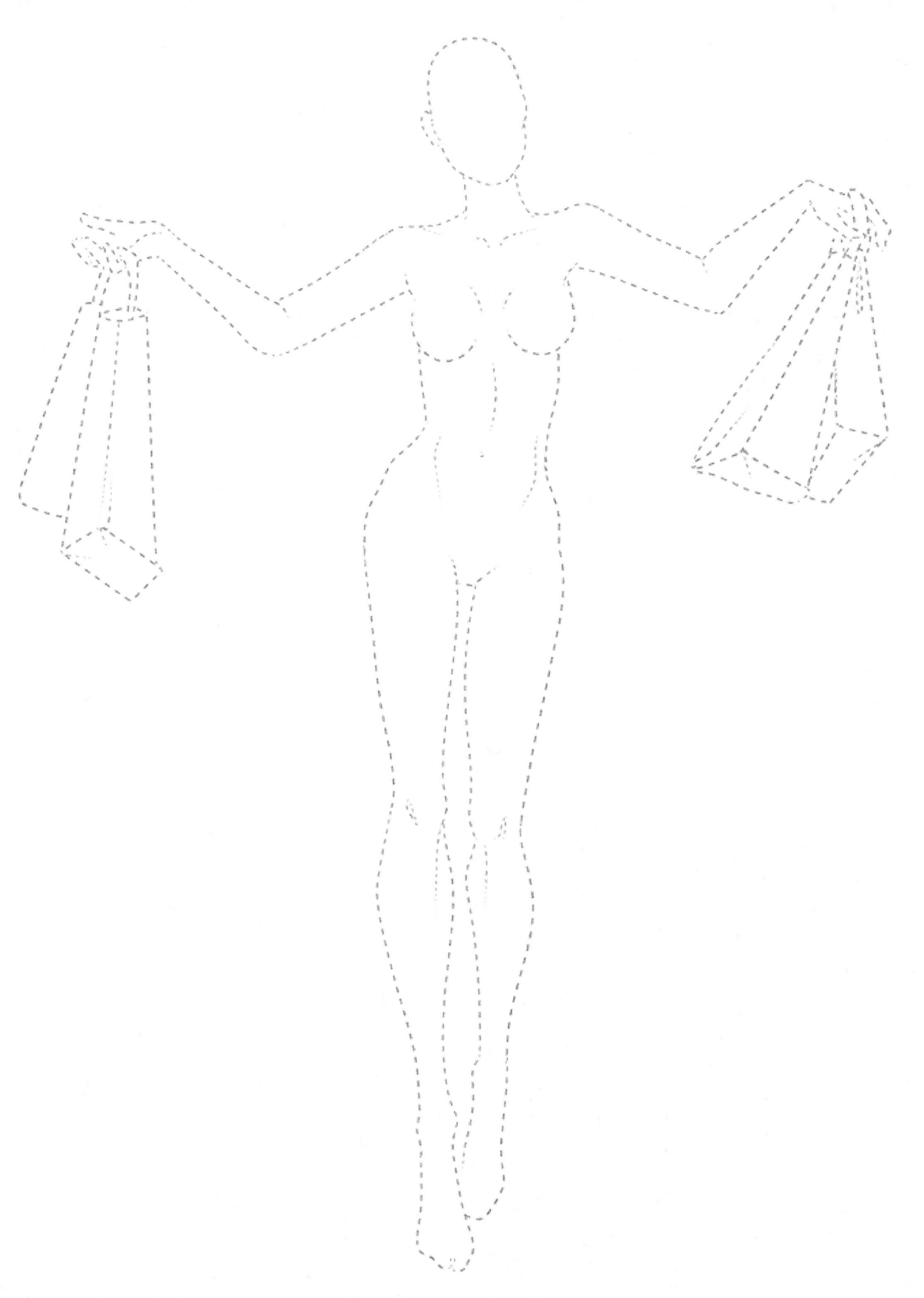

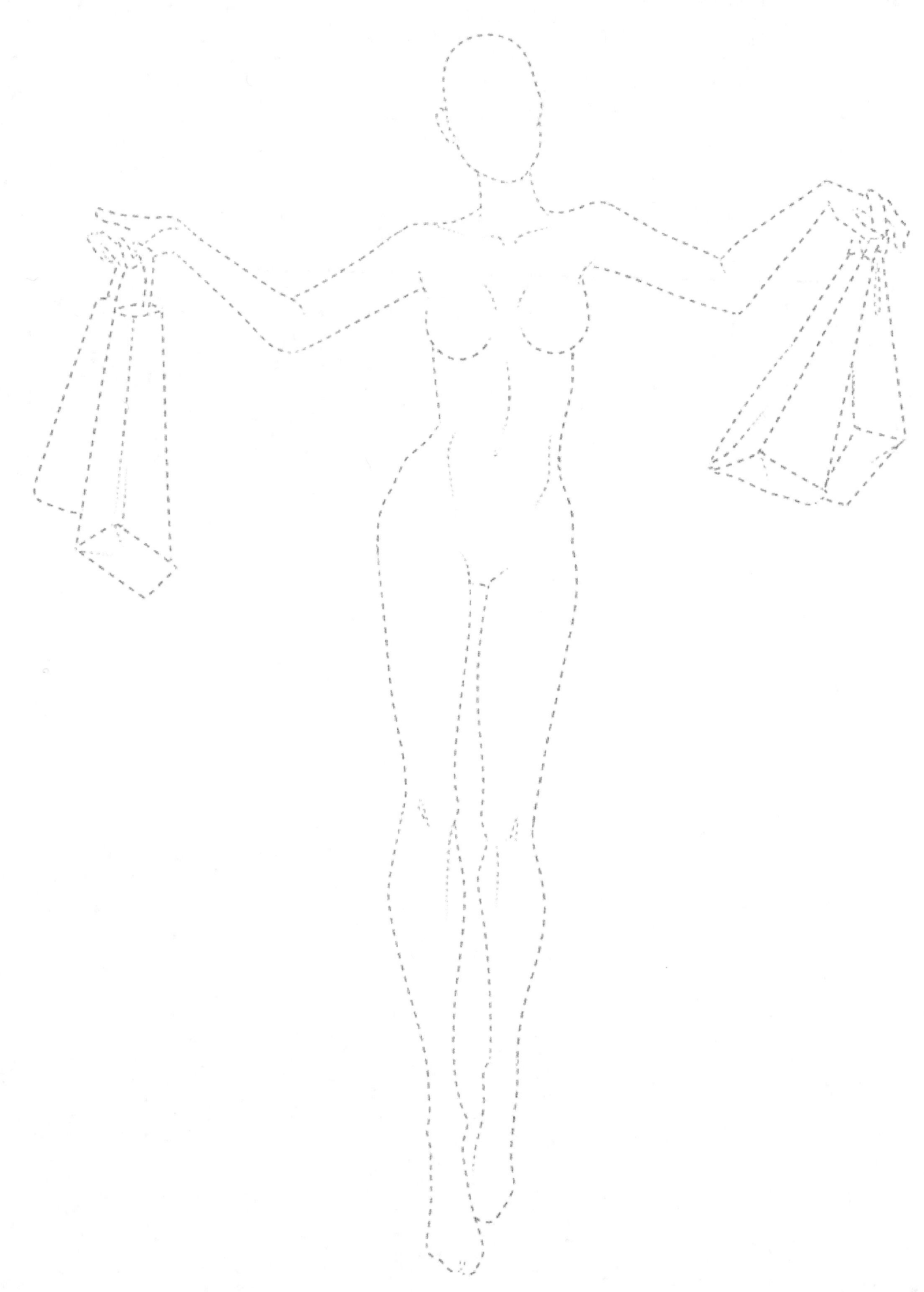

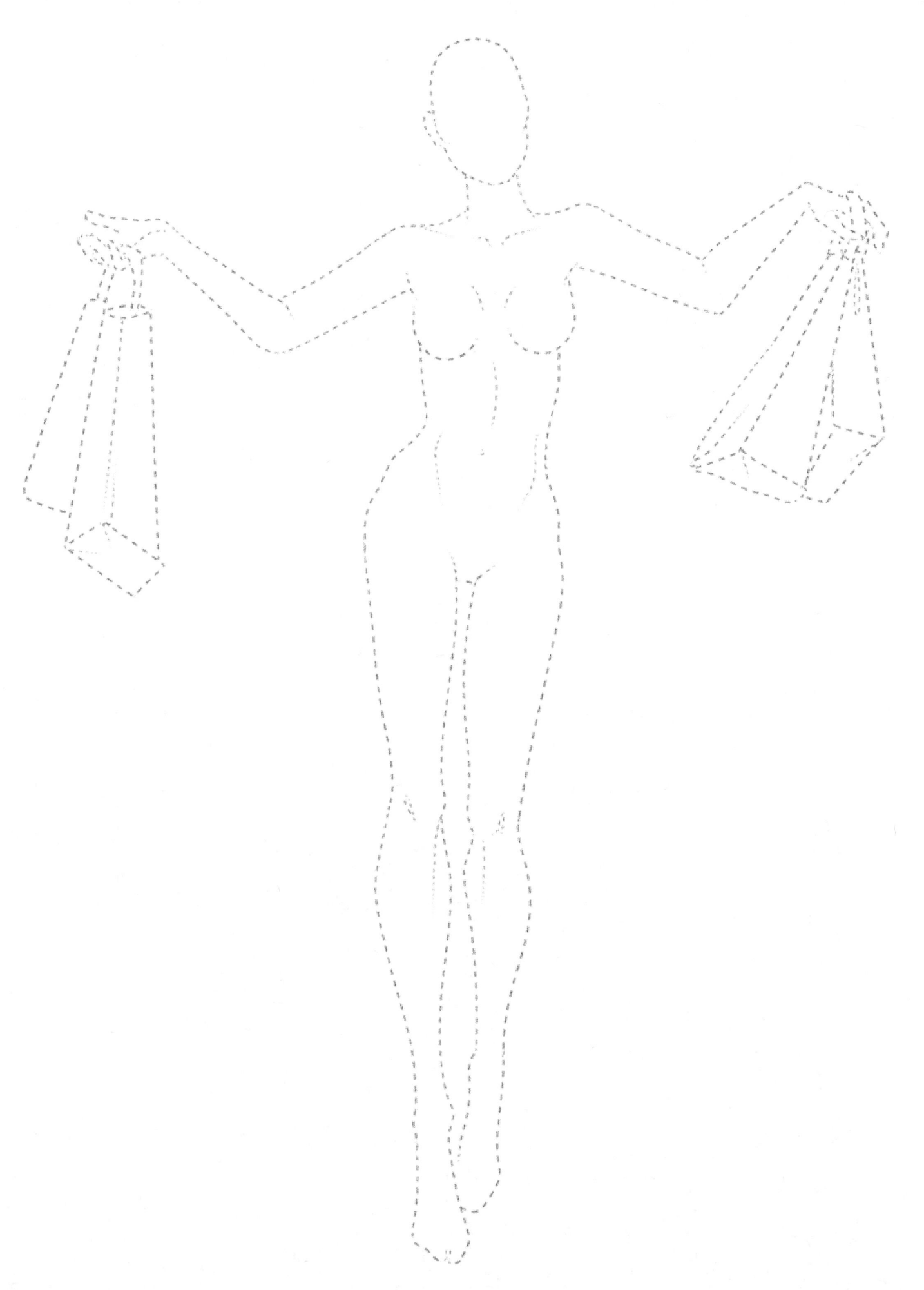

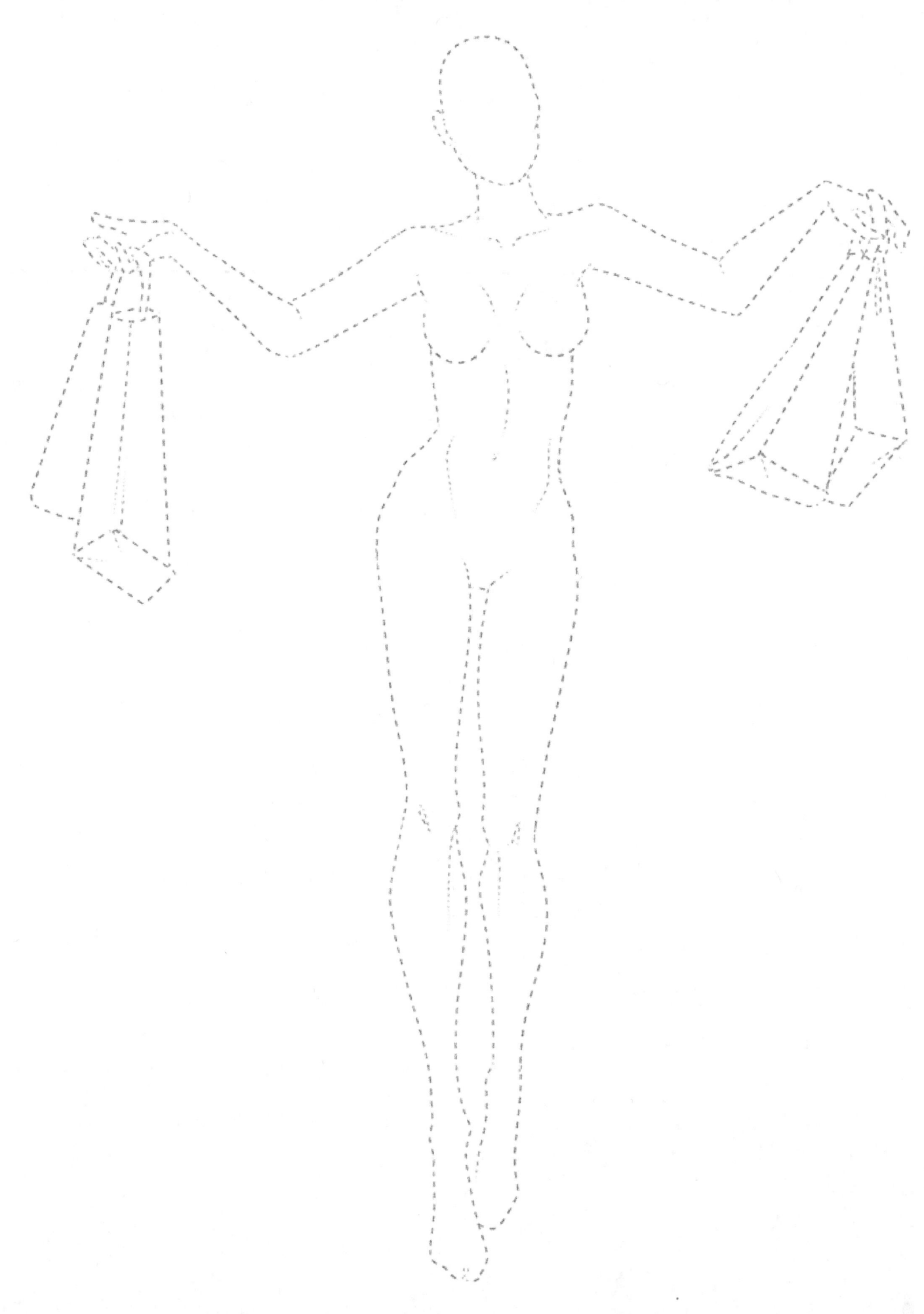

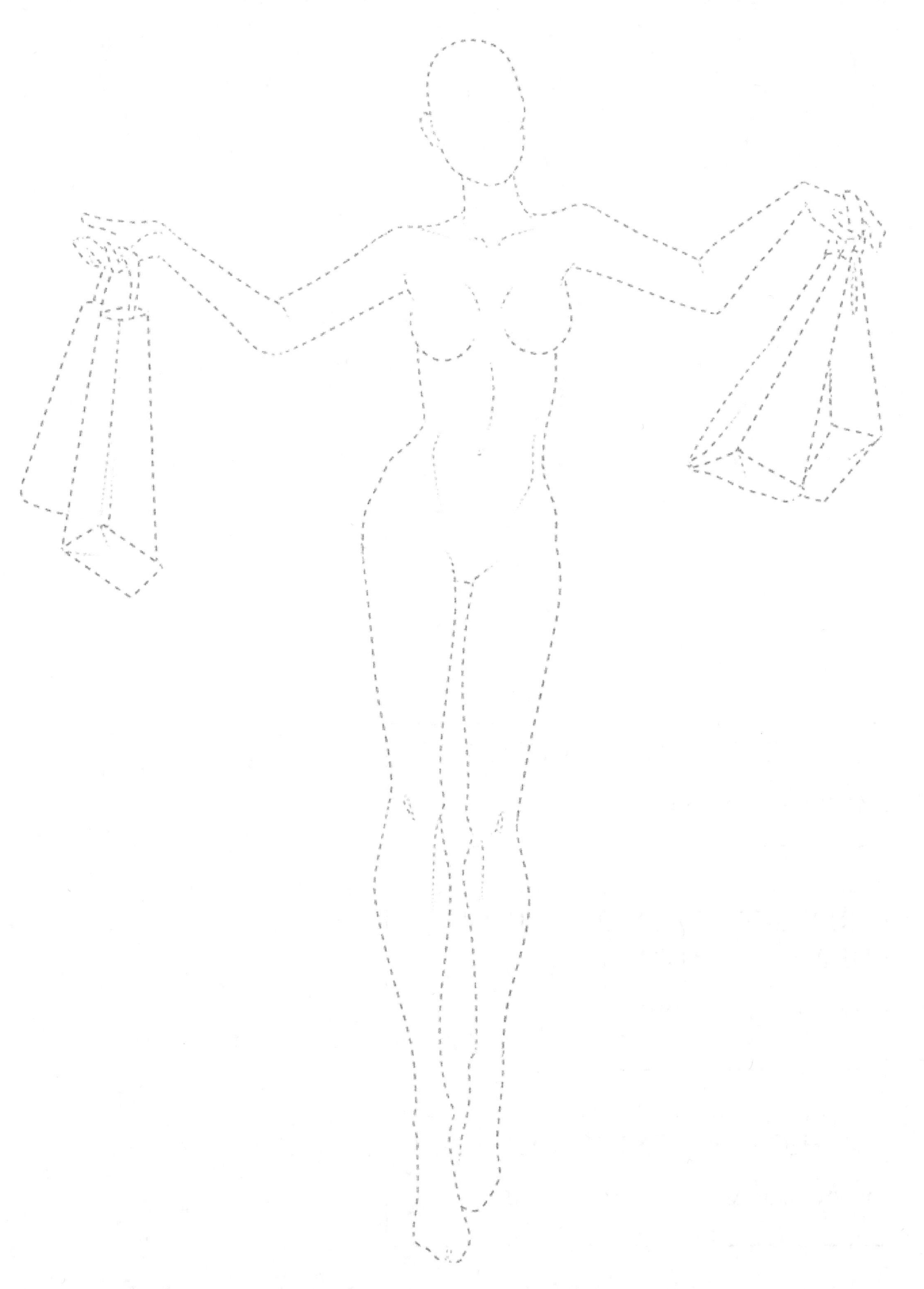

DOWNLOAD FASHION CROQUIS:

WWW.IFASHIONTEMPLATES.COM

FREE STEP-BY-STEP FASHION DRAWING TUTORIALS:

WWW.IDRAWFASHION.COM

FASHION DESIGNING COURSES:

WWW.ACADEMY.IDRAWFASHION.COM

MORE FROM US:

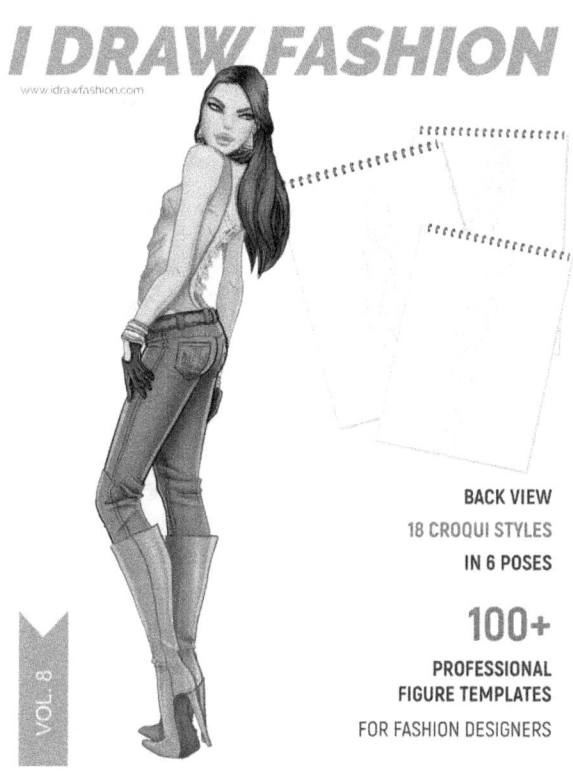
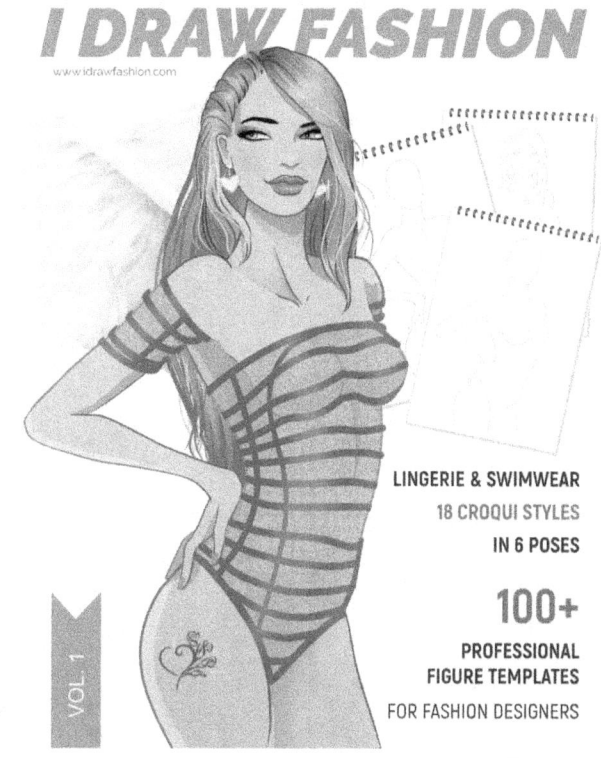
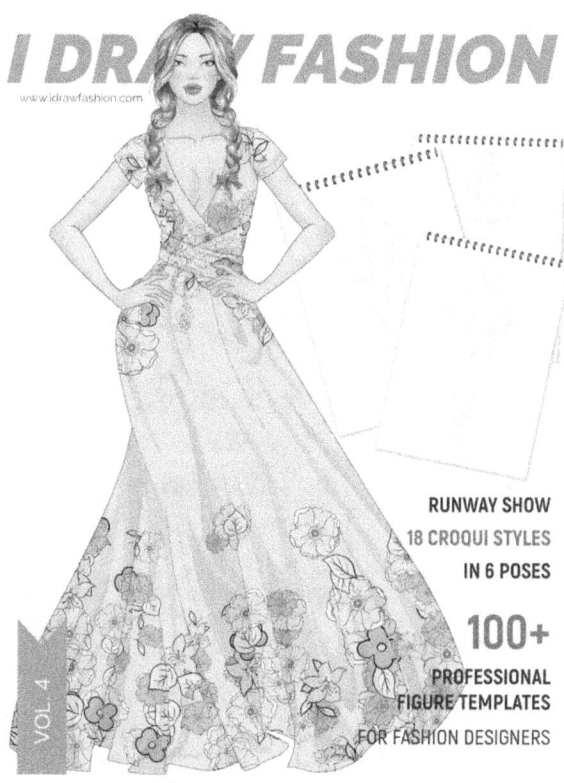
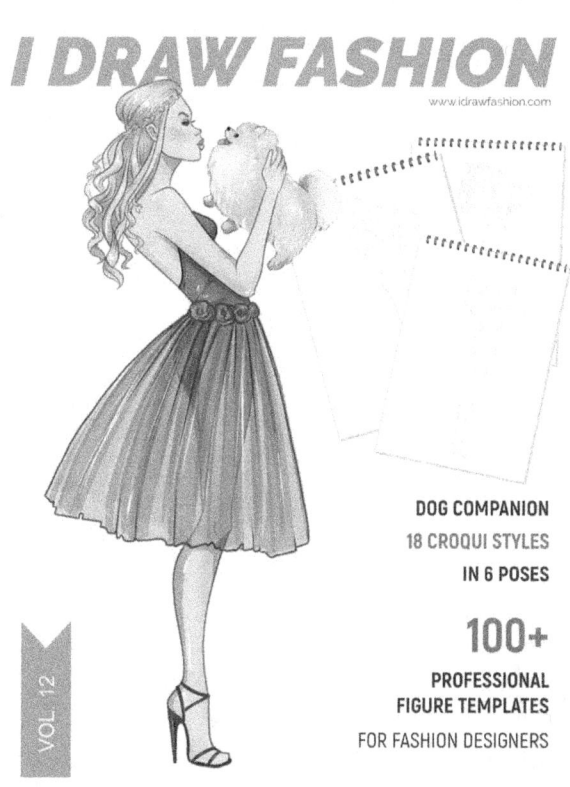

www.ingramcontent.com/pod-product-compliance
Lightning Source LLC
Chambersburg PA
CBHW081434220526
45466CB00008B/2390